Psychosocial interventions in the criminal justice system

proceedings

**Reports presented
to the 20th Criminological Research Conference
(1993)**

European Committee on Crime Problems

Criminological research, Vol. XXXI

Council of Europe Press, 1995

French edition:

Les interventions psychosociales dans le système de justice pénale

ISBN 92-871-2748-4

Publishing and Documentation Service
Council of Europe
F-67075 Strasbourg Cedex

ISBN 92-871-2749-2
© Council of Europe, 1995
Printed in the Netherlands

CONTENTS

PSYCHOSOCIAL INTERVENTIONS
IN THE
CRIMINAL JUSTICE SYSTEM

20th Criminological Research
Conference
(1993)

OPENING ADDRESS

by
Mr U. GATTI
Chairman of the Conference,
Institute of Psychology and Criminal Psychiatry
Genoa University
(Italy)

The reason behind the choice of theme for this Conference was the need to resume and intensify the scientific debate on psychosocial interventions within the criminal justice system.

Co-operation between the human sciences and the justice system, once considered as a vital element in improving the penal system and in making it more effective and humane, has been in the throes of a deep crisis since the seventies, with the result that scientific research on this subject has been neglected for some considerable time.

Research on the effectiveness of treatment, acceptance of the right of prisoners not to be subjected to personality manipulation, society's crime-related fears, which gave rise to demands for greater security, and significant changes in the breakdown of the prison population resulted in a substantial shift in criminal justice policy, followed by an increasing refusal to allow social operators to intervene in the criminal justice field.

The impact of this refusal was all the greater because it was shared by progressives and conservatives alike who, for different or even diamctrically opposed reasons, advocated diminishing the importance of psychosocial interventions in the criminal justice system.

In practice, rejection of the rehabilitative ideal did not result in the anticipated changes: prisons are increasingly overcrowded, the justice system is increasingly slow and inefficient, the social climate of prisons has worsened considerably and staff morale has deteriorated. Only recently have people again begun to question the claim that co-operation between human sciences and the justice system is impossible. A new phase seems about to begin, although it is still in embryonic form.

What we are currently seeing is not so much a new method of treatment in traditional terms as a growing awareness of the validity of psychosocial interventions which are more limited in scope or designed to meet particular needs. It is still difficult to put forward the ambitious objective of eliminating the causes of crime with therapeutic interventions, and there has been ample evidence of the contradictions and distortions of the "medical model". Today, psychosocial interventions are being developed in the light of new perspectives, and have been diversified accordingly. They aim to improve the social climate in prisons, meet specific individual needs, create mechanisms for moving people out of the prison system and motivate staff to work ultimately for aims which are not necessarily punitive in character. In addition, new intervention areas have been developed within "restitutive justice", with qualified psychosocial operators working for victim-offender reconciliation and compensation.

The objective of eliminating recidivism can be considered in new terms, with greater attention paid to individuals' needs, rights and deliberate choices.

In the light of these new realities, it was deemed worthwhile devoting a Criminological Research Conference to these issues in order to reactive the scientific debate, assess recent studies and evaluate the advantages and potential of psychosocial interventions as well as the associated risks of distortion and undesirable side-effects. The new operating conditions and contexts determined the choice of the term "psychosocial interventions" as opposed to more traditional terms such as "treatment and rehabilitation". This change suggests that new prospects for co-operation between the human sciences and the justice system are opening up. In the light of these considerations, we can redefine the areas of scientific debate and empirical research, which do not just concern the effectiveness of measures in terms of recidivism, but also the well-being of persons connected with the criminal justice system, in whatever capacity, plus the ethical and deontological aspects of interventions of this type, the completion of a whole series of psychological programmes in coercive contexts and the conditions and resources required for such measures to be put into practice.

So the area for debate and research is extremely broad, and for this reason themes connected with the problems of minors and psychiatric testing and treatment, to which the Council of Europe has already devoted a considerable amount of attention, have been excluded from this conference, which will focus mainly on the following five themes:

1. "Psychosocial assessments before and after sentencing", with a view to debating the different forms which this practice takes in the different legal systems;

2. "Psychosocial interventions aimed at resolving the conflict between the perpetrator and the victim, for example within the framework of mediation and compensation programmes", in order to identify the advantages, limitations and requirements of the new concept of restitutive justice;

3. "Evaluating psychosocial interventions in prison and other penal contexts", with the aim of drawing up an assessment that challenges convictions originating in the simplistic analyses of the seventies;

4. "Implementing psychosocial interventions linked to community sanctions (probation, day centres etc)", placing particular emphasis on practical constraints, different forms of organisation and staff support.

5. "Problems of therapeutic interventions for specific categories of offenders, for example with regard to sex offences, violence in the family, and drug addiction", in order to analyse psychosocial interventions in a typically clinical perspective.

Each rapporteur will comment on problems associated with the observance of human rights and on the practical problems facing professional operators in the course of their interventions. Each rapporteur will give a particular connotation to the term "psychosocial interventions" within his or her specific field of research and action, and will give a summary of developments in the given field and relevant research findings.

We hope that the facts and opinions submitted and the subsequent debate will help to further knowledge in this area and stimulate experimentation with new forms of intervention.

PSYCHOSOCIAL INTERVENTIONS IN THE CRIMINAL JUSTICE SYSTEM

20th Criminological Research
Conference
(1993)

INTRODUCTORY REPORT

by
Mr R. HOOD
General Rapporteur,
University of Oxford
(United Kingdom)

I.   The Context

The time is ripe for a reconsideration of the role of psycho-social interventions throughout the penal sphere. Indeed, it is over a quarter of a century since this subject was aired in a Council of Europe Conference.[1] The growing dissatisfaction with the outcome of the neo-classical 'just deserts' paradigm, the concern that a "new penology" is emerging with an increased emphasis on the management of so-called dangerous groups, set against the burgeoning claims that "treatments work", have set the debate alight again.[2] But, as with all such oscillations of the penal pendulum, there are dangers that such claims will be inflated, the lessons of the past ignored, and some of the benefits which have flowed from the adoption of the "justice model" reversed.

As always, it is necessary to define terms. What is meant by "psycho-social intervention"? Professor Lösel understandably takes the pragmatic view that it is best applied to "all those kinds of psychological treatment that go beyond 'pure' punishment, incapacitation or deterrence and are directed towards positively evaluated changes in the offender (eg. may reduce recidivism)". But does the use of the word 'positively' rule out **individual**, as opposed to **general**, deterrence? Are not aversive regimes such as "boot camps" psycho-social in their objectives? And what about surveillance and control? Electronic monitoring is surely a form of psycho-social intervention. Furthermore, such interventions may have aims other than the hoped for reduction in recidivism: as Professor Debuyst notes, psycho-social assessments may be employed in determining the offender's motivation and therefore as a tool for determining the seriousness of offending behaviour or for assessing "risk" in relation to conditional release. Likewise Mrs Roberts points to a number of criteria other than reconviction which influence the Probation Service when deciding to intervene in offenders' lives. These include the provision of services which aim to divert offenders from custody so as to reduce the prison population, to conserve scarce resources or reduce costs, or simply to offer concrete help to the disadvantaged. As Professor Snare's paper shows, interventions may also be aimed both at helping the victim and at reconciling offender and victim, the purpose of which might have more to do with "systems management" and avoidance of the criminal justice system than with changing the future conduct of offenders. Lastly, interventions may aim to create an acceptable climate for humane punishment and for reducing conflict in penal institutions through a therapeutic environment which reduces tensions and violence both among prisoners and between prisoners and staff. In their study of the therapeutic prison at Grendon Underwood in England, for example, my colleagues Genders and Player concluded that the regime substantially undermined the normal prison culture as well as improved the psychological well-being of prisoners, both of which were constructive "irrespective of whether or not [they led] to the abatement or reduction of criminogenic behaviour".[3] It is clear, therefore, that the Rapporteurs for this conference have, from their varying perspectives, indicated that psycho-social interventions have a number of different aims which therefore need to be assessed by different criteria.

II.   The "What Works" Literature

There has been a tendency for social scientists to imply that the attack on the "rehabilitative ideal" arose directly from, or was inherently dependent upon, Martinson's assertion that "nothing works". This is a distortion. As is well known, the assault on the "medical model" and, in particular, on the use of indeterminate sentences and parole procedures, preceded Martinson's work by a number of years. Indeed, it was probably as a *result* of disenchantment with the 'rehabilitative ideal' that Martinson's work got the attention it did. Earlier studies which had come to much the same conclusions had not been interpreted in the same way.[4] The claim that "nothing works" was always an over-simplification which has been used as a shibboleth by those who now claim that "appropriate" interventions are effective. There are three reasons why the "nothing works" formulation was, and remains, misleading which need to borne in mind when reviewing new evidence.

First, it was a misnomer. Nobody has ever established a satisfactory base-rate of recidivism following non-intervention against which to judge the outcome of **any** intervention. The term "nothing works" merely applied to the generalization that no specific forms of punishment or treatment could be identified which, when the type of offender was controlled for, produced rates of reconviction which were significantly lower than expected. Given the fact that the 'norm' or 'base-rate' of post-conviction relapse is affected by many factors other than any *added* element of intervention, such as the offender's motivation to desist, opportunities both legal and illegal, social supports, individual deterrent effects, and various other post-institutional circumstances, it is perhaps not surprising that "treatment effects" were shown to have a marginal impact at the best. This was especially true where, as Ted Palmer reminds us, the "various standard or traditional programs with which [treatments] were compared may have been quite good as well" and where, as was often the case, the intervention itself was on a scale which could only marginally impact upon the life history of the offender. It has, therefore, been suggested that there was little reason to expect much difference between the effects on recidivism between "the incidental learning opportunities" provided by such sanctions as probation or imprisonment or community service or restitution.[5]

Secondly, psycho-social interventions may well have an impact **within** the treatment situation on attitudes, self-concept, mental states and behaviour, but nevertheless be "overwhelmed" by post-intervention factors. As Lösel points out, interventions have a greater impact on attitude measurements than they do on recidivism. Without knowledge of the circumstances of the post-intervention period it is not possible to know whether reconviction or desistance from offending is due to "treatment" or "post-treatment" effects or the interaction between them. Debuyst reminds us that "the relationship between conduct in prison and behaviour after release is difficult to interpret, for the progress possibly made during a prison term is of debatable value in that the subjects fall back into their former habits or attitudes once they have returned to the previous social situation". These issues still need to be properly explored.

14

Third, as is well known, overall "nothing works" findings hid differential effects on offenders with different characteristics. Those who were classed as "amenable" responded comparatively well and the "un-amenable" reacted poorly, producing an average "no effect" finding. What was left unexplored was whether, given legal and ethical limitations, it would ever be possible to ensure that interventions only deal with those who are amenable, and what the consequences would be for the non-amenables (and for institutions) if they were all classified and dealt with together.

The issue raised by the claim that "nothing works" has been, to put it bluntly, whether "treatment" should be written off as unattainable or, even if attainable, regarded as undesirable in a coercive setting. Alternatively, should psycho-social interventions be intensified, made more distinctive, more differentiated and related theoretically to the problem of criminality, and appropriately resourced, staffed and researched? Is so, this still leaves the question of how such knowledge should be employed in the penal context. It is one thing to engage in an *empirical* argument about whether various sorts of interventions in offenders' lives which are intended to change their behaviour in future in fact do so. It is another matter altogether to argue that decisions about how offenders should be treated — the length and form of intervention and decision-making processes relating to release from custody — should be based on the attempt to maximise the effectiveness of such interventions. If, indeed, there is convincing evidence that psychological or social interventions lessen the probability of recidivism, how can they be applied in ways that do not lead to the abuse of discretion by those who administer the interventions and to the violation of offenders' rights? Is it now the case that "the principles of effective intervention" can be applied, in practice, "within a variety of just sanctions"? This is a key issue in the context of the materials presented to this conference. Unlike earlier discussions, which were usually concerned with the effectiveness of different **legal** penalties, such as probation compared with community service, intensive supervision compared with ordinary probation etc., the studies now cited are largely, as Lösel points out, concerned with different modalities of treatment — for example, cognitive-behavioural learning approaches as compared with psychotherapy. This obviously poses the question of how far different interventions are compatible with different legal punishments and how far their effectiveness varies according to the legal prescriptions for those punishments.[6]

III.   The Recent Evidence

Many of the claims that interventions can be effective rest on the findings of a series of *meta-analyses* which, it is argued have advantages over so-called *narrative accounts* in which the reviewer uses his or her judgement to sum-up the findings of a variety of inquiries. Meta-analysis is a statistical method which combines the results of a number of small scale studies in order to estimate both the size and statistical significance of the effect that may be attributable to 'treated' populations as opposed to their controls. The validity of these findings inevitably depend on the appropriateness of this statistical technique in a field so complex and differentiated as legal punishment. Professor Lösel's paper raises some serious problems. He shows that studies are combined, even though they have dealt with different populations under quite different legal controls — such as juveniles under prevention programmes and young people in custody — and with different follow-up periods. Yet in medical research where meta-analyses are widely used, it is agreed that studies which are combined must be "similar with respect to the disease and the exposure or intervention being studied, and the characteristics of the subjects must be sufficiently similar to make combining the results of such studies reasonable".[7] This raises the question of what an 'overall' effect of 1 per cent age points really means? Does it convey more than that it is worth while to make **some** efforts? The meta-analysts themselves agree that "the essential statistic produced by meta-analysis — effect-size — is still problematic".[8] Furthermore, "studies (...) with theoretically and methodologically sound tests of treatment and effect, more adequate outcome criteria, higher generalisability (...) [larger samples, and longer follow up periods] (...) and so forth, exhibited lower effects" (Lösel).

It appears, therefore that care should be taken in using and interpreting meta-analyses. This is not to deny that it is a useful technique under the right conditions: but it can only be as good as the studies which it combines. The question therefore is whether these conditions have been fulfilled and, indeed, whether they can be fulfilled. To what extent are the underlying methodological problems being addressed? It appears that experimental designs are still the exception; that the 'content' and organizational context of the programmes being evaluated are more often than not inadequately described, let alone adequately monitored; that the interventions are often complex, so that it is not possible to disentangle the contribution of different elements to the overall outcome; and that criteria of success are often differently specified (e.g. there is often no measurement of recidivism which takes into account the seriousness of offences). While Lösel believes that there is sufficient evidence to reject the "nothing works" hypothesis, he nevertheless concludes that "the effects are only moderate and in no way completely consistent". The conference will undoubtedly want to review the advantages and disadvantages of these statistical attempts to assess *en masse* a variety of studies of psycho-social interventions.

Bearing all this in mind, a consensus appears to be emerging that programmes which are based on cognitive behavioural principles — sometimes called "pro-social modelling and reinforcement" — show the largest and most consistent effects. Such programs are said to have been designed specifically to address the problems which give rise to crime; to be effective in residential and penal settings, although their impact tends to be greater in community settings; to be appropriate for property offenders but perhaps less so for violent or sex offenders. Where this approach, as designed by Robert Ross, has been tried in England, such as in Herefordshire and Worcestershire (described by Mrs Roberts) and in the "Reasoning and Rehabilitation" programme in the Mid-Glamorgan Probation Service, the results appear undoubtedly promising.[9] Findings elsewhere have claimed reductions in recidivism of 50 to 80 per cent for even "high risk" offenders, although the precise definition of that term shifts, of course, in relation to the population being studied. It is not for the first time that high hopes for penal interventions have been raised. Penal history is littered with discarded panaceas. A sober assessment is therefore needed of theory, practice, and research findings. It may be that these positive findings are due, at least in some measure, to "selection effects" of the offenders and staff; to measurement effects of various kinds; or simply to short-lived experimental "Hawthorne effects". It should be borne in mind that Ted Palmer, one of the leading supporters of the revival of rehabilitation, concluded that "although several methods seem promising (...) none have been able to produce major reductions when applied broadly to composite samples of offenders (...)".[10] No doubt, the conference will need to ask to what extent, and under what conditions, a cognitive behavioural approach can validly claim to be effective.[11]

For example, cognitive-behavioural programmes aimed to help violent and sex offenders to "manage their anger" and "manage gender relations" are growing apace. For example, in England and Wales, such offenders are required to "address their offending behaviour" through making positive efforts and progress in such programmes before being released on parole. Yet according to Professor Elchardus, none of the three classes of therapeutic options for violent offenders — neurological, cognitive, and psychodynamic — have been shown to be incontestably superior to the others (except chemical treatment of brain lesions). He describes the North American approach at the Phillipe de Pinel Institute which combines cognitive and psychodynamic approaches. And he gives praise to Dr Balier's psychoanalytic treatment of violent patients at Varces. However, there appears to be no data on which to assess their effectiveness. Clearly there is a need for more scientific evaluations in this field.

Nor is Professor Snare able to point to any empirical research which confirms the claims made for victim-offender mediation that "the offender will become aware of his wrongdoing, be held accountable and understand the harm of his action which can then be undone by his effort". Indeed she concludes that the impact of this approach on the reduction of recidivism appears to be most "unpromising". It has also been easier to demonstrate the high level of satisfaction with the help given to victims by victim support schemes and the satisfactory completion of restitution payments than it has been to demonstrate any substantial diversion of cases from the criminal justice system. This is particularly disappointing in view of the current prominence in the academic literature of such restitutive-rehabilitative notions as "reintegrative shaming".[12] Again, the conference will need to consider how research on this subject can be stimulated and effectively carried out.

IV.   Ethical, Professional and Practical Issues

The Rapporteurs raise important issues in relation to the conditions: ethical, social, professional and practical, under which psycho-social interventions might take place. For example, Professor Debuyst draws our attention to the tension between the role of diagnosis in determining responsibility, and therefore liability for punishment, and its role in assessing personality with a view to proposing methods of treatment — especially where the material is used to assess how the prisoner has dealt with "problems" in the very "abnormal environment" of the prison. This is especially pertinent where release from confinement is based on assessments of "risk" which are linked to the response to a behavioural programme. Indeed Professor Elchardus insists that the judge "must never be able to direct the therapy, which remains the exclusive responsibility of the physician". This is because it is bound up with consent to treatment on the one hand and medical ethics and independence on the other. Treatment clinics, he insists need "a negotiated independence from the judicial and prison authorities".

17

Unless merely "offered" with full consent and no penalty for non-participation, all treatment programmes inevitably necessitate assessments of needs and responses which can put pressure on clinicians "to push his nosographic [classificatory] categories in the direction desired by the judicial (and parole) authority, and again to justify a particular measure by the necessities of treatment". To what extent does this apply to other types of non-clinical intervention?

The crucial issue of staff morale and involvement in programmes which aim to change offenders is emphasised in Mrs Roberts' paper. She points out that the "complex and potentially contradictory" aims within which probation services operate have created a "practitioner resistance to evaluative methods". In this regard she pinpoints the necessity, from a practical point of view, of creating systems whereby data is routinely collected with a view to the evaluation of practice, and, from an organisational standpoint, of securing staff commitment, developing skills and generating what she calls "a culture of curiosity" so as to create "an information community". Professor Snare raises the important question of whether professional skills need to be developed in order to achieve successful mediation or whether the task is best left to the layman: this is certainly a good subject for research.

The conference will undoubtedly need to discuss whether the concept of "treatment" is appropriate within a criminal justice setting. It is common these days to adopt the terms "offender programme" or "rehabilitative services" but this does not necessarily resolve the issue. This may be especially problematic in relation to the intervention claimed to be the most "appropriate" and effective: namely cognitive-behavioural programmes. They are, of course, based on assumptions of what constitutes "pro-social" behaviour and on theories of knowledge and constructive reasoning: they emphasise a psychological rather than a sociological *aetiology*. This raises more than the issue of class bias — for example, the expectation of "correct attitudes" and responses from sex offenders in relation to questions of gender. It is for this reason that Elchardus urges us to reserve the term "treatment" for issues of health not of social values: "learning and conditioning techniques, however useful they may be, should be considered more as educative, or even normative, psycho-social interventions than treatment in the strictest sense of the word". Indeed, he believes that in environments like the prison, the fact that treatment is meant to be related to the goal of reduction in recidivism "undermines the relationship between therapist and patient".

Finally there is the perennial question of how to maintain the integrity of interventions over time. Indeed, the leading proponents of the behaviourist approach, Gendreau and Ross, recognise that there remains a problem in translating "the principles of effective intervention" so that they can be "implemented and maintained successfully in the real world". The famous "anthropological laboratories", now "assessment and treatment units", set up with such high hopes in Belgian prisons earlier this century, provide a good example. As Debuyst informs us, there is a danger that they will merely become aids to prison management: useful tools for dealing with "difficult prisoners".

Bearing all these problems in mind, what is required of research? All but thirty years ago, in my paper on "The Effectiveness of Punishments and Treatments" to the Second Conference of Directors of Criminological Research, I suggested that "research must be a continuous process of evaluation and re-evaluation" as the form and use of sanctions change. I stressed then that we needed more knowledge of what the "contents" of the "treatments" delivered were and what they meant to those to whom they were applied.[13] And, of course, it is necessary to investigate how such interventions affect behaviour when offenders are faced both by problems of the kind they formerly succumbed to and by entirely new problems. Research on psycho-social interventions therefore needs to be integrated with longitudinal studies of criminal careers. In other words, we need to develop an interactionist, more "dynamic", research strategy in order to understand the varying impact of those factors, including psycho-social interventions, which shape the reactions, choices and behaviours of those who have experienced penal sanctions.[14] The problems of evaluating the impact of psycho-social interventions on the lives of offenders remain as difficult as ever. At least, it is once again acceptable to discuss them.

NOTES

1. See the report presented in 1964 to the Second Conference of Directors of Criminological Research Institutes by Roger Hood on "Research on the Effectiveness of punishments and Treatments", in *Collected Studies in Criminological Research*, Vol. 1 (Strasbourg, 1967), pp. 73-113; and the report to the Fourth Conference in 1967 by Richard F. Sparks on "Types of Treatment for Types of Offenders", in Vol. 3, (1968), pp. 129-269. The subject of the Seventh Criminological Colloquium held in 1985 was "Studies on Criminal Responsibility and Psychiatric Treatment of Mentally Ill Offenders", but this was not concerned with the scientific evaluation of treatment methods, see *Studies in Criminological Research*, Vol. 24 (Strasbourg, 1986).

2. See for example John Braithwaite and Philip Pettit, *Not Just Deserts*, (Cambridge UP, 1989); Nils Christie, *Crime Control as Industry*, (Routledge, 1992); Sir Leon Radzinowicz, "Penal Regression", *Cambridge Law Journal*, Vol, 50, (1991), pp. 422-444; Malcolm Feeley and Jonathan Simon, "The New Penology: Notes on the Emerging Strategy of Corrections and its Implications", *Criminology*, Vol. 30, (1992), pp. 449-474; Paul Gendreau and Robert Ross, "Revivification of Rehabilitation: Evidence from the 1980's, *Justice Quarterly*, Vol. 4 (1987) pp. 349-406; Ted Palmer, "The Effectiveness of Intervention; Recent Trends and Current Issues" *Crime and Delinquency*, Vol. 37, (1991), pp. 330-346.

3. Elaine Genders and Elaine Player, "Rehabilitation in Prisons: A Study of Grendon Underwood", *Current Legal Problems*, 1993, pp. 235-256; also, *Grendon: A study of a Therapeutic Prison*, Clarendon Studies in Criminology, (Oxford Uni. Press, for the coming 1994). For a useful review of inmate responses to prison regimes see, Kenneth Adams, "Adjusting to Prison Life", in M. Tonry (ed), *Crime and Justice*: An Annual Review of Research, Vol. 16, (1992), pp. 275-359.

4. See James Q. Wilson, *Thinking about Crime*, (Basic Books, revised ed. 1983), pp. 162-163. Wilson noted the earlier reviews of research by Hood (see fn 1 above); Walter C. Bailey, "Correctional Outcome: an Evaluation of 100 Reports", *J. Criminal Law, Criminology and Police Science*, Vol. 57, (1966), pp. 153-160; and Leslie T. Wilkins, *Evaluation of Penal Measures*, (Random House 1969), See also, Leon Radzinowicz and Roger Hood, "The American Volte Face in Sentencing Thought and Practice", in C. F. Tapper (ed.), *Crime, Proof and Punishment: Essays in Memory of Sir Rupert Cross*, (Butterworths, 1981, pp. 127-143.

5. See D.A. Andrews, I. Zinger, R.D. Hodge, J. Bonta, P. Gendreau and F.T. Cullen, "Does Correctional Treatment work? A Clinically Relevant and Psychologically Informed Meta-Analysis", *Criminology*, Vol. 28, pp. 369-404 at pp. 373-4.

6. See S.P. Lab and J.T. Whitehead, "From Nothing Works" to "The Appropriate Works"; The Latest Stop on the Search for the Secular Grail", *Criminology*, Vol. 28, (1990), pp. 405-417, at pp. 407-8. Also, Andrews et al., "A Human Science Approach or More Punishment and Pessimism: A Rejoinder to Lab and Whitehead", *Ibid.*, pp. 409-429, at p. 421.

7.   See for example C. H. Hennekens and J. Buring, *Epidemiology in Medecine*, (édité par S.L. Mayrent), Little rown, 1987, pp. 264-269.

8.   P. Gendreau and R. Ross, "Revivification of Rehabilitation", quoting the conclusion reached by M. W. Lipsey, in an unpublished paper in 1986, *op. cit.* p. 391.

9.   P. Raynor and M. Vanstone, "'Straight Thinking on Probation' Effectiveness and the Non-Treatment Paradigm", Paper presented to the British Criminology Conference, Cardiff, 1993.

10.   Ted Palmer, "The Effectiveness of Intervention: Recent Trends and Issues", *Crime and Delinquency*, Vol. 37, (1990), pp. 330-346, page 340.

11.   Gendreau and Ross stated in 1987: "We have made only tentative progress in examining the conditions under which the principles of effective intervention can be implemented and maintained successfully in the real world", *op cit*, p. 395.

12.   See J. Braithwaite, *Crime, Shame and Reintegration*, Cambridge Univ. Press, 1989, esp. pp. 152-168.

13.   *Op. cit.*, pp. 82-89 and 102.

14.   An approach of this kind has been developed by Dr. Ross Burnett of the Oxford Centre for Criminological Research in a study entitled *The Dynamics of Recidivism*, recently completed for the Home Office.

PSYCHOSOCIAL INTERVENTIONS IN THE CRIMINAL JUSTICE SYSTEM

20th Criminological Research
Conference
(1993)

PSYCHOSOCIAL ASSESSMENTS BEFORE AND AFTER SENTENCING

by
Mr Ch. DEBUYST
Louvain University, School of Criminology
(Belgium)

Introduction

A report on psychosocial assessment (before and after sentencing) is generally consistent within an overall approach directed towards making possible the rehabilitation of the offender. The purpose of the assessment is to identify the characteristics which should be taken into account in order to achieve rehabilitation and, possibly, to devise an approach based on social and psychological help. Simultaneously and incidentally, the risk of recidivism is assessed directly or indirectly. Such an approach gradually became established around the 1950s. Since then, the policy based on rehabilitation (diagnosis/treatment) has given way to other policies: one punitive (just deserts), another based on the concepts of "negotiation" and "commitment". The question which therefore arises is "What, at the present juncture, can we still gain from a report on the theme of assessment?"

Let us start with two remarks. In one scientific tradition, psychosocial assessment is the essential first stage of any intervention, the argument being "first find out and then intervene". At the present juncture in the real world, however, is psychosocial assessment such an essential preliminary? The second remark: in this field, the Anglo-Saxon tradition differs from that of continental Europe. The **former** tradition, based essentially on the practice of probation, is one of help and supervision designed to enable the offender to avoid being sent to prison (that is how the practice of probation started). Its essential feature is a commitment made by the different parties: the judge, the offender and the person responsible for giving help. Psychosocial assessment was at one time not a prerequisite; it became one only in the 1950s (Criminal Justice Act of 1948). The **latter** tradition, on the other hand, has its roots in the scientific attitude adopted by the first criminologists (the Italian positivists), and is based on the idea that there is necessarily a link between the information collected, the diagnosis arrived at and the measures taken. For very specific reasons, this method is put into practice primarily in the prison system — ie after sentencing.[1]

We thus see our report taking shape: **initially**, we shall focus on psychosocial assessment **before sentencing**, essentially in the Anglo-Saxon tradition, where the experience is greatest and the scientific research most plentiful; **subsequently**, we shall turn to continental Europe. We shall see, as we discuss the subject of personality, the difficulty of introducing psychosocial assessment before sentencing, and we shall then consider psychosocial assessment in the prison system, where it has played an important role. We did not think there was any point in devoting a chapter to "the risk of recidivism", as this concept will be encountered in both parts of the report in connection with the question of psychosocial intervention.

Assessment before sentencing (the pre-sentence report) with special reference to the Anglo-Saxon tradition

Anglo-Saxon countries have a considerable advantage in that criminal trials are divided into two phases: a finding as to guilt, followed by determination of the nature and severity of the sentence. In these circumstances, psychosocial assessment, (social inquiry report prior to sentencing) naturally has its place at the beginning of the second phase, avoiding possible objections to the "assessment" of a person not yet found guilty.[2] Another reason for the "advantage" is that the practice of probation, already an old-established one, naturally necessitated **psychosocial assessment prior to the verdict**, as a choice had to be made between two measures: probation and imprisonment. This part of the report has two sections: in the first, we shall set the scene with a general discussion on the scope of the pre-sentence report; in the second, we shall endeavour to review the literature relating to this theme.

A.   **General discussion: Psychosocial assessment, between a concept based on help/supervision and one based on diagnosis/treatment**

1.   The **Criminal Justice Act** of 1948 introduced a change of perspective; earlier, the probation accent had been on help and supervision. Under the influence of developments in clinical criminology, which enhanced the standing of the diagnosis/treatment policy (between 1945 and 1965), the pre-sentence report became a true psychosocial assessment including a study of the offender's personality. The instructions found in various circulars since 1948 (Thorpe, 1979) show that the report should contain information on the subject's character, personality and social and family background. It should also provide information on the educational establishments attended by the subject, his pattern of employment and any plans regarding training and employment. Lastly, it should also provide information on the offender's family and friends, so as to give the court an idea of the influence they might have had on his criminal career. Very briefly, going along with Bottoms and Williams (1984), one might say that such a report fits in with the diagnosis/treatment policy.

2.   At the time when this policy was being very much called into question by the results of probation, which were considered inconclusive, Bottoms and Williams (1984) carried out a particularly critical analysis. According to them, the term "diagnosis", commonly used by the proponents of casework, is based on the idea that sufficient causal explanations can be found for human behaviour; on the other hand, the term "treatment" implies a belief that such causes can be manipulated so as to change someone's behaviour. The result of these two assertions, which are debatable, is that the client is under the impression that he has been relieved of any responsibility for his act; in addition, the concept of "choice" or "free will", a presupposition for probation work, becomes ambiguous and contradictory.[3]

Their criticism of the pre-sentence report based on the diagnosis/treatment paradigm continues: it contains, they claim, constant references to personal traits, such as: "The client is an anxious, immature person".

26

The probation officer no doubt has the impression that he has made an objective judgement relating to a personality trait (especially if he uses the results of psychological tests). In fact, it is a moral judgement, perceived as such by the subject and by the other parties (judge and social workers). Such "judgements" place the subject in a position of dependency or rebellion and confuse the other protagonists. This criticism undoubtedly raises the question of a "psychological language" that is difficult for a layman to understand and interpret.

What should be in a pre-sentence report? According to these two authors, one should revert to the earlier period, when the emphasis was placed on help and supervision. The language of the report should be detailed and precise, and should refer to the subject as a real person, living in the real world (ie without interpretations, which are always debatable). The best way of preventing the client from re-offending is to help him to achieve a stable situation. For such help to exist, firstly the client has to request it, and secondly it has to take an extremely tangible form. The pre-sentence report should therefore be prepared with the client and envisage such forms of help. It may possibly point to alternatives to prison: day training centres, adult probation hostels, etc (the directors of such establishments will be more willing to play a part than they would be if the intervention was presented to them as "treatment"). At the end of the report, the probation officer may make recommendations. However, these should be agreed beforehand, implying that the client is willing to co-operate in their implementation. In the authors' view, it is important to confront the subject with a choice. If he chooses the solution which allows him to remain at liberty, he has to go along with the form of help thus organised. If he does not wish to do so, he may "opt for" prison. As one can see, the concepts of "help", "responsibility" and "commitment" are all involved. It should be added, however, that the approach of Bottoms and Williams is valid for only part of the offender population. In dealing with offenders, one still has to make an important distinction (Bottoms, 1977): in the case of minor offences, one can apply alternative measures, with assessment linked to the idea of help and with an attempt to involve the offender; in the case of what are described as "violent" crimes, one has to think in terms of imprisonment and the risk of recidivism.

3.   The ambiguity of psychological language and the resulting uncertainties involved in interpreting it indeed constitute a problem. Nevertheless, such an assertion does not resolve matters. The important question is whether the person drafting the report sees himself as an "expert" or as a "mediator" between the different protagonists. In the latter case, he must take particular care to ensure that his report and conclusions are comprehensible. Thus information on the **responsiveness** of the subject, whatever the factors to which it is linked, constitutes a **reality** which it would be difficult to ignore in every case. Nevertheless, the personality questionnaires that are frequently used call for comment. They generally contain a number of questions to which the subject must reply. For example, "Do you have more difficulties in life than other people? Yes/No". The questions are divided into categories and, on the basis of the replies given, scores are arrived at for these categories (eg neurosis, extroversion, immaturity, autism, etc). The results obtained in this way are "objective" in the sense that they are based on assessments made directly by the subject. Yet such results are also subjective, in the sense that the subject is presenting his own perspective on the

various questions put to him, and this perspective is inevitably coloured by the conditions of the test, the context as a whole (is the subject simply a defendant or already a convicted prisoner?), his understanding of language, his past experience, etc (Debuyst, 1989). It must also be said that the categories within which the questions are grouped (neurosis, extroversion, etc) are **constructs** whose validity is always debatable. If used in a certain way, adjectives like "immature" and "anxious" strike the person concerned as an abuse of authority or as a "judgement". Despite the criticisms expressed by Bottoms and Williams, such questionnaires are still interesting. The replies are "ways of reacting" which the subject understands. Within the framework of a clinical relationship, the overall results or scores should be **broken down** in order to see, together with the subject, the types of reaction which he is displaying in certain situations and to discuss them with him. They yield "useful information" that makes it possible to pinpoint the "ways of being" revealed by the replies and to take them into account in the organisation of help with a view to achieving at the "social stability" of which the two authors speak.[4] That is why it is difficult to disregard any psychological or psychiatric information. The problem is to decide how such information should be used.

B.   **The pre-sentence report and its application; review of the literature**

This review relates to pre-sentence reports as envisaged in the Criminal Justice Act of 1948. The question of sentencing will inevitably arise, as will that of the role played by the pre-sentence report in the sentencing process.[5] Moreover, it should be noted that we shall not take into account the changes brought about by the statutory provisions introduced in Great Britain in 1990 and 1991, to which only a brief paragraph will be devoted.

1.   **Number of cases in which a pre-sentence report is requested, account taken by judges of the recommendations made and usefulness of the reports**

A report drawn up years ago and covering 453 cases before one court[6] between 1955 and 1960 showed that pre-sentence reports were submitted in 74 % of cases; 20 % contained no recommendations (Bottemley, 1973). Since that time the number of reports has increased considerably, partly because of the increase in crime. In 1981 Hall Williams recorded an annual total of 250,000, to be seen against the 500,000 serious offences dealt with by the courts each year. According to this information, probation officers spent one quarter of their time drafting such reports (Hall Williams, 1981), which might explain why even at that time the system was "over stretched". The overall figures should not hide the fact that the demand for pre-sentence reports varies, depending on the offence and on how necessary judges consider them. In his survey of motoring offences, R Hood (1972) noted that a pre-sentence report was requested only in 2.7 % of cases, or in 17 % of cases involving one of the four "major" offences.[7] This does not mean that, in the case of such offences, judges did not acknowledge that personality traits might be at work: in the survey, 30 % of them said that people who drove while under the influence of alcohol or failed to stop after an accident had an "unstable personality" or "emotional problems" (Hood, 1972). However, the consensus among judges is that both the proper administration of justice and the interests of the offenders require cases to be settled rapidly and that detailed examination would therefore not be helpful.

In most pre-sentence reports, the probation officer makes suggestions. The authors note that judges take up these suggestions in 75 to 85 % of cases (cf Bottemley, 1973; Thorpe, 1978). However, regional surveys have found, in certain circumstances, sudden slumps in judges' confidence in pre-sentence reports (cf Marsland, 1977, quoted by Thorpe). Moreover, differences may arise depending on whether cases are serious or not, or whether the judges are from "town" or "country" (cf Hogarth, 1971). Another angle to consider is whether the courts, after taking a decision without a pre-sentence report, tend to change it once they become aware of the report's contents. One study (cf Hood and Taylor, 1968) showed that 44 out of 92 cases involving changes, resulting in an increase in the number of probation orders and a decrease in the number of fines and prison sentences. A request that the judges explain the changes did not produce very clear replies.[8]

The answer to the question of whether the existence of pre-sentence reports has helped to make probation a success has varied over time: surveys carried out between 1955 and 1960 gave positive findings. Where the judge followed a recommendation of probation, the success rate was 80 %. Where the report recommended imprisonment, but the judge nevertheless decided to order probation (as happened in 13 % of cases), probation was successful in 50 % of cases. Where no pre-sentence report had been drawn up and the judge decided to order probation (as happened in 11 % of cases), probation had a 46 % success rate (Jarvis, 1965, quoted by Bottemley, 1973, page 165). Later evaluations were less positive: an increase in the number of pre-sentence reports led neither to a marked fall in recidivism, nor to a decline in the number of offenders in prison (Hood, 1966; Davies, 1974), indicating that neither objective was met.

2.   Information sought and information used by judges

Research in the countries of the Anglo-Saxon tradition casts serious doubt on the idea that the purpose of the psychosocial report is (or should be) to bring together all the information that is objectively desirable in order to understand the offender and his behaviour, irrespective of the prevailing conditions and the reasons for compiling the report.

Most authors agree that the amount of information used is **small**. Social psychologists state that, in the reaching of a decision, only a few factors can be taken into account at any one time, and that the events immediately preceding the decision, which are clear in the mind, therefore assume special importance (Fitzmaurice, 1986).

The information considered **essential** by a majority of judges includes the **offender's** family background, previous offences and employment history. It also includes the way in which **offences** were planned and premeditated (Hogarth, 1971).

As for the priorities given to these various types of information, a great majority of judges, whatever their approach to crime and sentencing, consider that greater weight should be attached to the offender's criminal record than to his background or life history. Judges with different approaches require equally full information, but of different types: judges whose concern is for offenders to be rehabilitated are more discriminating and demanding in their requests for information about the offender (family and social background, life history, etc), whereas those taking a punitive approach do not regard information about family background as essential. They show a need instead for information about everything concerning the offence itself (seriousness of personal injury, sense of guilt, the offender's attitude towards his act, etc) (Hogarth, 1971). As for the types of information used by probation officers in substantiating their recommendations, although they were the same, Wilkins did not find the underlying patterns of thinking to be the same: each had his own personal approach and style. A later survey (Gottfredson, Wilkins and Hofman, 1978) found that the type of offence and the offender's criminal record were virtually always taken into account; 80 % of probation officers took account of psychological and psychiatric data, and 70 % took account of statements made by the offender. Then came the subject's attitude, his employment history, etc (Gottfredson, 1990). Thus, the judges and probation officers dealing with the same cases have different views as to what kinds of information are useful. As can be seen, each professional group within the penal system has its own perspective; when considering a particular policy, this is an important variable which must be taken into account (cf Mair, 1990).

3.   **Statutory provisions in England in 1990 and 1991**

In the light of the facts which we have just recalled, it is possible to understand the important changes brought about by new statutory legal provisions (Green paper, **Punishment and supervision in the community**, HMSO, 1990, and Criminal Justice Act 1991). In the first place, there has been a change in the contents of the pre-sentence report, where the principal consideration is no longer rehabilitation or assistance, but the fairness of the decision taken by the judge (the penalty imposed must be commensurate with the seriousness of the offence). In accordance with the wishes of certain judges, the report must now therefore include information about the offence and the offender's attitude to it and about any expressed desire of the offender to mend his ways. Also, the report must contain a detailed programme of supervision and spell out the means by which the desired result is to be achieved. This presupposes a detailed knowledge of judicial practice and of the resources available, as well as a readiness to take them into account. Under the new provisions, account must also be taken of the possibility of incidents likely to jeopardise public safety (Wasik and Taylor, 1991). The probation officer is no longer expected to make recommendations. He presents information to the judge, who weighs it up; the value of the information lies in the fact that it enables the judge to decide whether it would be justified to sentence the offender to a term of imprisonment. The psychosocial report must therefore take into account the (very concrete) reasoning in which the judge will engage in that connection in each case.[9]

4.   Pre-sentence assessment, risk of recidivism, and psychosocial intervention

In this context the question of recidivism risk inevitably arises, although it is only indirectly connected with our theme and we shall touch on it only in connection with the subject of psychosocial intervention.

a.   We shall start by briefly considering two more general questions. The idea of the recidivism risk associated with an individual is giving way to that of the recidivism risk associated with a category of offences or individuals. With many approaches, the recidivism risk is no longer determined through examination of the individual but in the light of the type of offence or individual involved and of whether measures such as incapacitation are appropriate (cf Von Hirsch, Cohen, etc, quoted by Nikolopoulos, 1993). This question does not interest us directly, although the trend described is a very clear one. What we are interested in is the studies that are being done on delinquent careers and on the probability of a subject's embarking on or persisting in such a delinquent career (high-risk subjects). Previous offences, especially those committed at an early age, are regarded as being very important pointers to the future. In addition, many authors have compiled groups of characteristics as a basis for making predictions about future offences. One such author is Farrington (1992), who considers this method to provide a very effective tool for dealing with different age groups. The following should be taken into account: the age of the subject; his intelligence; the audacity that he displays; whether he has parents with a criminal record; his standard of early education. The question is whether information relating to such points (or factors such as traits suggesting a criminal personality) can be used as a check-list for identifying subjects likely to embark on a delinquent career. As emphasised by Farrington, this question raises that of the underlying theory. The answer will be "yes" if the theory interprets the subject's delinquent career as the expression of delinquent potential that becomes apparent very early and manifests itself directly in action. The answer will be more cautious, and account will be taken of circumstantial data, if a different meaning is given to the delinquent career: very often, an offence committed at an early age paves the way for subsequent offences; also, offences tend to become more serious, the offender becomes branded as a criminal, etc. The correlation between antisocial personal traits at different ages is not very high: only half of antisocial children become antisocial adults (Farrington, 1992). For that reason, one should try to identify those factors which may trigger such changes. Thus, in psychosocial assessment, when one is operating with the factors making up such predictive "models", it is important to know how to use them: should one simply use them for diagnostic purposes, in order to arrive at certain conclusions about the risk of further offences, or should one take them into account in the course of intervention on the grounds that they throw light on certain reactions which are likely to occur?

b.   This second approach is reflected in the results of research into the use of the concept of recidivism risk by probation officers

A study using a qualitative method (Dozois, Poupart and Lalonde, 1984), showed that the concept of recidivism risk was an important one for probation officers, who spontaneously rated their clients on a recidivism risk scale. The nature of the

31

offence and previous criminal record were the main factors in their "diagnosis". Repeated violence might denote either a malevolent disposition or a worsening of the problems that the subject was encountering. However, the nature of the offence and criminal record were not sufficient. It was important to see whether there was a pattern of violence, whether or not a subject was able to exercise some form of control. Psychiatric information, such as data relating to the personality, was also considered useful. The last important factor was the ability or the wish of the offender to mend his ways. The practitioners took the view that the offender would have a better chance of mending his ways if he had either the means of resolving his problems or the desire to change his behaviour appreciably, or both.

For them, the information collected became part of their practical knowledge; in and through their practical work they learned ways of handling specific problems. Even if a certain routine set in, the manner of proceeding varied from case to case, as negotiations were constantly taking place between the practitioners, the client, the other parties involved and the authorities. As far as they were concerned, therefore, the preparation of pre-sentence reports was not a "bureaucratic" activity as it was linked to a practical situation that required changes of attitude and involved the different protagonists in negotiations. A further study, also Canadian (Martel, 1990), mentions the development of a "tool" that enables probation officers to "measure" the risk associated with each offender — a questionnaire with 58 questions covering the key aspects of their future client's life (present and past lifestyle), the aim being to determine the degree of supervision needed by each offender. With a tool of this kind, one can actually predict the types of conflict likely to arise in real — as opposed to stereotyped — situations.

Continental Europe: the difficulty of introducing psychosocial assessment before sentencing and the priority given to assessment within the prison system.

The problem is that, since the Italian positivists, psychological and social assessment, in continental Europe has become firmly anchored within the prison system (ie after sentencing), the desire to organise pre-sentence assessment has encountered major obstacles which we think should be analysed.

A. **Personality evaluation before the verdict and the difficulties of taking it into consideration**

1. **The French experience with personality evaluation and its "non-development"**

France was, like Belgium, one of the countries where, between 1950 and 1960, the question of personality evaluation before the verdict was most hotly debated[10] — in connection with the introduction of probation to the penal system.[11] The discussions led to Article 81 of the new French Code of Criminal Procedure (1958). This article allowed the investigating judge to "carry out, or have carried out, an enquiry into the personality of the accused and his material, family and social situation". Personality evaluation was thus clearly provided for. For criminologists, this was a way of taking scientific data into criminal proceedings and determining the sentence most appropriate to the subject's rehabilitation (Ancel, 1981).[12]

Under Article 81, a personality evaluation was optional in the case of a misdemeanour ("délit"), seeming to suggest that it was mandatory in the case of a felony ("crime"). However, the Court of Cassation pointed out that Article 81 did not constitute an exception to the basic rule that investigating judges had a right and duty to close an investigation once they deemed it to be complete (Silvert et al, 1992; Durviaux et al, 1992).[13] It may thus be said that non-application of Article 81 means that the investigating judge does not consider a personality assessment necessary and that the trial court finds that it has sufficient information. A survey by Mrs Coppard-Briton of recourse to Article 81 in the district of the Rennes Court of Appeal between 1961 and 1967 showed that judges ordered personality evaluation in only 10 % of serious criminal cases at the investigatory stage, and that only 7 to 8 % of these files contained a medico-psychological report (Moutin, 1979). There are numerous reasons besides the resistance of judges for what Pinatel has called the "non-development or downgrading of assessment" (Pinatel, 1981). Moreover, Pinatel underlines the paradox that, just when personality evaluation became possible and the nature of it was specified, criminological theory, under the influence of "interactionism" and "anticriminology", cast doubt on the very principle. In our opinion, this situation cannot be explained by the grey areas in criminological theory.

2.   **The difficulties experienced by psychologists responsible for assessments before the verdict**

Besides resistance on the part of judges, and no doubt of certain theoreticians, personality assessment has brought problems for many psychiatrists and psychologists. We shall see this at two levels: in the discussion of what personality assessment implies with regard to professional ethics and treatment; and, more broadly, in the relationship between psychiatric reports and personality assessments. The relationship between the two has always been ambiguous. The situation in this respect is very different from that found in the countries of the Anglo-Saxon tradition.

a.   **Personality assessment raises a question of professional ethics and integration into the penal system**

We find this clearly expressed by Dr De Greeff (1957), who from the very outset questioned the ability of the penal system, as it exists, to realistically take into account personality reports: "A properly performed personality assessment would in practice be unusable by the judge (...) As it gets to grips with the offender's true personality, the assessment will reveal the complexity of that personality and will become uncertain and hesitant. A judge, especially a competent judge, knows that when taking a decision he cannot commit himself as regards the future and must be able to change his mind — which, in the penal system, is virtually impossible. Irrespective of this "capacity" of the system, De Greeff considers that it is impossible, even in a two-stage trial (eg in Great Britain), to present a really thorough medico-psychological and social assessment, for such an assessment places the defendant in a situation of great inferiority vis-à-vis the court. One might well say that, given the intimacy of the details which it contains, it would be damaging to anyone. De Greeff said that one should make do with an assessment that is fairly simple but sufficient, in most cases, to bring out the essential points. The same difficulty arose in Italy when consideration was given to the idea of having, besides the psychiatric assessment, a **criminological assessment** of the defendant's personality as regards psychological characteristics not attributable to pathological causes. The promoter of the idea, Prof Pisapia, has had doubts about it: given the amount of information which would have to be gathered, could such an assessment be made before the decision as to guilt or innocence was taken? (Pisapia, 1981).

b.   **Questioning the diagnosis/treatment relationship**

Here again, the matter is not straightforward. We shall refer primarily to Dr M Colin, who stated his position by taking as his starting point a definition of clinical criminology which is rather unusual: "clinical criminology concerns interaction with the offender, with his sociopathic background and with the authorities and bodies assuming responsibility for him" (1961). In other words, he did not embrace the idea of an assessment based on personality characteristics revealing how the offender came to commit the offence. In more general terms, the important question was whether the professional was an **expert** asked by society to provide an expert opinion or, on the contrary, someone who, through being in contact with the accused and with the authorities or bodies responsible for him, became a **mediator** between these various parties (Colin, 1973). He adopted the latter position, adding two ideas: (a) that "the emphasis laid on personality disorders is legitimate only in so far as a sociological analysis is an essential complement prompting awareness of collective responsibilities"; (b) that the concept of diagnosis (or preliminary assessment) should be challenged, since generally speaking "anything which precedes therapy is an obstacle to therapy". This did not mean that the problem of diagnosis did not arise. It meant instead that its function "is not to be a preliminary step, but rather to accompany the subject throughout therapy". At this point he quoted Dr Diatkine, according to whom "the therapist should not feel bound in the conduct of treatment by any plan derived from preliminary assessments; what he discovers day by day can be deduced from a preliminary diagnosis, however carefully made. Each structure achieves a balance in many ways, depending on the effects of the object and narcissistic cathexis, on the situations modifying this cathexis and on the many steps taken by the subject to avoid (or provoke) dangerous situations" (quoted by Colin, 1973). That really questions the logical connection between preliminary diagnosis and intervention.

c.   **The ambiguous relationship between psychiatric report and personality assessment**

In France, within the framework of Article 81, the distinction between the two appears at first sight to be very clear. The **psychiatric report** seeks to determine the criminal responsibility of its subject; the **personality assessment** seeks to throw light on the defendant's personality provides information as a basis for both understanding the defendant's motives and devising a method of treatment (Leyrie, 1977).[14]

On reflection, however, the situation is less clear. P Moutin (1979) emphasised that judges became confused in particular by the fact that, with the 1958 Code of Criminal Procedure, the standard question of responsibility was superseded by a set of broader questions: "Does the psychiatric and psychological assessment of the subject reveal mental or psychological abnormalities? If so, describe them and state to what disorders they are related. Is the offence with which he is charged related to such abnormalities? Is his condition dangerous? Is the subject amenable to a sentence imposed by the court? Can the subject be cured or rehabilitated?" (Moutin, 1979). With this broadening of the field, judges could not see any clear difference between psychiatric report and personality assessment. In making little use of Article 81, they appeared not to want to change their habits and confined their attention to the problem of responsibility proper (Moutin, 1979). Here again we see the importance of a variable which the Anglo-Saxons stress: judges' acceptance of new ideas (Mair, 1990).

On the other hand, many psychiatrists also have a critical attitude. What they are required to do in preparing their reports locks them "into a web of specific watertight questions, on a subject made up of parts which overlap and coincide" (Thys and Korn, 1992a). In practice, two attitudes manifest themselves amongst psychiatrists: some are willing to prepare reports, and adopt traditional psychiatric methods as being the only approach that the courts understand; others refuse to do so, and at the same time, avoid all contact with the courts (Rasch, 1981). A Belgian study of 261 reports prepared by 22 psychiatrists between 1965 and 1975 (Thys and Korn, 1992a, 1992b) confirms this, emphasising the traditional nature of the reports, which were based on a logic that was nosographic, causal and linear, and in which family determinisms dominate" — in other words, the reports were prepared on "positivist" lines. Two questions arise: should there not be a brief psychiatric report covering essential points ("obvious" mental illness that rules out a trial), and should the problem of responsibility be left out, for there are few who accept that a firm line can be drawn between the normal and the pathological (Rasch, 1981)? This points once again to the ambiguous relationship between psychiatric report and psychosocial assessment.

d.   Psychiatric report, criminological assessment and underlying social problems

A fourth difficult point concerns the underlying social problems. Let us consider Italian legislation. Under the old 1930 Code, a psychiatric report, as well as covering issues of responsibility, could raise the question of recidivism risk, but only if the existence of an actual "disorder" was stated. This necessarily meant that any information on the accused's character, criminal habits or personality was excluded (Canepa, 1981). The inclusion of such information in the personality report or criminological assessment may therefore be regarded as a step forward. However, owing to the way in which such assessments have to be carried out, they tend to increase the unfairness of the penal system (Bandini, 1981).

Studies carried out in Genoa on 260 cases of murder or attempted murder between 1961 and 1975 showed, on the one hand, that many psychiatrists were reluctant to state that someone was "a threat to society", restricting their assessments to "the ability to understand and to want to do something" (ie the problem of responsibility), and, on the other, that judges requested assessments following such offences far more frequently in the case of the well-to-do than in that of poor people.[15] Introducing a criminological assessment (in addition to the psychiatric assessment) would result in the social classes not "covered" by the psychiatric assessment being singled out for a criminological assessment based on the idea of recidivism risk, which would be a way of bringing a particular form of social control to bear on these classes (Bandini, 1981). This is a final point to be borne in mind.

We add, at the end of this general survey, the critical remarks with which Moutin and Bernard (1983) concluded their paper: "Like the American N Morris, we regret the fact that the psychiatrist (like the psychologist on many occasions)[16] is not properly used in the criminal justice system, being used more in diagnosis than in treatment", and they add that one of the preconditions for remedying the inadequacies of the past system is "greater and better participation by the subject".

B. **Psychosocial assessment as a continuous process; the transfer of information from one authority to another within the penal system**

From French experience it seemed obvious that a personality assessment before sentencing should produce a body of information that would follow an accused/sentenced person through the penal system — including the prison system, where it was important to have information available quickly (Pinatel, 1981). The problem had already arisen in Great Britain: in principle, the pre-sentence report, although written at the request of the court, served as a source of information for other bodies. It was important that the person writing the report should bear these **hypothetical** addressees in mind, the court judge being only the first user.[17]

The problem is how to select information that will be useful to the "hypothetical addressee" who will eventually decide about conditional release. In more general terms, how to select and handle the information in such a way that it is put to optimum use throughout the process. Two approaches would appear to be practicable: the first was suggested by the American authors Gottfredson and Gottfredson (1990) and the second has been adopted in the Netherlands (Blankevoort, 1990).

a. In order to introduce a measure of consistency where inconsistency generally reigns, Gottfredson et al suggest that all psychosocial assessments should contain the same core of information useful to all potential users. That would be the standard part of the report; the other parts would be left to the writer's discretion. The standard part should focus on the likely risks associated with the subject (violent or suicidal behaviour). By way of example, they list the following questions (taken from a prison file): Has the subject had serious health problems? Is there a drug or alcohol problem? Does the subject appear to have had any serious physical disability? Has the subject displayed particular emotional problems? In other words, it is a matter of throwing light on likely "abnormal" reactions, the "normal" person being defined as having an ability to see things in an objective light and to act accordingly (De Greeff, 1931). However, this approach of Gottfredson and Gottfredson entails one difficulty: it should not be forgotten that a court or prison environment is in itself "abnormal" in respect of the adjustments it demands of the people in contact with it. If "normal ability to react" is taken as a criterion, therefore, it is important to remember the rule laid down by the German psychiatrist K. Schneider (1955): the "normality" of a reaction should be seen in relation to the characteristics of the environment concerned; "An **abnormal** reaction to a **normal** situation must not be confused with a **normal** reaction to an **abnormal** situation". Obviously, the prison environment (or, more generally, the judicial environment) is "abnormal".

b. A **second** approach, adopted in the Dutch system, is to make the rehabilitation officer responsible for conveying information from one environment to the other.[18] The writing of the pre-sentence report is then the first stage in a relationship between officer and "client" continuing throughout the penal process, in which the former takes into account the diversity of the environments concerned (Blankevoort, 1990). "The relationship with the rehabilitation officer becomes established during the police investigation. If need be, he accompanies his "client" both before the public prosecutor

37

and the investigating judge. If the term of imprisonment is lengthy, he maintains contact within the prison, possibly with a view to preparing a report designed to secure release on parole". The relationship (between rehabilitation officer and prisoner) is one of confidence based on mutual effort: the prisoner must accept certain demands imposed on him from outside, and the rehabilitation officer must be able to negotiate solutions with the judge, the public prosecutor's office, etc, with the agreement of his "client". We talk here of a field of manoeuvre or an "inter-system", based on a relationship of assistance, in which the "client" plays an active part and in which the pre-sentence report effectively constitutes only a first step (Blankevoort, 1990). Under this arrangement, the pre-sentence report contains a certain amount of initial information known to the "client" and which may change during the process of interaction, in which the rehabilitation officer really does play the role of a mediator — and to some extent an "external" mediator. One can well imagine, however, that such a position raises problems in the case of an administration trying to rationalise and harmonise its procedures.[19]

C.   Psychosocial assessment in the prison context

On the initiative of Ferri and Lombroso, prisons became (or were destined to become) veritable "anthropological laboratories". Lombroso had already raised the question as to how conditional release could be effected and prisons be successfully run unless a study was made of individual crimes. As early as 1917, the Belgian psychiatrist Vervaeck had created anthropological laboratories in Belgian prisons, effectively turning them into places where crime could be dealt with rationally and effectively (Pinatel, 1963). It was in this setting that some of our present clinical knowledge was acquired (particularly between 1930 and 1960). This tradition, derived from the Italian positivists, is attributable to the fact that until the 1950s it was considered that the percentage of prison inmates with psychological problems was higher and[21] that individual care was accordingly called for. Subsequently medico-psychological and social assessment came to be regarded as a necessity given the recognised right of prisoners to be helped to re-establish themselves in society. This idea is expressed in Resolution (73) 5 of the Council of Europe Committee of Ministers on standard minimum rules for the treatment of prisoners: "As soon as possible after admission and after a study of the personality of each prisoner with a sentence of suitable length, a programme of treatment shall be prepared for him in the light of the knowledge obtained about his individual needs, his capacities and dispositions". (**Human rights in prisons**, Council of Europe, 1986, page 183). The same text also provides that "Prisoners shall be involved in the drawing up of their individual treatment programmes" and that "The programmes should be periodically reviewed." It must be admitted that in many countries the reality falls short of this ideal. On this issue we can only comment briefly and possibly make reference to other reports.

a.   Assessment and programme of treatment

The need for medico-psychological and social assessment has been met in different ways. In some countries, the response has been to send offenders, particularly those convicted of serious offences, to a national centre for an opinion in the light of which they can then be transferred to prisons with an appropriate regime; in Italy, this is Rome-Rebibbia (inaugurated in 1955); in France, the Centre d'observation at Fresnes, etc. In other countries, such as Belgium, every prison of any size has an "anthropological laboratory", since 1960 renamed assessment and treatment unit. Reviewing the different arrangements for medical, psychological and social assessment, whether it be Rome-Rebibbia, Fresnes, the Belgian prisons unit or — subsequently in Belgium — the Centre d'observation pénitentiaire (Dr De Waele), one finds that the aim is **either** to obtain as much information as possible in all areas (psychiatric, psychological and social) (with regard to Rome-Rebibbia, see Michiels, 1957) **or** to develop, on a sound methodological and theoretical basis, a tool that will yield the most detailed and most enlightening information about the offender. The assessment form that was developed by Dr E De Greeff and used in all Belgian prisons was based on a study of different psychological functions (intellectual, emotional, volitional) with a view to understanding what kind of outlet the individual offender found in the offence committed by him (De Greeff, 1955), while the assessment record developed by Dr De Waele was built around the offender's life history (De Waele, 1975). The scope of the investigations created problems: apart from the decisions to be taken within the prison context, such assessments served a mainly scientific purpose. Their most positive feature was that they constituted the framework for a type of clinical criminology which subsequently led to a more discriminating, less simplified view of delinquent behaviour.

Apart from this approach, with assessment being the major activity of the medico-psychological centres operating within the prison context, what is left? One ought really to make a further exhaustive study of what is happening in different countries. In any event, it would seem that the situation falls far short of fulfilling the aims set by Resolution (73) 5 and mentioned above.

As part of a general approach, assessment no longer seems to be the necessary starting point for all intervention. The punitive policy has undoubtedly become the predominant one. In addition, however, the most interesting initiatives often take place outside the assessment framework or use assessment only as a back-up (therapy or various activities). Besides these shifts, resources are much scarcer than they used to be, so that the work often consists merely of responding to urgent requests (still an important activity). There are several reasons for this: staff cuts, increasing numbers of prisoners, changes within the prison population (which now includes a not inconsiderable percentage of people imprisoned on drug-related charges, so that different approaches are needed). Problems of prison management (where the prisoners are only one factor) assume major importance. In this context the systematic use of psychosocial assessment might once again make sense in the preparation of prisoners for release, to the extent that such preparation consists essentially of resolving, on the initiative of the subject and with his cooperation, the various problems which ought to be solved before he is released (family, job, psychological, financial and other problems). Some authors have spoken in this connection of socio-clinical assessment focusing on the prisoner's release (see G Houchoun, J François et al, 1977). It must be admitted, however, that such an approach is difficult to implement as it arouses considerable resistance in the prison context — resistance not only on the part of the institution and the prison staff, but also on the part of the prisoners themselves (cf Gibbons; 1986, Debuyst, 1988). An analysis of these questions lies outside the scope of this paper.

b.   Conditional release and predictive tables

The final type of psychosocial assessment concerns the probability of recidivism after conditional release. On the whole, it is recognised that tables for predicting behaviour after release have never given satisfactory results (cf Quisey; 1984, Lievens, 1981), one reason being that the recidivism risk is generally over-estimated. The recent work of Webster et al (1985) and Gabor (1986) have not shed much new light on the subject.[21]

Independently of this general question, a comparison has been made in this area of **the effectiveness of forecasts based on clinical diagnosis and that of forecasts which might be described as statistical** (based on criteria deemed relevant). The latter appear to give more accurate predictions. Numerous studies have brought this out, and a more recent one confirmed it (Hassin, 1986): the error rate for forecasts based on clinical diagnosis was 44.9 %, compared to 30 % for those based on the statistical method. The error rate for forecasts based on clinical diagnosis was higher in the case of positive forecasts than for negative ones. This weakness would appear to lie in the fact that the clinician does not take into account enough the type of population group to which the subject belongs and which he will inevitably encounter again after his release. Moreover, clinicians appear to have a more tolerant attitude towards certain social categories: women, prisoners of western origin (Europe and North America) and people with a high cultural level. On the other hand, decisions based on statistical predictive tables disregard such individual factors and therefore appear to be fairer. However, there is reluctance to use such tables unreservedly, for the error rate is still 30 % (made up principally of inaccurate positive forecasts) and, as they do not take individual factors into account, forecasts based on them may overlook the influence of an important variable that a clinical investigation would easily reveal.

Which variables give the most accurate predictions? The best indicators of recidivism are those which relate to the period before imprisonment: age; previous convictions; type of offence; age at first conviction (Goffredson et al, 1990). Hassin (1986) found such variables to be discriminatory; those supposed to be more psychological (personality characteristics) or sociological (social environment) were in reality correlated with those regarded as discriminatory, so they might very well not be taken into account (if the only purpose was to predict recidivism). One interesting question is whether conduct in prison is a good pointer to behaviour after release. According to Gottfredson et al (1990), research carried out by O'Leary and Gasler shows only a tenuous connection between indiscipline in prison and behaviour after release. However, an important qualification is necessary here: there was a lack of correlation mainly in the case of first-time prisoners; among recidivists, 58 % of those whose behaviour in prison was negative re-offended after release, whereas for those whose conduct was reported as positive the figure was only 38 % (p. 253). The relationship between conduct in prison and behaviour after release is therefore difficult to interpret[22], for the progress possibly made during a prison term is of debatable value in that the subjects fall back into their former habits or attitudes once they have returned to the previous social situation. It is therefore really essential to take the subject's social environment into account, especially if support is to be given on conditional release.

General conclusions

1.   As part of a policy of psychosocial intervention, assessment as traditionally conceived is very much in question. This is not just because crime policy has been dominated by a repressive tendency for the past twenty years and would appear to be less concerned with rehabilitation. It is also because the "assessment-diagnosis-decision on treatment" model of which it was a part no longer appears fully appropriate. Other models have assumed a certain importance (help/supervision, just desserts). This does not mean that psychosocial assessment is no longer of interest, but its scope and content have been changed.

2.   Moreover, the idea of assessment creates the impression that the subject is being turned into a "passive object" of examination and investigation. This type of relationship may make sense if the subject sees the value of the investigations, and if these yield information that is useful to practitioners (it has been found that probation officers attach considerable importance to psychiatric and psychological information). It must not be forgotten, however, that the transfer of the information is not a simple matter and that the conclusions which may be drawn from it are rarely obvious: the results of psychological tests represent "reconstructions" and, by that very fact, involve a degree of interpretation.

3.   It would seem, therefore, that such information is rather an input for the various protagonists in a policy of interaction based particularly on the idea of the offender's involvement in the solutions proposed to him within the penal system (with the possibility of his refusal to become involved, which does not mean an end to the interaction). This idea of involvement or participation, which has been frequently stressed, is based on the fact that punishment makes sense only if it is accepted and that an assistance programme can be effective only if the subject participates in it.

4.   If we compare the Anglo-Saxon tradition with the tradition of continental Europe, we find that in the former psychosocial assessment (with the pre-sentence report) takes place before the verdict and that, following substantial research into judges' use of such reports, the emphasis has been placed on the need to transmit information which will enable the judge to justify, with full knowledge of the facts, the decision taken (alternative measures or imprisonment) — and to do so taking into account the possibilities effectively available to him. In continental Europe, where psychosocial assessment has not become established before sentencing and generally takes place in the prison context, it has emerged more clearly as a form of scientific inquiry or research directed towards obtaining knowledge of the offender's personality and behaviour, with the advantages and drawbacks which such an attitude entails. Advantage: a more detailed knowledge of the offender's behaviour, which is not without importance. Drawback: a risk of irrelevance within the penal system and of being taken into account only cursorily or occasionally, even in the prison context.

5.   It would be interesting to consider the role of the new forms of "assessment" in the context of policies other than the one traditionally known as the "diagnosis-treatment" policy, which, at any rate, will keep its importance. It has to be recognised,

41

however, that the delinquent's "just deserts" are generally considered to be linked to the damage caused to society, other relevant elements of the situation being neglected. It would therefore be important to take more seriously account of the delinquent's perceptions as well as of the psychological mechanisms which influence the terms in which problems of responsibility and its attribution are formulated (as is the case, inter alia, in social psychology and attribution theory).

NOTES

1   This report relates only to adult offenders, and not to minors. Similarly, we confine ourselves to "normal" adults and make only occasional references to psychiatric reports.

2   This argument is not decisive. However, in England pre-sentence reports may be drawn up before the trial, on the initiative of the probation service (cf Thorpe, 1979, page 9; Hall Williams, 1981, page 120), and, although this happens far less frequently, the content of such reports is no different from that of reports prepared at the second stage of the trial. In addition, the fact that criminal trials are not divided into two phases has not prevented the Dutch rehabilitation service from using pre-sentence reports (cf Lamers, 1950).

3   The authors add that treatment cannot truly be focused on the client (or felt by the client to be focused on himself): the diagnosis concerning his personality is made without his opinion really being asked, and the treatment flows from the diagnosis as an inevitable consequence (page 218).

4   This is also a way of avoiding esoteric language or an interpretation whose meaning may not be obvious to those who must use the report. The following are some of the specific charges levelled by judges against pre-sentence reports (cf Hogarth, page 239): too long (20 %); too many technical terms (14 %); recommendations not sufficiently specific (11.5 %); too much information about the offender's childhood (8.5 %); not enough information about the facts (8.5 %), etc. The Belgian clinician E De Greeff (1953) has also touched on this question and spoke about his experience as a young physician-anthropologist at a main prison. He describes how terms like "schizoid", "paranoiac", "introversion", "biologico-social", etc, gave rise to sceptical and disagreeable remarks on the part of the staff, and how he had to use as few scientific terms as possible in his explanations, whereupon the staff became really interested. He concludes that assessments should be couched in language that is acceptable to people who are intelligent but not used to the jargon, and that reports should be drafted with a wide readership in mind but without a lowering of standards (page 602).

5   We are thus confronted with abundant literature which is not easy to manage and which, moreover, seems to wax poetical on a subject that has little to do with the most topical current issues. Other papers presented at this conference (particularly that of Mrs J Roberts) will go into greater detail.

6   The Cornwall Quarter Sessions.

7   That is to say, driving while banned from driving (temporary suspension of licence), driving while under the influence of alcohol, dangerous driving, and failure to stop after an accident.

8   We have here one of the key ideas of Fitzmaurice et al (1986): people have very limited access to their own mental processes (page 39); most of the time, they view the problem in terms of self-justification.

9   Much the same argument has been put forward by a Swiss jurist, Gisel-Gugnon (1978). At present, the question to be asked is whether the social and related sciences can provide information which will help in a system of justice that aims to heal to take positive measures taking into account the sense of justice of the social group, the victim and the offender (Debuyst, 1992).

10   See the special issue of the *Revue de droit pénal et de criminologie* (Journal of Criminal Law and Criminology) on personality assessment (1951), the proceedings of the *Cycle européen de Bruxelles* on the same subject (1952), the *first course given by the Société internationale de criminologie*, Paris, (1952), and the first French criminology congress, Lyon (Collin et al, *Examen de personnalité en criminologie* (Personality Assessment in Criminology), published by Masson, Paris, 1960).

11   In France, 1958. In Belgium, 1964. It should be noted that the Belgian law on probation also called for social inquiry reports (cf Quarré, 1985).

12   Personality evaluation models were described which would take their place in a new type of criminal trial — cf the school of thought represented by Versele (1949). Any other school of thought, which involved a more thorough theoretical treatment, one finds the theory of criminal personality as developed by J Pinatel; this also seemed to provide a model which could serve as a basis for assessment before verdict, and certainly before treatment (cf Pinatel, 1963, 1989).

13   There were four similar judgments by the Court of Cassation in 1960, confirmed by a judgment of 7.11.1989. Some authors described this as the emasculation by the Supreme Court of the spirit of the reform (cf Pinatel, 1981, page 112).

14   One could offer another definition, given by a psychologist: in the execution of his task, the expert (psychologist) must do three things: determine personality characteristics (using tests), explain how the offender came to commit the offence, possibly in the light of those characteristics (ie enable the court to understand), and give advice (ie suggest ways of educating the offender so that he stops behaving in an antisocial manner) (C. Duflot-Fabori, 1988, page 69 et seq). Matters are complicated by the fact that the psychologist, as an auxiliary expert, may become involved either by taking part in the preparation of the psychiatric report (after the physician has called for additional examinations) or in the context of Article 81: preparation of a personality assessment report.

15   Judges requested an assessment in 87.5 % of cases involving subjects who had received higher education, in 62.1 % of cases of people with a certificate of secondary education and in only 34.8 % of cases for people who had a certificate of primary education or no educational qualifications (Bandini, 1981, page 85).

16   The comment in parentheses is the author's.

17   A questionnaire designed to determine whether the report was really used *after* the court verdict showed that this happened in 40 % of 521 cases. This implies that in almost one case in two the report served as a tool for several users (Thorpe, 1979).

18   We would point out that the rehabilitation services were initially private charitable organisations, so that the rehabilitation officer appeared to be outside the official judicial system (cf note 4).

19   A change in the system ended this possibility by bringing rehabilitation officers into an executive organ of the penal system, with a responsibility for drawing up social inquiry reports at the request of the Ministry of Justice and for ensuring that alternative measures were carried out. They lost the opportunity to give help at an early stage, which had enabled them to get to know subjects as soon as they entered the penal system and to organise the rehabilitation of prisoners on release. With regard to psychosocial assessment, the rehabilitation officer thus became an "expert", providing social inquiry reports, and lost his strategic position in the system which had allowed him to be a negotiator acting in his own right (cf Blankevoort, 1990). In the Netherlands, the pre-sentence report originated in the first quarter of the century, prompted by the wish of charitable organisations to help offenders to avoid prison sentences. To this end, the organisations used to prepare reasoned reports predicting offenders' rehabilitation prospects. The court officer would agree to suspend prosecution if the accused placed himself in the care of the rehabilitation organisation in question (cf Blankevoort, 1990).

20   A report of the Netherlands Prison Commission (1947) put the percentage at over 50 %, and as high as 80-90 % in the case of recidivists (Baan, 1953), which would seem to be extremely high and at odds with the subsequent impression gained regarding such persons.

21   See the criticisms made in the *British Journal of Criminology* by Monica Walker (1987, No. 2, page 231, and 1989, No. 1, page 29).

22   We draw attention to the conclusions of a study by Le Blanc (1983) on the effectiveness of the treatment in an institution for young offenders (Boscoville, Quebec). The value of the study lies in the fact that it was based on the use of a set of tests (primarily personality questionnaires) to which the young people were subjected on entering and leaving the establishment. There were marked improvements in various respects, so it was reasonable to believe that the period spent in the institution had had a positive influence on the subjects' personalities and on their psychological potential for integration. When the subjects were re-examined one and a half years after release, however, it was found both that the recidivism rate was relatively high and that the same personality tests showed the subjects to have fallen back to their initial scores for most of the traits covered.

BIBLIOGRAPHY

Baan P.A.H. (1953), L'examen médico-psychologique et social des délinquants, R.D.P. et Cr., n° 6, p. 583-592.

Bandini, T., (1981), L'évaluation de la dangerosité en psychiatrie légale, Ann. intern. de Crim., v. 19, n° 1-2, p. 81-90.

Blankevoort V. (1990), L'équilibre entre aide et surveillance. Où se situe la probation? L'intervention psychosociale au sein du pénal, 1re conférence intern. du CREPO, Ottawa.

Gisel-Bunion M. (1978), L'individualisation d'une peine mesurée sur la culpabilité du délinquant, Edit. Université, Genève.

Bottemley A.K. (1973), *Decision in the Penal Process*, London, Martin Robertson Edit.

Bottoms & Williams (1984), A non-treatment paradigm for probation practice, in Mc Anany, Thomson & Fogel, *Probation and Justice. Reconsideration of mission*, O.G.& H Publ., Cambridge, Mass., pp. 2O3-249.

Canepa G. (1981), L'expertise de la personnalité de l'inculpé, Ann. intern. de Crim, p. 11-20.

Carré Ph. (1985), Le dossier de la personnalité et la procédure pénale belge, La Criminologie au Prétoire, Faculté de Droit, U.L.B., Edit. Story, Bruxelles.

Colin M. (1961), Examen de personnalité et Criminologie, Paris, Masson et Cie.

Colin M. (1973), La criminologie clinique, (Canepa et Szabo Edit.). Journées d'études C.I.C.C.I., Gênes.

Debuyst C. (1988), Préparation à la sortie: aspects psychologiques, dans: La libération conditionnelle au croisement des disciplines, Compte rendu du Colloque, Liège, 22-38.

Debuyst C. (1989), Criminologie clinique et inventaires de personnalité. Utilisation quantitative ou qualitative. Déviance et société, vol. XIII, n° 1, p. 1-21.

Debuyst C. (1992), Les paradigmes du droit pénal et les criminologies cliniques, Criminologie (Montréal), V. XXV, n° 2, p. 49-72.

De Greeff, (1931), La notion de responsabilité en anthropologie criminelle, R.D.P. et Crim. n° 4, p. 445-460.

De Greeff, E. (1953), L'examen médico-psychologique et social des délinquants, Rev. D.P. et Crim., n° 6, p. 599-605.

De Greeff E., (1955) Bilan d'une expérience. Trente ans comme médecin-anthropologue des prisons de Belgique, revue Esprit, n° 4, pp. 649-674.

De Greeff E. (1957), l'examen médico-psychologique et social du délinquant, R.D.P. et Crim., n° Spécial, p. 183-196.

De Waele J.P. (1975) L'analyse des données en criminologie clinique, Gênes, Journées intern. de Crim. cl. comparées.

Durviaux L. & Hicter A. (1992), Le dossier de personnalité en France, (Sem. Ecole de Crim. Univ. Louvain).

Dozois J., Lalonde M. & Poupart J. (1984), Dangerosité et pratique criminologique en milieu adulte, Criminologie (Montréal), V. XVII, n° 2, p. 25-51.

Duflot-Favori C. (1988), Le psychologue, expert en Justice, P.U.F., Paris, .

Gibbons Don C. (1986), Correctionnal treatment and intervention theory: bringing sociology and criminology back in *Inter. J. of therapy and comp. crim.*, vol. 30, 255-277.

Gottfredson M. & Gottfredson D. (1990), *Decision making in criminal Justice*, Plenum Press, N.Y. & London (1re edit., 1987).

Gisel-Bugnon (1978), L'individuation d'une peine mesurée sur la culpabilité, Libr.de L'Université, Georg et Cie, Genève.

Farrington D., (1992), Criminal career research in the United Kingdom, *Brit. J. Criminol.*, n° 4, pp. 521-536.

Fitzmaurice C. & Ken Pease (1986), *The psychology of judicial sentencing*, Manchester Univ. Press.

Hall Williams, J.E. (1981), The evaluation of the personality of the accused in the english system of criminal justice, Ann. internat. de Crimin, vol. 19, n° 1-2, p. 115-125.

Hassin Yael (1986), Two models for prediction recidivism. Clinical versus statistical, *Br. J. of Crim.*, vol. 26,3, p. 270-286.

Hogaert J. (1971), *Sentencing as a human process*, Univ. Toronto Press.

Hood R. (1972), *Sentencing the motoring offender*, London, Heinemann,.

Hood R. (1966), a study of effectiveness of pre-sentence investigations in reducing recidivism, *Br. J. of Crim.*, vol. 6, p. 303-310.

Houchon G., François J. et coll., (1977), Programme de recherche socio-clinique en milieu pénitentiaire, Cah. de Crim. et de path.sociale, n° 12, U.C.L..

Lamers, E. (1950), L'examen scientifique du délinquant aux Pays-Bas, Cycle européen d'études au sujet de l'examen médico-psychologique et social des délinquants, Belgique, Imprim. des Services pénitentiaires.

LeBlanc M. (1883), Boscoville: la rééducation évaluée, Montréal, Hurtebise.

Lievens P. (1981), l'apport de la psychiatrie à l'utilisation du concept de personnalité dangereuse, in Dangerosité et justice pénale (C. Debuyst Ed.) Coll. Déviance et Société.

Leyrie J. (1977), Manuel de psychiatrie légale et de criminologie clinqiue, Edit. Vrin, Paris.

Mair G., (199O), Evaluation des effets des stratégies de diversion sur les attitudes et les pratiques des agents du système pénal, 19e conférence des recherches criminologiques, Conseil de l'Europe.

Martel J. (1990), Aperçu des pratiques concernant l'intervention psychosociale au sein du pénal, la conférence internat. du GREPO, Univ. d'Ottawa.

Michiels J.M. (1956), Le centre national italien d'observation à Rome-Rebibbia, Rev.D.P. et Crim., 1956-57, pp. 5O7-517.

Moutin P. (1979), La criminalité, Univers de la Psychologie, T. VI: La psychologie appliquée (deuxième partie): le crime et la Justice. Paris, Editions Lidis, 1979.

Moutin P. et Bernard K. (1983), Les limites de l'expertise psychiatrique et de l'examen médico-psychologique dans le procès pénal, Bulletin de Psychologie, (Université de Paris), n° 359, Janv.-avril, p. 376-383.

Nicolopoulos G., (1993), Les points de résistance de la notion de dangerosité, Th.Doct. (prom. G. Houchon), Ecole Crim. U.C.L.

Pinatel J. (1963), Criminologie, Tome 3 de Bouzat et Pinatel, Traité de Droit pénal et de Criminologie, Paris, Dalloz, p. 472-518.

Pinatel J. (1981), L'examen médico-psychologique et social de l'inculpé suivant la loi française, Ann. intern. de Crim., vol. 14, n° 1-2, p. 107-114.

Pinatel J. (1989), De la recherche clinique à la clinique criminologique, in Nouvelles approches de criminologie, (Ottenhof et Favard Ed.), Edit. Erès, Toulouse, p. 255-264.

Pisapia G. (1981), L'expertise criminologique et ses perspectives de réalisation en Italie, Ann. intern. de Criminologie, vol. 19, n° 1-2, p. 21-31.

Quinsey V. (1984), Politique institutionnelle de libération: identification des individus dangereux. Une revue de littérature, Criminologie (Montréal), v. XVII, n° 2, p. 53-78.

Rasch W. (1981), The mission of the psychiatric expert, Ann.intern. de Crim., vol. 19, n° 1-2, p. 71-80.

Schneider K. (1955), Les personnalités psychopathiques, Paris, P.U.F., (édit. allem., 1950, 1re édit., 1923).

Silvert N; et Vermeersch C. (1992), Le dossier de personnalité dans et à la suite de la réforme du Code de Procédure pénale française (Sémin. Ecole de Crim., Un. de Louvain).

Thorpe J., (1979), *Social inquiry reports: a survey*, Home Office research study n°48.

Thys P; & Korn M. (1992 a), A propos de l'expertise mentale: analyse d'une cohorte d'expertises psychiatriques concluant à l'irresponsabilité, Déviance et société, v. XVI, n° 4.

Thys P & Korn M. (1992 b), Irresponsabilité pénale et dangerosité sociale supposée. Une approche du raisonnement amenant les psychiatres-experts à recommander l'application de la loi belge de défense sociale, R. de D.P. et de Crim., Mars, p. 285-300.

Versele, C.S. (1949), Le dossier de personnalité, Rev. de D.P. et de Crim, p. 309-357.

Wasik M. & Taylor R. (1991), *Blackstone's guide to the criminal Justice Act 1991*, London, Blackstone Press Lim.

PSYCHOSOCIAL INTERVENTIONS
IN THE
CRIMINAL JUSTICE SYSTEM

20th Criminological Research
Conference
(1993)

PSYCHOSOCIAL INTERVENTIONS AIMED AT RESOLVING
THE CONFLICT BETWEEN
THE PERPETRATOR AND THE VICTIM,
FOR EXAMPLE WITHIN THE FRAMEWORK OF
MEDIATION AND COMPENSATION PROGRAMMES

by
Mrs A. SNARE
Institute of Criminology and Criminal Law
University of Copenhagen
(Denmark)

CONTENTS

1.   Introduction

The terms of reference for this subject matter are by no means clear-cut, but interesting as they are, deconstructionist efforts would hardly be of immediate assistance in the present context. Conceptual clarifications follow when seen to be needed. Our point of departure is the relation between victim and offender, and although not explicitly stated in the title of the report, the primary focus is the interests of the aggrieved party.

No longer does it seem reasonable to introduce the subject of crime victims with words to the effect that they are totally forgotten in the administration of criminal justice. The background for the shift is partly related to the fact that a number of studies have shown that victims of crime quite often feel neglected, lost or even abused in their encounter with the system. The effect, referred to as secondary victimisation or "second injuries", indicates that apart from the harm suffered by reason of the offence, the victim is caused more suffering by the police investigation, prosecution and trial.

The subsequent development can be portrayed in two directions. Firstly, reforms within the criminal justice system as well as initiatives by outside organisations have been implemented which directly aim at assisting victims in the aftermath of victimisation[1]. In that regard, we are dealing with a very wide spectrum of crime victims and consequently a far-reaching diversity of possible supporting interventions. There are victims, such as those of sexual/violent assaults, whose situation is deemed to require very special facilities in order to counteract the oft-reported humiliating confrontation at police stations or in court. Although the demarcation line is not absolute, other crime victims are in a much less vulnerable position but nonetheless in a situation needing improvement.

Secondly, the surfacing of the victim is also attached to the promotion of the (re)emergence of a justice model framed in notions of participatory justice, compensatory justice, restorative justice, or reparative justice. Linked to this conceptual framework is the progression of conflict resolution mechanisms; conceived as alternatives or supplements to the traditional justice recourse under headings such as mediation, reconciliation, negotiation and reparation or restitution programmes.

1.1.   Scenario

Mrs. Hansen, still employed despite the high unemployment rate in Denmark, arrives home to find her suburban house in disarray and she gets a brief glimpse of a young man rushing out through the back-door. His 9 to 5 o'clock job is also over for the day. The police actually respond fairly quickly to her call and show up in a few hours to make a report. (In this case the officer even tries to secure some fingerprints which enhances our burglary victim's trust in the workings of the system.)

Mr. and Mrs. Hansen prepare the list of stolen belongings for the insurance company, which pays them a visit in order to confirm that reported losses seem reasonable in light of the couple's living standard. The "surveyor" also suggests that they install some additional locks. In fact, it turns out that this visit is the most personalised encounter that Mrs. Hansen has with any authority-sounding agency.

Although by chance, the police solve the case. (In Denmark, 24.827 burglaries in the category "villa/house" were reported to the police in 1992; with a clearance rate of 12.3 percent.) In due time the young man receives a suspended prison sentence with supervision. However, Mrs. Hansen is unaware of the proceedings, though according to procedure asked by the police about any compensation claims; she was not needed as a witness at the trial and none of the goods were found. True enough, she did read in her local paper that the police had caught a burglar who had been active in the neighbourhood. That is all; she lost her "case" to the state, as Nils Christie (1977) phrases the issue.

How did Mrs. Hansen (and her family) fare after being burglarised? Well, life continued pretty much like before but still the intrusion left its scares. She reluctantly entered her house, did not want to be at home alone and experienced a loss of control and of belief in an orderly society. For a period of time her quality of life was rather deeply affected; she felt deprived and strongly mistrusted other people.

Could the story be told in a different way involving less debilitating or possibly even positive effects?

2.   A restorative justice approach

Lately we have witnessed the growth of initiatives aimed at counteracting perceived major deficiencies in the ordinary handling of criminal events by adopting a different course of action. The more recent roots of a restorative justice approach have been traced to the development of community — based access to "informal justice", to criticism of the ineffectiveness of formal criminal sanctions in terms of individual as well as general prevention, and to the already mentioned advancing focus on the crime victim (Messmer & Otto 1992:1). Advocates propose to provide a strategy for conflict resolution which is more human, more just, more beneficial to society and which does not exclude the victim.

A multifaceted heritage is evidenced in the various goals attached to victim-offender mediation programmes, which under different labels and in the course of a few years apart have been implemented in Europe, following a North American start. The Canadian and U.S. victim offender reconciliation programs (VORPs) are often viewed as the beginning of a spreading movement (see e.g. Coates 1990).

Britain in 1979 started its first reparation scheme — the standard British term for victim-offender mediation — while the Norwegian conflict resolution boards and Finnish municipal experiments began their history shortly after. Germany in the mid-80s established its first Täter-Opfer-Ausgleich projects, and in France at the same period mediation services were organised as referrals from the prosecution office or in the shape of neighbourhood dispute centres. Other nations have followed the same route, but as of yet a country like Denmark lacks experience in this practice of resolving conflicts. (See further various geographical surveys in Messmer & Otto 1992 and Galaway & Hudson 1990.)

It can not be ruled out that national denominations reflect actual differences in background and purposes, but the more noteworthy observation is that new means of conflict resolution has gained increasing acceptance in countries with different legal traditions and acute problems. Thus the joint search seems to entail issues related to critical features of modern civilization.

2.1.   Marked by variety

The current state of affairs regarding victim-offender mediation is characterised by a great diversity concerning:

—   organisational framework in relation to the existing criminal justice system, for example, with regard to at which stage of the penal process cases are referred to mediation (pre-trial, post-conviction but prior to sentencing, or after the sentence, with the possible addition of recruiting "conflicts" directly from the public);

—   level of institutionalisation whereby at one end of the spectrum there are disparate community projects (although frequently organised in a network) with almost none, some or full public funding and, at the opposite end, the Norwegian total integration of victim-offender mediation into a separate law (passed in 1991; in force on Sept. 1, 1992), which requires all 450 plus municipalities in Norway, either individually or in cooperative efforts, to establish a local forum for conflict resolution;

—   the background of mediators, generally defined as a third neutral party, who occupy a range from local, trained volunteers to semi-professionals, with usually a social work/ probation occupation;

—   mode of operation with reference to the practice of case handling and mediation procedures; and, finally,

—   operational philosophy as judged by what is perceived as the ultimate programme objective(s).

Any attempt at assessing victim-offender mediation is hampered by the conflict of aims (or diversified rationales) built into this movement. The varied background and aspirations have, on the one hand, helped to gather support from many different quarters due to the idea's "something for everyone appeal", also featured as its "motherhood and apple pie" nature (Dignan 1992b). On the other hand, tensions arise when attempts are made to balance what appear as opposing concerns or expectations.

Initiatives can be reviewed from (at least) four main vantage points: offender advantages, victim needs, system adjustments, and community involvement combined with added societal dimensions. In other words, which interests are being served by victim-offender mediation?

2.2. The offender in focus

From the outset an offender-oriented perspective largely prevailed in many European projects advocating alternative fora for conflict settlement, while the North American VORP model to a higher degree is seen to have stressed the aim to secure resolution between victim and offender by encouraging direct communication between the two as the beginning to a greater understanding and some form of mutually agreeable restitution.

In particular the early British reparation schemes have been criticised for placing too much weight on diversion of offenders from the traditional criminal justice system as the main objective (see e.g. Davis 1992a/b; Dignan 1992; Marshall & Merry 1990; Marshall 1992).

Likewise in Norway; among the six initial goals for the establishment of conflict resolution boards, the first four (pragmatic) reasons refer to offender-related gains and added thereto are the more ideologically directed considerations for the victim and the strengthening of local community competence in decision-making (Nergård & Halvorsen 1990).

Another common characteristic is the original widespread concentration on juveniles as the practical target group for mediation efforts as in the case of the two countries mentioned above and elsewhere. (See reports from several countries in Messmer & Otto 1992).

The focus on young (first time, property) offenders underscores the aim to divert from prosecution those considered eligible. In time several projects have included adults too, but it rather seems to be a rare exception when programmes exclusively deal with adult offenders. In Norway the attorney general eliminated the upper age-limit of 18-year-olds in 1989 during the experimental phase, and the Conflict Resolution Board Act confirmed this standpoint (Holmboe 1992:85). Yet in practice the Norwegian arrangement is likely to basically remain a juvenile-focused option. Moreover, the 1988 Juvenile Justice Act in Austria promoted mediation for young offenders throughout the country (Pelikan 1992), and the Juvenile Court Act in Germany has in 1990 been revised to expressly incorporate this response as a new judicial measure (Wandrey 1992).

Is victim-offender mediation most of all to be conceived as an area of juvenile justice reform? Overall, in Europe and North America, delinquent youths are especially in the limelight when intervention occurs at a pre-court stage as a possible substitute for future official proceedings.

Apart from implementing less repressive measures than ordinary penal interventions, a rehabilitative or educational motive has accompanied the new direction. The idea is that the offender will become more aware of his or her wrongdoing, be held accountable and understand the harm done which then can be undone by own effort. And these resocialisation strivings are not limited to the procedure in which offenders are diverted but also apply to mediation programmes which operate at post-adjudication stages, for instance, as part of achieving a more lenient sentence or probation.

In sum, based on an operating philosophy of minimal intervention/mitigation and socio-pedagogical influence, a pro-offender stance is recognised as having largely dominated reform efforts. The question has been raised whether many reparation and mediation services have opted for the offender model to an extent that they are in danger of being looked upon as an offender's charter (Guy 1993).

The degree to which the goals (of diversion, mitigation and/or education) have been achieved is highly debatable. The little available information there is on recidivism does not offer an affirmative answer as to a crime reducing effect, and the possible diversion impact is countered by numerous worries about a "net widening" or multi-sanction end result. This is a recurrent theme in the literature, but definite evidence is hard to find. One common impression hinges on that the official wish is to see conflict resolution "as a little more" than simple discontinuation of prosecution (e.g. Pelikan 1992:172).

Originally, one tenet of victim-offender mediation initiatives also expressed the aim to pose as a viable alternative to imprisonment. At the very best mixed evidence is reported (Coates 1990), while others underline that abolitionist concerns have not been met (e.g. Falck 1991; Weitekamp 1992).

2.3. Victims, restitution and participation

Perhaps not exactly in the forefront, but victims' needs and interests have been supported by the mediation approach in consequence of the awareness of their downgraded situation in the traditional legal framework. A parallel concern, as mentioned, is evidenced in reforms within the criminal justice system itself which deal with victims' reintegration into criminal proceedings and rights to be heard as well as compensated.

One key aspect is the question of compensation to victims of crime. This can take the form of financial assistance through state funds, but here the point of discussion is restitution based on a direct relation between the individual offender and victim. In turn, repayment can be secured through the court (criminal or civil remedy) whereby the offender is ordered to pay a specified sum to the victim or through a settlement negotiated in a mediation facility.

The terminology in use, however, can easily be confusing and particularly when addressed in a multi-purpose perspective. Thus in the 1970s, Galaway and Hudson (1978) made a clear distinction between restitution as an offender — oriented sanction and compensation as more directly victim — related, involving a state agency which through the use of tax money makes a payment to the victim to cover losses resulting from victimisation[2].

In time restitution through either monetary award or personal service is conceptualised as an obligation towards the victim.

Accordingly, nowadays "making good" by the offender is often succinctly approached as a redress that can be offered to satisfy the claims of victims. However, while in a new package restitution represents age-old justice systems which viewed crime as an injury more to the individual victim than to society (Van Ness 1990:7; Weitekamp 1992:81)[3].

The objective has moved further than to have the offender repay a victim for losses incurred; traced as a "gradual emancipation of mediation in relation to a simple reparation procedure" (Bonafé-Schmitt 1992:184). In that context "reparation" in the British scheme was meant to carry an expansive connotation of something more than just material compensation, that is, the inclusion of "putting things right", apology and explanation so that personal and symbolic dimensions received top priority as a way to deal with the emotional needs of victims (Marshall 1990:86). The broader outlook than focusing only on the concrete restitution requirement entails a process orientation and an inter-active component (Trenczek 1990:109).

A crucial dimension in the mediation programmes is therefore the personal participation of the victim in the disposition decision. Once more it can be remarked that within the criminal justice system itself, attention has been paid to giving the injured party a role in the proceedings. In the mediation frame, expanding the victim's role entails one more step away from his or her peripheral position. Negotiations are set up to ensure a definite say in the undertaking and choice of outcome. (See below.)

The participatory or interactive aspect of a mediation meeting is not restricted to the victim's situation but also encompasses the offender's involvement. In this light initiatives adopt the view of criminal acts as conflicts rather than legal entities, mirroring Nils Christie's thesis of returning issues to their proper owners (Christie 1977; 1981). Based on the development of an "ethnography of dealing with conflicts" in everyday life, this kind of reasoning underlies the Austrian model towards reappropriation of delinquent acts which are handled according to the logic of the criminal code (Pelikan 1992:166).

From the perspective of penal theories, compensation in the sense of reparation or restitution can serve several purposes and may be viewed as being retributive, reparative or rehabilitative. Its potential for serving and restoring the victim is acknowledged, but confusion still remains as to whether, for example, a reparation sentence is intended as primarily a service for victims or as a penalty for offenders (see e.g. Galaway 1992 on the New Zealand provision).

The actual practice has received some unfavourable evaluations. With respect to the early restitution projects in the U.S., Emilio Viano sees the opportunity for assisting victims but comments that:

> "Too often, however, the focus of restitution has remained the offender and the benefits to be derived by the correctional system. The victim is again treated as incidental to the plan and in the long run is vastly shortchanged" (Viano 1978:98).

The opinion that victims have been "used" is frequently voiced concerning the British start. Tony Marshall, one amongst many critics, also conveys scepticism on the part of the victim support movement which "remained cautious about the idea for a long time, suspicious that reparation schemes might be "using" victims to benefit offenders primarily" (Marshall 1992:18). Criticism of the early pre-trial models

> "revolve around the central allegation that whatever aims they might subscribe to in theory, in reality diversion is the overriding objective, and all other goals, including that of reparation, are subordinated to it. As a result, it is claimed that at every stage of the process, the balance of interests between victim and offender is overwhelmingly loaded in favour of the latter, while the victim's interests are systematically neglected" (Dignan 1992a:454).

In particular the selection of cases is under attack when victims' access to mediation is restricted by the constraints of criminal justice definitions — not too minor a case as to be simply dropped but at the same time not too serious as to require prosecution. Meanwhile victims' evaluation of the triviality or seriousness of an incident does not necessarily correlate with the legal rank-order (Warner 1992:204).

2.4.   System reliance and tensions

Embedded in the problem to reconcile the individual parties' interests are obstacles related to the working relationship between programme goals and the law enforcement apparatus.

Accordingly, the concern over the imbalance of victim and offender needs, respectively, in mediation and reparation schemes has been combined with criticism against the priority of system-interests. The charge amounts to that whilst sympathy may be abundant for victims in comparison to offenders, the management of criminal justice is geared towards the latter.

It has been argued, as mentioned above, that the decision to recommend a case for referral often appears "to have little bearing on the needs of the victim", and as long as mediation programmes are dependent on funding and enough case material, they submit to the overriding goal of assisting the regular system (Dignan 1992a). Reconcilement with an engulfing environment of traditional justice has on the British scene been judged as the most crucial problem since "other agencies were often exceedingly *keen* to use the new facility, but for their *own* ends" — that is, from the perspective of offender rather than victim concerns (Marshall 1992:21; italics orig.)[4].

From a different system vantage point, alternative conflict resolution mechanisms are discussed in terms of their success to unburden the courts of their "mass litigation" of penal matters (as expressed by Bonafé-Schmitt, 1992:179). Or these interventions are in a management perspective broadly conceived to provide for a more friction-free running of the regular operation by dealing with certain cases, but without necessarily focusing on concerns of either party.

Regarding the unloading aspect, existing information on the quantity of out-of-court mediated cases does not appear to confirm a large impact in easing clogging. Notably, officials have argued that the mediation procedure causes a greater work load than the normal handling.

Not infrequently, with Norway as a prime example, the greatest obstacle from the beginning and onwards has, in fact, simply been "too few cases" since neither the police nor the public have opted for this type of conflict resolution (Nergård 1993:91).

One matter is a very high approval rate of the idea of mediation activities by criminal justice institutions as shown in a German survey (Kerner et al. 1992) and by legislative action as in Norway, where the promulgated law signals overwhelming political endorsement despite the results provided in a requested evaluation study of a ten-year experiment which do not present much sign of success (Falck 1991; Nergård 1993). Or more generally, public and official supportive views concerning restitution are documented (e.g. Bae 1992; Hudson 1992).

A totally different matter is the hurdle of overcoming objections from law enforcement agencies and gaining resolute support. It is very unusual that difficulties in cooperation and issues of cooptation are not dealt with in national reports on the state of affairs in victim-offender mediation (see Messmer & Otto 1992).

A problem of getting sufficient referrals, whether due to reluctance on the part of referral authorities or other factors such as lack of resources, has placed mediation programmes in a marginal position when viewed in the light of many high expectations.

However, the number of cases is an ambiguous measure of success if the primary task is to work with victims and offenders. In comparing British "police-based" schemes with "court-based" ones, the evaluation is made that number-wise the former are more effective but content-wise the latter are in closer affinity with the potential of mediation (Marshall 1990:88-89). The issue is then phrased as getting the "right" kind of cases, and suggestions are made to include more serious criminal violations as suitable for mediation.

Inter-agency tensions also bring forth the question of whether new practices of solving conflicts between victims and perpetrators ought to take place within or outside the ordinary justice system. Some reformers propose an utmost independent base (e.g. Marshall 1990) while others are less inclined towards cutting institutional links due to the potential dangers in an entirely informal justice system (e.g. Trenczek 1990). Even in the U.S. with a fairly settled practice, it is unclear where victim-offender reconciliation fits into the system and programmes are very unsystematically applied at the discretion of criminal justice administrators (Coates 1990; Haley 1992; Weitekamp 1992).

In short, the uncertainty surrounding the proper position of alternative conflict resolution fora surfaces in three, partly distinctive forms. First, there is the question of integration or separation between pure victim support services and mediation/reparation tasks. Second, frictions exist between the informality of these procedures and guarantees of due protection by the law. (The allotted space does not allow an exploration of legal restraints.) Third, we have, on the one hand, the notion of mediation in conjunction with the workings of the regular system and, on the other hand, the vision of "neighbourhood justice".

2.5. Community engagement and beyond

The ideal of independently run community conflict resolution entails yet another facet of victim-offender mediation. In its pure model, disputes totally "bypass" the legal apparatus since the parties seek to solve any confrontations on their own by the mediating aid of local residents. This effort has been summarised in the following words: "to avoid the systematic recourse to the law, the police, social workers and so forth (...) [and] for people to learn again to communicate directly with one another, to negotiate and to free themselves from the dependence of the welfare state (...) (Bonafé-Schmitt 1992:194).

The "Norwegian case" well illustrates the dilemma of wanting to create — at the same time — a penal alternative and an informal local solution (Holmboe 1992:30). Ideas of decentralisation, community empowerment and familiarity with local values and norms as well as wanting to actively involve the victim and the perpetrator backed up the creation of conflict resolution boards. Simultaneously the experimental projects were to provide an alternative method of handling delinquent youths.

This joint venture is still contained in the adopted statute (konfliktrådloven), but opinions diverge as to whether this institutionalisation in the criminal justice system is a step in the right direction and a sign of revitalisation (Nergård 1993) or whether community mediation centres are more or less side-tracked (Falck 1991). An optimistic view holds that "the case" is yet not lost but that the situation demands active and self-conscious board members (Christie 1991).

The problem of sticking to founding ideas about a locally organised forum (thought to receive a substantial number of offences which have not been reported to the police or different types of "neighbour" disputes) and remain ideologically consistent is also evident in the Finnish development (Grönfors 1992). There as elsewhere the pragmatic question of collaboration rules in terms of "how to get cases for mediation" (Iivari 1992; with the noted complication that in Finland the majority of mediated cases continue to court due the legal duties of the prosecutor).

The trust in laymen mediators from the community might represent the minimal preservation of the original conceptual framework.

3.   Strategy of conflict resolution

It has been emphasised that "(...) restorative justice is based conceptually on methods that are more than just a label for a certain type of intervention. We are talking about mediation" (Messmer & Otto 1992:10). In the same vein, the point is made that the traditional aims of diversion, reform and restitution can be pursued in several different ways which do not exhibit the real innovative character of victim-offender mediation, namely the need for the parties to meet face to face with the aim of "reconciliation" (Marshall 1992:18).

The two terms, mediation and reconciliation, are often used interchangeably, though the latter can tend to convey higher value-laden emotions than reaching a satisfactory mutual agreement (Trenczek 1990:122; Kerner et al. 1992:30). In the North-American genesis, the concept of reconciliation has a religious foundation, but many programmes there are now discomfortable about its connotations, preferring at the very least to speak of conciliation rather than a re-establishment of a prior non-existent relationship between victim and offender.

On a rather different level, it should be recognised that the ideal mediation strategy does not accept "speedy justice" as a significant goal. There is little or no evidence that the programmes have generated quicker outcomes than the ordinary recourse, and much criticism of the cooperation with official agencies concern the fact that not enough attention is paid to the circumstance that victims' needs can not pre-determined.

If the mediation strategy shall be carried out in what is thought to be a fulfilling manner, the endeavour can be very time-consuming in contrast to expedient goals attached to this option. It has been noted that "efficiency will always conflict with the slower process of fair negotiation" (Schwartz & Preiser 1992:287). Some large, state-funded operations in the U.S., handling both civil and criminal cases, have so large caseloads that effective mediation appears to succumb to rapid processing (Haley 1992:129). A similar quality concern has been raised with regard to the surprisingly rapid implementation of victim-offender mediation within juvenile penal practice in Germany (Kerner et al. 1992:48).

3.1.   Mediation as psychosocial intervention

The core element in our context is a face-to-face encounter where the involved parties are actively involved in the process and resolution.

Several existing programmes, however, do not employ immediate interaction as the most important prerequisite for an operation. (See e.g. Dignan 1992a who reports that one third of settlements in the studied reparation scheme are reached without the parties meeting each other.) Even when principally devoted to personal communication, the accepted procedure might involve the mediator as a "go between".

The degree to which indirect mediation is looked upon as problematic largely depends on the primary objective set for an undertaking and the amount of resources at hand to choose between cases. That is, does "shuttle diplomacy" undermine the genuine meaning of conciliation and does it extract too much time from handling personal confrontations (Marshall 1990).

The interactive encounter also takes on a different quality when inside a correctional setting, mediation is arranged as an option whereby "unrelated" victims meet offenders of the kind of crime they have experienced (e.g. household burglary). Victims are then given the opportunity to voice their concerns and perpetrators get a better chance to understand the personal consequences their acts have generated.

Direct mediation is usually seen as the desired form, and as such it is foremost "an interpersonal negotiation strategy" whereby persons actually relate to each other. In condensed form:

"negotiations within the framework of mediation are cooperative ventures related to different interests and perceptions during a course of permanent interaction. This holds for the joint response to jointly identified issues at stake. Available alternatives in issue definition must be open to affirmation or denial by participants. Definitions on relevance, on what is considered important, should be part of the clients' negotiation competence" (Messmer & Otto 1992:11).

From a psychosocial viewpoint, it should be stressed that in theory emotional aspects are seen as important — or more — than material ones. In that regard one study points to that victims express dissatisfaction when offenders do not show much understanding during their encounter (Kerner et al. 1992:36)

The mediation process places high value on subjective meanings as well as the particularities of individual situations; therefore encouraging the expression of competing scenarios and endings. Using Jürgen Habermas' terminology, the foundation rests on communicative rationality (as opposed to procedural or substantive/material rationality). Thereby the involved people in an open dialogue come to a solution that is acceptable to them.

Consequently or at least according to a Weberian "ideal type", negotiation/mediation procedures have been identified by their orientation towards dealing with "cases" based on the relational-dimension and the crucial premise that instead of accepting orders from above that demand compliance, normative rules are to be decided upon by the parties themselves. Thereby to give a "voice" to the immediate actors is viewed as "a sensitive way of actualising the validity of social norms" (Trenczek 1990:121). And the empowerment of the participants, especially of the victims, stands out as intrinsic to the mediation process.

3.2. The role and training of mediators

Communication is the medium in victim-offender encounters, and the role of the mediator is to see to that both parties are, so to say, forced to get an understanding of the other side's experience of the conflict at hand and its aftermath. The task is also to facilitate the reach of a procedural outcome that satisfies the parties' conflicting points of departure.

An array of methods for settling disputes with the help of a third neutral party has frequently been used in a wide range of conflicts related to civil law. Mediation in respect to criminal offences is linked to and builds upon the settlement of other types of conflicts in a non-judicial manner through a consensual process, be that neighbourhood, divorce or labour disputes. Most of these efforts, however, involve people who know each other in advance, often intimately, but resolving conflicts between perpetrators and victims open up for mediation between total strangers (Coates 1990).

The question can then be raised whether it is possible to simply take over any prepackaged method of conciliation in the new area of applying mediation. While attempting to formulate guidelines for social workers' "new profession" in Austria, it was decided that this was not feasible. Christa Pelikan analyses the challenge posed when different categories of conflicts have to be taken into account, along the lines of incidental, fairly loose or close personal relationships, and then additionally differentiated according to the central object at issue — "money" as opposed to "honour" (or pride) (Pelikan 1992:174-77). Various mediation strategies have to be investigated in the search for the most appropriate intervention tool in view of the needs and prerequisites of specific cases.

Regardless of whether the third party is a trained local volunteer or a qualified social worker, sufficient intervention skills and ethical standards are needed. For a start, the mediator (or coordinator of the project) has to be able to persuade the parties in order to get them to agree to meet in the first place — and without using undue pressure. Interviews further point to that victims are dissatisfied when they have felt that the mediator was not being truly "neutral" but acted in the offender's interests (Kerner et al. 1992:36). (See also section 3.3.)

The training of mediators in casework and to make them able to evaluate each individual case does not cause controversy, nor does the promotion of skills needed to monitor and intervene in a face-to-face contact between the perpetrator and victim.

To develop specialisation in tools of psychosocial aid, however, raises the issue of the main purpose of victim-offender mediation programmes. Are the mediators to take on the role of clinical psychologists or any other counselling experts? Or is the lay element an integral part of the mediation movement?

Once more the diversity in programme implementation does not allow any definite conclusions. The tendency of many initiatives to want to include more serious offences would seem to indicate that an indepth awareness of traumatic reactions is required. The most appropriate response — independent of the outcome of the individual case — may be to facilitate, if needed, a transfer to already existing helping provisions, be that professional services or volunteer victim-support facilities.

Should mediators themselves be professionals? Support exists for a recognised training, adherence to a code of ethics and possibly some formal certification (Schwartz & Preiser 1992:288). Seen in the paradigm of informal justice, the answer is negative and the danger of having jurists just replaced by a market for other "thieves" is put forward (e.g. Falck 1991; Bonafé-Schmitt 1992:190-91).

3.3.   Mediator or probation worker

When victim-offender mediation is carried out by an established institution like probation, a rebalancing effort is required. That is, to engage as much in the victim's situation as in the offender's fate.

Observation studies conducted in Britain (at three centres) harshly criticise the mediation practice for selling a dubious product: non-material reparation with the inducement of a sentencing discount (Davis 1992). The criticism is based on that mediators are too willing to prepare "glossy" reports for the court, they couch the parties too much to get them involved, and in preparatory meetings the image of the victim is used to pursue a therapeutical change in offender attitude instead of relying on the parties' confrontation with each other (ibid.). The questions are asked why "offender and practitioner spend a great deal of time closeted together with no victim in sight?", and whether a drama coach would not do a better job since the final performance too often gave the impression of "two inexperienced actors (who) struggled with unfamiliar lines for the benefit of an unseen audience" (ibid.:456).

Disapproving comments about the way meetings between victim and offender are conducted also refer to their brief and perfunctory character — "a meeting was usually all it was, often just a quick apology and a thank you among two embarrassed and uncertain individuals" (Marshall 1990:88).

Due to a general lack of systematic participant observation research, it is not possible to assess the greater validity of the negative imagery presented of some probation-run programmes in the United Kingdom. However, the dilemma a mediator faces when wishing to maintain an active role while remaining impartial is widely acknowledged. Blurred goals accentuate the difficulty, and a career in working with individual welfare cases calls for a considerable readjustment process (Wandrey 1992:497).

4.   Effectiveness in settling offender-victim conflicts

Three circumstances lead to vagueness in dealing with effectiveness of mediation endeavours. First, one is constantly reminded that programmes described cover a wide range of approaches from dealing with financial restitution to those that focus on indepth, face-to-face reconciliation. Secondly, effectiveness is a highly ambiguous measure when not related to a specific desired outcome. And thirdly, the state of research is marked by the same amorphism as the field of victim-offender mediation itself.

There is plenty of literature covering the ideas behind a restorative justice approach and likewise a fair amount of descriptive studies on actual programmes. They deal with intake procedures and how cases are administratively prepared (for example whether the parties are individually interviewed — once or repeated times — prior to a mediation meeting or simply called on the phone to agree upon a time for settlement). Certain data are additionally recorded by the programmes on case profiles, but the disparate samples are often quite small and follow-up investigations limited.

A special problem is the fact that the trajectory of the mediation process itself features as very much of a "black box" (Messmer & Otto 1992:8). We know very little about what actually goes on inside the parameters of the negotiation encounter, apart from anecdotal illustrations.

Below the effectiveness of victim-offender of mediation will only be commented upon with respect to a few motivational variables. (Some other impact assessments have previously been touched upon.)

4.1.   Willingness to participate

The first step for a successful mediation outcome is the voluntary participation of both parties. Voluntariness, however, is a relative and not an absolute concept.

The offender's situation is not seldom marked by the classical choice of a lesser evil; to avoid further penal proceedings or hope for a lenient sanction. British data indicate much less cooperation by the few offenders who were not under threat of prosecution, and in the category of court referrals a substantial minority declined to take part in mediation (Marshall 1990:88; see also Davis 1992 on the problem of inducement). One U.S. commentator contrasts the rhetoric of voluntary participation with "a substantial element of coercion on offenders to participate" (Coates 1990:128).

Victims of crime are freer than offenders to opt out, and the planning of mediation projects centres around the question: are they willing to cooperate? Overall, a consistent high rate of agreement to participate has been reported, though practical difficulties normally result in a lower level of implementation.

Some German model programmes are noted for having 80 % to 90 % of the victims agreeing to be involved (Trenczek 1990:117; Kerner et al. 1992:34) but several cases fail to be effected (Hartmann 1992:218). Data from North America suggest that approx. 50-60 % of invited victims actually become involved in a face-to-face session (Coates 1990:129; Umbreit 1992:432). Given the chance, 6 out of 10 victims and nearly all offenders said "yes" to mediation according to British research, though actual meetings occurred in some 40 % of referrals (Marshall 1992:19). In Finland mediation could be arranged in nearly half of the referred cases (Iivari 1992:146) while French data give rates of 50 % to 80 % — a variation which can be explained by different methods of calculation, i.e. mediation sessions or simply acceptance to take part (Bonafé-Schmitt 1992:189).

Victims are generally more likely to refuse participation than offenders, but consent to mediation does not appear to be the kind of major problem that sceptics believed when the movement started.

The charge has been made that pressure might be placed on victims to take part, when programmes aim to secure non-prosecution or mitigated sentences after the offender has offered to make amends (e.g. Davis 1992). However, one reviewer of British mediation arrangements concludes that existing studies by and large do not report "that victims have actually been manipulated this way whether in pre-trial or court-based schemes" (Dignan 1992a:455).

Attempts have been made to identify the characteristics of acceptance or refusal. One German investigation suggests that victims "who had only suffered material damage, or were only slightly injured physically were more willing to cooperate than other crime victims and, victims and offenders who did not know each other before the offense were also more willing to cooperate than those who were acquainted with each other" (Kerner et al. 1992:35). On the other hand, a correlative analysis using two different mediation sites in Germany shows that variables which were significant for one project were not necessarily important in another (Hartmann 1992).

4.2.   Satisfaction

A simple criterion of success is to reach a mutually satisfactory solution. Most certainly, once a meeting takes place, it is very likely that the participants will find an agreeable settlement. Over 80 % or 90 % of the time are the figures derived from a spectrum of countries (Iivari 1992:146; Marshall 1992:19; Umbreit 1992:432 etc.).

Programmes also report an equally high level of offender compliance with the agreements. Findings further point to that the actual completion rate is considerably higher when offenders have negotiated restitution with their victim through a mediation process compared to when similar offenders have been ordered by the court to pay a certain amount of restitution (Umbreit 1992:439).

Economic compensation for the harm done is widely reported as the most common single requirement, or the payment takes the form of work by the offender (e.g. Marshall 1992:19; Nergård 1993:88; Trenczek 1990:117; Iivari 1992:146; Warner 1992:202 etc.). The end result is also frequently the mediation session itself; an apology and explanation offered by the offender and the opportunity to express own feelings will satisfy the victim (who might be covered by an insurance company or the damage did not involve a material loss).

The more elusive issue is naturally the victim's emotional satisfaction. Not unexpectedly, informal surveys tend to assert that victims are highly satisfied — and existing retrospective interview evaluations do support these impressions.

It appears that the psychological or emotional content of the mediation experience is the most satisfying dimension for the victims and more important than the restitution itself: "Material reparation tended to fade into the background, sometimes acting as a symbolic representation of the exchange and agreement. (...) In interviews, both victims and offenders were clearly most impressed by the relational aspects of the experience and emerged with more sympathetic understanding of another. (...) The experience of atonement coupled with acceptance by the victim was often emotionally cathartic for offenders" (Marshall 1992:20).

Data from the U.S. based on post-mediation interviews confirm the cited attitudinal positive results, and the downgrading of the financial compensation (Umbreit 1992:433-36). Talking to and confronting the offender were what victims liked the most about mediation, and more than 9 out 10 felt good about the session (ibid.).

In a follow-up study in a German project, too, victims' ratings of the mediation practice and the final result were strongly positive (Kerner et al. 1992:35-36). However, the overall level of satisfaction among these victims appears to be markedly lower than indicated by some U.S. results (Umbreit 1992); most notably with regard to being interested in trying mediation another time (61 % vs. 94 %).

In all likelihood there are many reasons that can explain different findings between various programmes and across national borders. Specifically, at times one can not help but wonder what victims really respond to. Thus it is reported from a Scottish project that: "Most victims were highly satisfied with the process and outcome of mediation ... and appreciated being consulted, their experiences listened to and receiving compensation of some kind" (Warner 1992:202). Yet here we are talking about a programme in which very few agreements involved direct mediation since victims usually did not wish to meet the accused.

4.3.   In demand: comparative research and failed cases

In the area of victim-offender mediation research, there is a definite need of studies which utilise comparative instruments. A major study is being carried out in the U.S. involving multi-sites, observation protocols, audio-taping of mediation sessions as well as other techniques — and most importantly based on control groups (Umbreit 1992). The three subgroups being compared consist of a) victims and offenders who participated, b) those who were referred but did not participate and c) a matched sample along several variables from the same jurisdiction who were never referred to the mediation programme.

Preliminary findings indicate that nearly 8 out 10 offenders in all three groups were satisfied with how the system handled their case, and the differences found in favour of mediation were not statistically significant (ibid.:438). For victims a significant difference in level of satisfaction was found between referrals and non-referrals. But, interestingly enough, it did not matter at all whether the victim actually participated or not in a mediation session − 8 out of 10 victims were satisfied in either group. On the other hand, with regard to perception of fairness in the case processing, the "referred but no mediation" group of victims scored the lowest: 39 % as compared to 85 % in the mediation sample and 64 % of "non-referrals" indicated that their case was handled fairly by the system (ibid.:439).

More indepth investigations of cases that never "made it" or "went wrong" would clearly be welcomed. Reasons for not wishing to participate have to be systematically explored, and unsuccessful mediation cases have hitherto carried too little weight in follow-up studies. Obvious difficulties arise in trying to contact and get interview consent from victims (and offenders) who rejected mediation or when deliberately a meeting broke up. Nonetheless, "successes" have to be compared to "failures" in order to provide a reliable information basis for policy decisions[5].

5.   Victim support provisions in the criminal justice system

Historically with reference to the classical, ideal penal law solution, we stand by the importance of cooling down conflicts and emotions. Spontaneous reactions are to be prevented and replaced by formalised means of social control. The victim-offender mediating strategy represents a move in the opposite direction. Rather than keeping the parties apart, they are encouraged to interact.

Victim support reforms implemented within the criminal justice system follow several different strands in addressing various needs related to being acknowledged and treated as a victim (see e.g. HEUNI 1984; 1989; Joutsen 1987).

At one level, improved provisions as regards the police encounter and court appearance are foremost a matter of higher public service attainments in order to deal with victims' identified dissatisfaction in terms of lack of information, practical arrangements and reassurance (Mayhew 1985).

For victims who are deeply affected by their victimisation more than a management issue is involved. The vulnerability of sexual assault victims have brought forth special consideration for protection during case proceedings through closed hearings, confidentiality and trials in camera. Entitlements to protective arrangements connect to a line of reasoning of keeping the parties separated in order to improve the wellbeing of the victim/witness or at least avoid additional suffering. The employment of legal representation to victims of sexual assault depicts another form of psychosocial service that recognises the fate of the harmed party. Keeping in mind that these interventions might prevent aggravated emotional conflicts between the victim and perpetrator, yet the profile connotates distance rather than interaction and, in particular, the concept of advocacy underlines a conflict of interests.

Victim interests in amends are acknowledged in the ordinary criminal justice system. State compensation schemes appear in much of Europe, and liberalisations as to which victims are worthy recipients as well as improved procedures have been introduced. There is also a tendency towards heightened awareness of compensating

71

non-financial damages in connection with personal injury; i.e. "to reinstate the self respect and self worth of the injured party" (SOU 1992:214). Greater use of restitution from the offender (as a civil action, condition of probation or compensation order) represents another means of satisfying the claims of victims.

Compared to compensation through state funds, court ordered restitution establishes a direct link between the victim and the perpetrator. Moreover, according to research findings the latter is favoured by the victims to the extent that they would settle for a lesser amount of money than received from state funding (Dijk, van 1984:83). Thus restitution from the offender brings its own psychological impact into the situation.

Participation within the criminal process and the role of the victim in decision-making depict one more area of concern in the official handling of cases. It has been documented that victims seem to want "a greater 'say' in certain issues (...), but (...) [have] little wish for more involvement in actual sentencing decisions" (Mayhew 1985:76). Rights to be informed and to make statements are therefore wanted in the regular recourse, while victim-offender mediation could offer a more suitable forum for actually finding a resolution.

6.   Different models of justice

Tenets in victim-offender mediation run counter to the main trends in criminal justice, and as such located in a broader frame with far-reaching efforts to establish a restorative justice approach which can deal with "society's need for socially integrative interventions" (Messmer & Otto 1992:1). The questioning of the legitimacy of current criminal justice practices seeks to introduce a paradigmatic shift away from retribution.

For sceptics a shift towards a paradigm of restorative justice is not in sight: "it appears unrealistic to expect that mediation can be established as a real alternative to criminal law. This is because it does not symbolise essential social norms and values in the same way" (Bussmann 1992:321). Others find that the aims of the traditional justice system can be met while avoiding its flaws (Wright 1992; Gehm 1992).

A review of the philosophical background and theoretical components underpinning a restorative approach to justice is not possible within the constraints of the present report. Only three themes are outlined in order to mark a vast range of perspectives.

First, the ethic of care in contrast to the rights standard of justice has been examined in psychological research on individual moral development (Gilligan 1982; Gilligan et al. 1988). Focus in "care justice" is placed on the preservation of relationships, with a preference for inclusive solutions to avoid turning the issue into binary choice with winners as well as losers.

Second, John Braithwaite (1989; 1993) presents a theory of reintegrative shaming to replace exclusionary and stigmatic criminal justice policies. His notion of inclusionary shame with the provision of both degradation ceremonies and ceremonies to decertify deviance (through forgiveness, apology and amends) is being discussed as a viable operational philosophy for victim-offender mediation programmes (Dignan 1992b).

Lastly, in the sense that participatory models are seen as part of a privatisation trend, they delineate a mistrust of the state machinery of justice, technocratic solutions and a division between the administration and those administered — and instead rely on society's or smaller groups' potential of self-regulation (Jung 1990).

NOTES

1.	Official recognition appears in international fora and attention can be drawn to the European Convention on the Compensation of Victims of Violent Crime (1983); the United Nations Declaration on Basic Principles of Justice for Victims of Crime and the Abuse of Power (1985); Council of Europe Recommendation No. R (85)11 on The position of the victim in the framework of criminal law and procedure; Recommendation No. R (87)21 on Assistance to victims and prevention of victimisation, and Recommendation No. R (91)11 dealing with, among other things, special provisions concerning children and young adults who have been the victims of sexual exploitation.

2.	In the 1970's, the prototype for formal restitution programmes was featured as a community-based, residential facility receiving offenders from prison who prior to arriving at the centre had been involved in face-to-face negotiations with their victims concerning the damages done and future payment schedules (Galaway & Hudson 1978:5).

3.	Contrawise to being a victim aid it has been argued that historically restitution was designed to benefit the offender or his kinship by the avoidance of more severe reactions by the victim's kin group (Edelhertz 1977, as cited in Galaway 1992:82).

4.	More generally the claim has been made that several established measures of victim assistance within the criminal justice system are adopted rather to support the smooth running of cases than to cater to victim needs. For example, concerning a growing emphasis on state compensation to crime victims, van Dijk suggests that this practice has allowed the criminal justice system to dismiss its own obligations to be sensitised to victims' need for respectful treatment (Dijk, van 1984:83).

5.	At times glorifying statements are somewhat overwhelming. The following was stated with regard to the beneficial impact of victim-offender mediation programmes in facilitating offender correction, as to victim satisfaction and for the community in general: "However sparse or subject to question, available evidence indicates that they have produced the benefits claimed. At least there is no evidence that any of the programs have failed to live up to expectations. In other words, in every instance where victim-offender mediation has been tried, by all accounts it has been successful" (Haley 1992:124).

BIBLIOGRAPHY

Bae, Imho: A Survey on Public Acceptance of Restitution as an Alternative to Incarceration for Property Offenders in Hennepin County, Minnesota, U.S.A. In: Messmer & Otto, 1992.

Bonafé-Schmitt, Jean-Pierre: Penal and Community Mediation: The case of France. In: Messmer & Otto, 1992.

Braithwaite, John: Crime, Shame and Reintegration. Cambridge: Cambridge University Press, 1989.

---: Shame and Modernity. British Journal of Criminology, Vol. 33, No. 1, 1993.

Bussman, Kai-D.: Morality, Symbolism, and Criminal Law: Chances and Limits of Mediation Programs. In: Messmer & Otto, 1992.

Christie, Nils: Conflicts as Property. British Journal of Criminology, Vol. 17, No. 1, 1977.

---: Limits to Pain. Oslo: Norwegian University Press, 1981.

---: Etterlyses: Selvbevisste konfliktråd. Nordisk Tidsskrift for Kriminalvidenskab. Vol. 78, No. 3, 1991.

Coates, Robert B.: Victim-Offender Reconciliation Programs in North America: An Assessment. In: Galaway & Hudson, 1990.

Davis, Gwynn: Reparation in the UK: Dominant Themes and Neglected Themes. In: Messmer & Otto, 1992.

Dignan, James: Repairing the Damage. Can Reparation be Made to Work in the Service of Diversion? British Journal of Criminology, Vol. 32, No. 4, 1992(a).

---: Reintegration through Reparation: A Way Forward for Restorative Justice? (paper) 1992(b).

Dijk, van Jan: State Assistance to the Victim of Crime in Securing Compensation: Alternative Models and the Expectations of the Victim. In: HEUNI 1984.

Falck, Sturla: Community Mediation Centres on the Right Track or Side-Tracked. In: Youth, Crime and Justice. Scandinavian Studies in Criminology, Vol. 12. A. Snare (ed.) Oslo: Norwegian University Press, 1991. (Shortened version in Messmer & Otto, 1992.)

Galaway, Burt: The New Zealand Experience Implementing the Reparation Sentence. In: Messmer & Otto, 1992.

Galaway, B. & J. Hudson (eds.): Offender Restitution in Theory and Action. Lexington, Massachusetts: Lexington Books, D.C. Heath and Company, 1978.

--- (eds.): Criminal Justice, Restitution, and Reconciliation. Monsey, New York: Willow Tree Press, 1990.

Gehm, John R.: The Function of Forgiveness in the Criminal Justice System. In: Messmer & Otto, 1992.

Gilligan, Carol: In a Different Voice. Psychological Theory and Women's Development. Cambridge: Harward University Press, 1982.

Gilligan, C., J.V. Ward & J.M. Taylor with B. Bardige (eds.): Mapping the Moral Domain. Massachusetts, Cambridge: Centre for the Study of Gender, Education and Human Development, 1988.

Grönfors, Martti: Mediation - A Romantic Ideal or a Workable Alternative. In: Messmer & Otto, 1992.

Guy, Jacqui A.: Restorative Justice or Offender's Charter? (paper) 1993.

Haley, John O. assisted by Ann M. Neugebauer: Victim- Offender Mediation: Japanese and American Comparisons. In: Messmer & Otto, 1992.

Hartmann, Arthur: Victim-Offender Reconciliation - Program and Outcomes. In: Messmer & Otto, 1992.

HEUNI 1984: Towards a Victim Policy in Europe. Finland: Helsinki Institute for Crime Prevention and Control, affiliated with the United Nations, Publication Series No. 2.

HEUNI 1989: Changing Victim Policy: The United Nations Victim Declaration and Recent Developments in Europe. As above. Publication Series No. 16.

Holmboe, Morten: Konfliktrådloven. Kommentarutgave. Oslo: Norwegian University Press, 1992.

Hudson, Joe: A Review of Research Dealing With Views on Financial Restitution. In: Messmer & Otto, 1992.

Iivari, Juhani: The Process of Mediation in Finland. In: Messmer & Otto, 1992.

Joutsen, Matti: The Role of the Victim of Crime in European Criminal Justice Systems. HEUNI, Publication Series No. 11, 1987.

Jung, Heike: Introductory Report. Privatisation of Crime Control. In: Collected Studies in Criminological Research, Vol. XXVII. Strasbourg: Council of Europe, 1990.

Kerner, H.-J., E. Marks & J. Schreckling: Implementation and Acceptance of Victim-Offender Mediation Programs in the Federal Republic of Germany: A Survey of Criminal Justice Institutions. In: Messmer & Otto, 1992.

Marshall, Tony: Results of Research from British Experiments in Restorative Justice. In: Galaway & Hudson, 1990.

---: Restorative Justice on Trial in Britain. In: Messmer & Otto, 1992.

Marshall, T. & S. Merry: Crime and Accountability: Victim/Offender Mediation in Practice. London: HMSO, 1990.

Mayhew, Pat: The effects of crime: victims, the public and fear. In: Research on Victimisation. Collected Studies in Criminological Research, Volume XXIII. Strasbourg: Council of Europe, 1985.

Messmer, Heinz & Hans-Uve Otto (eds.): Restorative Justice on Trial. Pitfalls and Potentials of Victim-Offender Mediation. - International Research Perspectives -. NATO ASI Series. The Netherlands: Kluwer Academic Publishers, 1992.

---: Restorative Justice: Steps on the Way Toward a Good Idea. In: Messmer & Otto, 1992.

Nergård, Trude Brita: Solving Conflicts Outside the Court System: Experiences with the Conflict Resolution Boards in Norway. British Journal of Criminology, Vol. 33, No. 1, 1993.

Nergård, T. B. & S. Halvorsen: Slik har det gått med konfliktrådene. En evaluering av forsøket med konfliktråd i norske kommuner. Diakonhjemmmets Høgskolesenter, Forskningsrapport nr. 31, 1990.

Pelikan, Christa: The Austrian Juvenile Justice Act 1988. A New Practice and New Problems. In: Messmer & Otto, 1992.

Schwartz, I. M. & L. Preiser: Diversion and Juvenile Justice: Can We Ever Get It Right? In: Messmer & Otto, 1992.

SOU 1992:84 Ersättning för kränkning genom brott (Compensation for criminal violation). Delbetänkande av kommittén om ideel skada. Stockholm: Statens offentliga utredningar, 1992.

Trenczek, Thomas: A Review and Assessment of Victim- Offender Reconciliation Programming in West Germany. In: Galaway & Hudson, 1990.

Umbreit, Mark S.: Mediating Victim-Offender Conflict: From Single-Site to Multi-Site Analysis in the U.S. In: Messmer & Otto, 1992.

Van Ness, Daniel V.: Restorative Justice. In: Galaway & Hudson, 1990.

Viano, Emilio C.: Victims, Offenders, and the Criminal Justice System: Is Restitution an Answer. In: Galaway & Hudson, 1978.

Wandrey, Michael: Organisational Demands on Mediation Programs: Problems of Realisation. In: Messmer & Otto, 1992.

Warner, Sue: Reparation, Mediation and Scottish Criminal Justice. In: Messmer & Otto, 1992.

Weitekamp, Elmar: Can Restitution Serve as a Reasonable Alternative to Imprisonment? In: Messmer & Otto, 1992.

Wright, Martin: Victim-Offender Mediation as a Step Towards a Restorative System of Justice. In: Messmer & Otto, 1992.

PSYCHOSOCIAL INTERVENTIONS
IN THE
CRIMINAL JUSTICE SYSTEM

20th Criminological Research
Conference
(1993)

EVALUATING PSYCHOSOCIAL INTERVENTIONS
IN PRISON AND OTHER
PENAL CONTEXTS

by
Mr F. LÖSEL
University of Erlangen-Nürnberg
(Germany)

Introduction

Psychosocial interventions in prison and other penal contexts are strongly related to the concepts of correctional treatment and rehabilitation. These concepts were very popular in the 1960s and early 1970s. They received powerful support in crime policy, although they soon became subject to criticism. From "conservative" and "punishment" positions, for example, it was argued that treatment is (a) insufficiently oriented toward deterrence; (b) not an appropriate compensation for guilt; (c) too insecure in protecting the public; or (d) too cost-intensive. Discussants from the "progressive" and "critical" camps warned, for example, that (a) crime is a social problem and not an individual pathology; (b) treatment is often based on a medical model of social deviance and continues stigmatisation; (c) the offenders become dependent on powerful social services; (d) there is insufficient legal control of informal decision processes and forced personality modifications; (e) treatment is basically in conflict with punishment and thus impossible in prison and other penal contexts.

There were arguments countering the above-mentioned points in detail (see, e.g., Egg, 1984). However, the increase in evaluation research dealt an even stronger blow to the concept of rehabilitation. Discussions on crime policy were dominated by the belief that there were hardly any substantial effects (Martinson, 1974: "nothing works") or that, at least, methodologically sound statements were impossible (see, e.g., Bailey, 1966; Brody, 1976; Greenberg, 1977; Lipton, Martinson, & Wilks, 1975; Logan, 1972; Sechrest, White, & Brown, 1979; Wright & Dixon, 1977). Although these analyses were generally thorough, there were nonetheless more positive evaluations of parts of the findings (e.g., Blackburn, 1980; Gendreau & Ross, 1979; Hood, 1967; Palmer, 1975; Quay, 1977; Romig, 1978; Sparks, 1968). Even Martinson (1979) later differentiated his message. However, treatment lost its status as a centrepiece of modern crime policy (see Christie, 1986; Kaiser, Dünkel, & Ortmann, 1982; Schüler-Springorum, 1986). Other concepts gained more attention, for example, selective incapacitation, deterrence, just deserts punishment, situational prevention, system diversion, or non-intervention.

How far the results of evaluation actually led to the "decline" of the treatment concept is not confirmed. That the expansion of rehabilitation measures slowed down, was, without doubt, also due to the other arguments mentioned above and to the combination of treatment with indeterminate sentences in some countries (e.g., the Netherlands, Scandinavia). On the other hand, it can be seen that the decline of the treatment concept in crime policy was reflected only partially in the actual practice. In the latter, there was also some continuity in the development of rehabilitation measures (e.g., Kaiser, Kerner, & Schöch, 1991). Similarly, research on offender treatment did not stagnate during the 1980s. In recent years, there is even a "revivication" (Gendreau & Ross, 1987), "re-emergence" (Palmer, 1992), or a "fresh breeze" (Lösel, 1992) in this field. It is indicated, for example, by a series of publications and conferences (e.g., Andrews, Zinger, Hoge, Bonta, Gendreau, & Cullen, 1990; Basta & Davidson, 1988; Egg, 1993; Gendreau & Andrews, 1990; Killias, 1992; Lipsey, 1992; Lösel, Köferl, & Weber, 1987, Lösel, 1993a; McGuire & Priestley, 1992; Palmer, 1992; Rowson & McGuire, 1992; Thornton, 1987).

There may be various reasons for this revival, for example: (a) Other fashionable concepts in crime policy also have not proved to be very successful. (b) More longitudinal research is available on psychosocial factors that play a particularly important role in the onset, continuation, and desistance of criminality. (c) Greater experience makes it possible to design programs more precisely and to implement them better. (d) Evaluations are performed more adequately and in a more differentiated manner. However, more basically, the fresh breeze in correctional treatment reflects the nature of evaluation. It is not a static diagnosis but a continuous process by which a system learns about itself (Cronbach et al., 1980). As Hood (1967) has stated, we must accept that treatment research will be a sequence of evaluation and re-evaluation and constant results will signify lack of progress.

This perspective is confirmed by recent meta-analyses that have substantially contributed to the renewed discussion of offender treatment. Meta-analysis is a method that integrates the state of scientific knowledge on an issue in the most comprehensive, systematic, unbiased, and differentiated way by using statistical procedures (e.g., Cooper, 1989; Glass, McGaw, & Smith, 1981; Hedges & Olkin, 1985; Rosenthal, 1991). Although meta-analyses are also confronted with many problems in detail (e.g., Bullock & Svyantek, 1985; Lösel, 1991; Matt, 1989), they offer advantages over traditional literature reviews: For example, the influence of subjective criteria on the selection and evaluation of studies is reduced. General trends across differing results and "blind spots" of research can be detected systematically. Computation of effect sizes, and not just significance, allows more valid aggregations of single studies, which often are based on samples that are too small to yield statistical power. The relationship between research methods and outcomes can be analyzed in detail. Alongside the estimation of a total effect based on a large number of subjects, quantitative differential analyses can be performed (on which measures are particularly effective, in which contexts, for which offenders, on which criteria, and so forth).

Since the mid-1980s, a series of meta-analyses on broadly defined "offender treatment" have been published, for example: integrations of 111 studies on the treatment of juvenile delinquents in residential settings (Garrett, 1985); 35 studies on diversion programs for juvenile delinquents (Gensheimer, Mayer, Gottschalk, & Davidson, 1986); 66 studies on community-oriented programs for juvenile delinquents (Gottschalk, Davidson, Gensheimer, & Mayer, 1987); 16 (18) studies on German socio-therapeutic prisons for adult offenders (Lösel et al., 1987; update: Lösel, 1993a); 50 studies on the treatment of juvenile offenders (Whitehead & Lab, 1989); 46 studies on rehabilitation programs for juvenile delinquents (Izzo & Ross, 1990); 154 studies on the treatment of juvenile and adult offenders (Andrews et al., 1990); 449 studies on the treatment of juvenile offenders (Lipsey, 1992a, 1992b); and 44 rigorously controlled studies on the treatment of juvenile or adult offenders (Antanowicz & Ross, in press). The analyses are not limited to formal juridical categories, which may be realised very differently, but are oriented more toward the psychosocial content of interventions. Most of the research integrated is based on experimental or quasi-experimental designs.

These and other studies form a very broad and relatively unbiased database for the evaluation of the effectiveness of psychosocial interventions in penal contexts. The present paper attempts to integrate the main findings, to evaluate how far the above-mentioned revitalisation is justified empirically, and to articulate problems and perspectives. Particularly, the following topics will be addressed: (a) overall effectiveness; (b) treatment modality (successful and unsuccessful programs); (c) influences of the treatment setting; (d) criteria of effectiveness; (e) design characteristics; (f) process evaluation; (g) offender assessment and treatment individualisation; and (h) organisational context. First, I will briefly discuss problems in characterising "psychosocial interventions" and at the end of the paper, I will make some suggestions for future research and practice.

Characteristics of Psychosocial Interventions

Evaluating psychosocial interventions or treatments in the penal system presupposes that we know what these measures are. The answer is more difficult than our implicit understanding would suggest. Typically, measures like individual or group psychotherapy, counselling, social skills training, socio-therapy, crisis intervention, case work, and so forth, are subsumed under this heading. They may be characterised by features like those proposed by Meltzoff and Kornreich (1970, p. 4) for the concept of psychotherapy: It is broadly defined as "the informed and planful application of techniques derived from established psychological principles, by persons qualified through training and experience to understand these principles and to apply techniques with the intention of assisting individuals to modify such personal characteristics as feelings, values, attitudes, and behaviours which are judged by the therapist to be maladaptive or maladjustive."

However, most studies of offender treatment and rehabilitation have included a variety of psychosocial interventions that go even beyond a broad understanding of therapy (e.g., Andrews et al., 1990; Lipsey, 1992). Although biomedical measures (e.g., pharmacotherapy or surgery) are clearly excluded (e.g., Gendreau & Ross, 1987), teaching, vocational training, or employment programs, for example, are included. Alongside more educational measures, legal categories are also used that indicate more or less "soft interventions" only indirectly (e.g. parole/probation, diversion, restitution, community service). Some of these can even have a deterrent character (e.g., sharp shock or getting tough programs).

In fact, the above definition also shows that, in principle, measures of punishment or deterrence could be subsumed under this heading. In basic research on learning, punishment (negative reinforcement) is one established principle for behaviour change. Various authors still recommend it for offender treatment (e.g., Jeffery, 1979; Brennan & Mednick, in press). In addition, from the perspective of the offender, social interventions that are conceived as "counselling," "social training," or "therapy" may also be viewed as "punishment" because they are experienced as stressful, time-consuming, and controlling. This problem is indicated in the typical role conflict in social work between help and control. There is much discussion in crime policy regarding which measures should be associated with which institutions. Nonetheless, it is questionable whether the offender possesses the differentiated perspective on the criminal justice system that experts presume. For example, many juvenile offenders seem to perceive interrogations by the police as being more stressful than the criminal proceedings themselves (Karstedt-Henke, 1991).

The subjective perspective of the clients also leads to fuzzy borders in ethical criteria of psychosocial interventions. According to the critics of enforced personality changes in treatment, voluntary participation or at least informed consent should be present as far as possible. This is also expressed in the above-mentioned definition: "(...) assisting individuals to modify (...)" However, it is not just in the penal system that participation in counselling, therapy, social training, and so forth is often only partially voluntary. It frequently involves a certain amount of informal or subjective "pressure" to participate in other contexts as well (e.g., demands from the family, school, employer). And as far as informed consent at the beginning of a measure is concerned, this can only be based on vague information and not on detailed knowledge.

Problems are also raised by the content of the underlying assumptions on psychological or educational principles. It is difficult to say what is and what is not an established principle. For example, adventure programs for young delinquents may seem to be theoretically adequate, because they address the sensation-seeking and lack of self-confidence of many offenders. However, the underlying hypotheses are not well-established principles, because it is unclear whether these programs really encourage learning processes that are incompatible with offending (e.g., Feldman, 1989). Furthermore, some adventure programs may even provide intensified contacts with deviant peers and activities that are part of the "problem behaviour syndrome" (Jessor, 1987). Insofar, it is not very surprising that these programs are found to be relatively unsuccessful (Winterdyk & Roesch, 1981).

Another problem is that, in practice, psychosocial interventions can often not be separated clearly from each other and from the institutional context. This is shown, for example, in evaluation research on socio-therapeutic prisons in Germany (e.g., Egg, 1993; Lösel et al., 1987). These model institutions are intended for adult criminals who are mostly categorised as recidivists with a serious crime record and personality disorders. There is no unified treatment concept. A common feature of the interventions is that they are applied not only on the individual level but also include group processes and organisational factors in the sense of social therapy. Mostly, treatment concepts cannot be assigned to one theoretical approach alone; increasingly, psychotherapy in the narrow sense is giving way to models of social training. Work and other contacts outside prison, intensive day pass and vacation opportunities, as well as purposeful preparation for release are some of the major design features. All this is to some degree the case in Germany's normal prisons. Insofar, from the perspective of process evaluation, more or less clear differences can be assumed only between "socio-therapeutic" and "regular" forms of incarceration.

However, socio-therapeutic institutions have not only a more favourable personnel-prisoner ratio than regular prisons but also more psychosocial service personnel. As Lösel and Bliesener (1989) have shown in a time-budget analysis, psychologists are in fact more occupied with tasks of treatment or counselling and less with security or discipline compared to their colleagues in normal prisons. Yet, even the involvement of trained psychosocial professionals is not a clear conceptual criterion. On the one hand, the effective role of lay workers, family members, and other mediators has become particularly apparent in psychosocial interventions. On the other hand, activities of the psychosocial services that are not aimed directly at the offender (e.g., staff training or organisational changes) can also make an important contribution to rehabilitation.

Taking into account the problems in delineating the borders of psychosocial interventions, the present paper applies the concept broadly and pragmatically. Similar to the above mentioned description, it refers to all those kinds of psychosocial treatment that go beyond "pure" punishment, incapacitation, or deterrence and are directed toward positively evaluated changes in the offender (e.g., may reduce recidivism). The paper will not introduce new conceptual differentiations, but rely on the categories that are already applied in meta-analyses and other integrations of evaluation research.

Overall Effect

The various meta-analyses have drawn different overall conclusions. These range from a negative (Whitehead & Lab, 1989), through an inconclusive (Gottschalk et al., 1987), to a rather positive evaluation of treatment effectiveness (Andrews et al., 1990). This is surprising, insofar as the overall effects are relatively similar. According to approximated comparisons (Lösel, 1992, 1993a), the mean effect sizes vary only between .05 (Lipsey, 1992) and .18 (Garrett, 1985).[1] So different studies like those on diversion programs (Gensheimer et al., 1986), community-based interventions with juveniles (Gottschalk et al., 1987), community and institutional treatments with juveniles and adults (Andrews et al., 1990), or sociotherapeutic prisons for adults (Lösel et al., 1987) all show nearly identical means (.10-.11). The data from Whitehead and Lab (1989), who did not compute an overall effect, also suggest a similar mean effect size of about .12. And even the two "extremes" may come closer if one bears in mind that Lipsey has computed a conservative inverse-variance weighted effect size (his Na-djusted mean is .085) and Garrett's mean is only .12 for the "more rigorous" studies. The most appropriate estimation of the overall effect size should be approximately .10 or 10 percentage points (Lösel, 1992, 1993a). This means that if, in the control group, 55 % exhibit recidivism or other negative outcomes, the rate in the treatment group will be 45 % (a 20 % reduction from a fictitious baseline of 50 % in the control group).

---

[1] For reasons of simplification, the present paper will only use correlation coefficients (phi, r_{m}) as measures of effect size (Cohen, 1988; Friedman, 1968). This is most adequate for categorical data (like recidivism). In the range of low and medium effects, these coefficients are approximately 0.5 of the d coefficient, which is frequently used for quantitative outcome measures. According to the Binomial Effect Size Display (Rosenthal & Rubin, 1982) a correlation of, for example, .20 is equivalent to a 20 % difference between experimental and control group. If, for example, recidivism in the control group is 60 %, then .20 indicates 40 % recidivism in the treated group. This absolute difference in percentage points could also be expressed as a percentage of a hypothetical control group with 50 % recidivism (e.g., Lipsey, 1992). An effect size of .20 would then represent a 40 % (20/50) reduction from the control group baseline. The coefficients reported in this paper should only be interpreted as approximations, because it is not clear how far, in some meta-analyses, coefficients depended on unequal marginal proportions, etc.

How far methodological problems are responsible for this effect will be discussed in more detail below. Nonetheless, it should be noted that the meta-analysis of rigorously controlled studies by Antanowicz and Ross (in press) has shown that 45 % of the programs were significantly successful. This is in line with the recent qualitative review from Basta and Davidson (1988). There may be a positive publication bias as some meta-analyses are only based on journal articles. However, the biggest study included unpublished papers (Lipsey, 1992). This revealed that the treatment group performed better in 64.3 % of the 449 studies (a highly significant effect).

At approximately .10, the main effect is small (see Cohen, 1988). It also can be rather meaningless, because the underlying primary studies are very heterogeneous. However, there are two important messages in this overall effect size. First, in spite of its very mixed database, it is significantly positive. Second, it is consistently lower than the overall outcome in meta-analyses on psychotherapy in general (e.g., Shapiro & Shapiro, 1983; Smith, Glass, & Miller, 1980; Matt, 1989). Although these are based on even more heterogeneous populations of primary studies (including different kinds of client problems), their main effects range from approximately .15 to .42 (d coefficients from .30 to .93) with a mean of about .33 (.70). Larger effect sizes are also found in meta-analyses on treatment in childhood and adolescence (e.g., Beelmann, Pfingsten, & Lösel, 1992; Casey & Berman, 1985; Weisz, Weiss, Alicke, & Glotz, 1987). The fact that the main effects are lower in offender treatment confirms the practical experience that it is particularly difficult to intervene in persistent antisocial behaviour (e.g., Kazdin, 1987; Lösel et al., 1987). Probably, meta-analyses in other fields are based on "softer" outcome criteria, shorter follow-up intervals, less disturbed clients, or so-called analog groups; and that client motivation, the treatment setting, and the post-treatment milieu are, at times, more favourable. However, a meta-analysis of Corrigan (1991) on social skills training in adult psychiatric populations has also shown that effects are lowest in offender groups compared to developmentally disabled, psychotic, and non-psychotic groups.

The small main effect calls for realistic expectations of success. However, as Rosenthal and Rubin (1982) or Prentice and Miller (1992) have demonstrated, even a small effect size may be of practical significance (e.g., when there is no better and/or less expensive treatment). Small effect sizes are not at all unusual in biomedical research that forms the basis for large scale interventions (Rosenthal, 1991). Also in criminology, widely emphasised relationships like that between social class and criminality are similarly low (e.g., Tittle, Villemez, & Smith, 1978). For this reason, more cost-benefit analyses are required in the field of offender treatment (e.g., Dünkel, 1987; Greenwood & Turner, 1985; Lösel & Köferl, 1989). For example, Prentky and Burgess (1992) have shown that institutional treatment of child molesters is cost-effective as compared to pure incarceration. The empirically based estimate of effect size was only .15 (25 % recidivism in treatment versus 40 % in the control group). In a preliminary cost-benefit analysis, even the .10 effect for German socio-therapeutic prisons did not seem to be discouraging, although the daily costs for each inmate are about twice as high as in normal prisons (Lösel, 1993b). For an adequate cost-benefit evaluation it is necessary to include a broad variety of costs and savings (e.g., time of institutionalisation, delay of recidivism, costs of stolen goods, damage, police work, prosecution and trial, re-incarceration, social welfare for families, loss of taxes).

Cost-benefit analyses are not included in the meta-analysis and they are very difficult due to a lack of monetary information on specific programs and justice procedures. However, from this perspective, the low overall effect should be viewed constructively. On the one hand, it disconfirms the popular slogan of a zero effect. On the other hand, it suggests that a careful selection of the most adequate kinds of intervention may be particularly relevant in offender treatment.

Types of Treatment

Variations in outcome due to the kind of treatment are up to now the most important differential effect. In Lipsey's (1992) large-scale study, treatment modality explained 11 % of the variance of effect sizes. Both in measures within as well as outside the juvenile justice system, more strongly structured, cognitive and behaviourally oriented, and multi-modal treatments directed toward concrete skills are more successful than, for example, nondirective counselling, client-centred groups, or less-structured casework. For the 112 studies that applied multi-modal (41), behavioural (39), or skill-oriented (32) treatments, the mean effect size was .11. This is twice as high as Lipsey's overall effect size.

The differential findings from Andrews et al. (1990) point in the same direction. These authors have formulated theoretically based criteria for "appropriate treatment" that draw on three principles:

1. The risk principle concerns the selection of an appropriate level of service: High-risk clients require the intensive measures of high-level services. When risk of repeated offending is lower, one should not "take a sledgehammer to crack a nut."

2. The need principle refers to constructs that the present state of empirical knowledge views as "criminogenic" factors. The offender's needs include, for example, changing antisocial attitudes and feelings, reducing antisocial peer contacts, enhancing family relationships and supervision by parents, identification with pro-social models, strengthening self-control, improving social skills, reducing drug addiction, improving cost-utility ratios for pro-social behaviour, and so forth. In contrast, general concepts such as modifying self-images, reducing anxieties, strengthening peer contacts (which might be antisocial), or reducing nonspecific personality problems seem to be less promising targets.

3. The responsivity principle refers to an adequate matching of kinds and styles of service to the abilities and learning styles of the offender. It involves principles of successful intervention, such as anti-criminal modelling, teaching concrete skills, or use of authority. The mainly cognitive-behavioural measures include, for example, role playing, graduated practice, reinforcement, making resources available, verbal guidance, and cognitive restructuring. In contrast,unstructured group activities among delinquents, sharp shock treatments, permissive milieu therapy, and unstructured psychodynamic or nondirective approaches are seen as less appropriate.

Treatment measures that meet these three principles are clearly more successful (.32) than unspecified (.10) and inappropriate (-.07) service or pure criminal sanctions (-.08). The latter two even show negative mean effects (less recidivism in the control group). Correlations between effect size estimates and type of treatment approach .70. Thus, the study from Andrews et al. (1990) clearly suggests that the generally low overall effect mentioned above results from putting together the substantial outcome from successful programs with the low or even negative effect sizes from less adequate forms of treatment. According to the Binomial Effect Size Display from Rosenthal and Rubin (1982), the effect for appropriate programs indicates a mean of 34 % recidivism in the treated group versus 66 % in the untreated (32 percentage points difference). On the other hand, the negative effects for inappropriate programs underline the danger that treatment can even be worse than doing nothing (e.g., McCord, 1978).

There may be some implicit circularity in the categorisations from Andrews et al. (1990). However, other meta-analyses have also produced differential effects of treatment type. For example, Garrett (1985) has reported behavioural programs to be more effective than psychodynamic approaches. Although this relative efficacy diminished when only more rigorous studies were taken into account, a cognitive-behavioural approach seemed to be more successful than any other. In Gottschalk et al. (1987), behavioural measures were more likely to be effective than, for example, unstructured case work or probation. Izzo and Ross (1990) have found stronger effects in cognitive programs versus noncognitive ones. And in the meta-analysis from Antanowicz and Ross (in press), successful programs differed significantly from unsuccessful ones on the following treatment factors: sound conceptual model, need principle, responsivity principle, role playing/modelling, social cognitive skills, and multifaceted treatment. The study did not confirm the risk principle as a moderator.

In contrast to these meta-analyses, Lösel (1993) has reported a homogeneous effect of socio-therapeutic prisons. The effect sizes of the various comparisons with the outcome of normal prisons did not differ significantly. This may have been partially due to sample overlap, as some institutions were evaluated several times. However, there are also other reasons for the homogeneous results: In the primary studies, it was not a specific kind of treatment but "the whole institution" that was evaluated. It is questionable whether there were clear conceptual and practical differences in the treatment implementation. The socio-therapeutic institutions use a combination of social training, therapeutic techniques, vocational training, work, intensive day pass, vacation, release preparation, and so forth that might result in a rather similar impact. As in other complex correctional institutions, it would be worthwhile to evaluate the separate effect of specific treatment elements.

Whitehead and Lab (1989) have also found no strong differences in the outcome of various types of intervention. Only system diversion programs were more successful than non-system diversion, probation/parole/community corrections, and institutional/residential programs. One reason for this could be that a formal and not a content-oriented classification of interventions was used. On the other hand, the authors also did not find significant differences when classifying for behavioural versus non-behavioural interventions. This discrepancy with other research integrations might be explained by differences in the meta-analytical method and study sampling. However, it also suggests cautiousness in making too broad conceptual generalisations. Pure behavioural programs with reinforcement techniques and so forth may improve the direct adaptation to institutions; however, they are not sufficient for behavioural changes in other contexts (e.g., Feldman, 1989). For the latter, multi-modal approaches including cognitive components seem to be necessary (Gendreau & Ross, 1987).

One example of the most promising types of treatment is the social-cognitive skills training developed by Robert Ross and his colleagues (e.g., Ross, Fabiano, & Ross, 1986). The major components of their program include (a) teaching of self-control in action (e.g., thinking about negative outcomes); (b) stimulation of meta-cognition (e.g., reflection on the linkage between own perceptions and specific behaviours); (c) social skills training (e.g., coping with provoking situations); (d) practice of interpersonal problem-solving (e.g. understanding needs of others); (e) teaching of creative thinking (e.g., non-criminal behavioural alternatives); (f) training of self-critical thinking (e.g., role-taking); (g) teaching pro-social value orientations (e.g., experience of their function for social life); (h) training of emotional control (e.g., anger and aggression); (i) promotion of helping behaviour (e.g., service for more deprived people); and (j) enhancement of empathy for victims (e.g., perspective taking). For details of cognitive-behavioural programs see, for example, Hollin (1990), Morris and Braukman (1987), or Novaco (1975).

Although most research integrations show relatively positive results on cognitive and behavioural forms of treatment, these approaches should not yet be emphasised too uncritically. Mayer et al. (1986), for example, who analyzed social learning treatments only, have reported no significant correlations between specific characteristics (e.g., modelling, behavioural contracting, token economies) and effect size in the control-group studies. Antanowicz and Ross (in press) have found no significant differences between successful and unsuccessful programs in specific factors that are relevant in the cognitive-behavioural approach (e.g., social perspective taking, self-control, problem-solving, victim awareness, token economies, contingency contracting). This was not primarily due to proved ineffectiveness, but to the fact that only a few rigorously controlled evaluation studies were available for many treatment characteristics. This shows that more replications of controlled evaluations of specific interventions are necessary (see, also, Palmer, 1992). Even in "big" meta-analyses, differential effects are often based on only a few studies. They are only partially derived from theories and generally harder to reproduce than main effects. Furthermore, classification of specific forms of treatment is sometimes questionable.

The differential success of treatment modalities also should not be viewed too technically. An even more important message from the meta-analyses is that efficient treatment must be based on theoretically sound concepts (i.e., empirically tested theories of criminal behaviour and its modification). Relatively successful measures are particularly those addressing features that are also relatively well tested correlates of persistent criminality in etiological research. For example, the contents of cognitive-behavioural programs are supported by many findings on cognitive deficits, impulsiveness, criminogenic thinking patterns, and so forth (e.g., Farrington, 1992;

Goldstein, 1990; Loeber, 1990; Moffitt & Silva, 1988; Novaco, 1975; Wilson & Herrnstein, 1985; Yochelson & Samenow, 1976). Consequently, in their attempt to develop a comprehensive theory of criminality, Gottfredson and Hirschi (1990) emphasise lack of self-control as a core concept (see, also, Lösel, 1975). However, skill- and capacity-oriented programs may fall theoretically and practically short, when, for example, major environmental pressures and social disadvantages or motivational problems are disregarded (see Palmer, 1992). Thus, successful intervention clearly needs a comprehensive theoretical foundation and a corresponding multi-modal program design.

Settings

In many discussions on crime policy, it is almost taken for granted that treatment in the community is superior to treatment in an institutional setting. Although it is often not very clear what is meant by "community" (Mair, 1990), several meta-analyses confirm this point of view. Andrews et al. (1990) have found a significant difference in mean effect size between programs in community versus institutional/residential settings. In Lipsey's (1992) study, programs in public facilities (criminal and non-criminal justice), custodial institutions, and the juvenile justice system had smaller effect sizes than those implemented in private, ambulatory, informal, or mixed settings. Larger effects in the primary studies on community-related measures have also been reported in Izzo and Ross (1990) and Whitehead and Lab (1989). In contrast, Antanowicz and Ross (in press) have found no significant differences compared to institutional contexts. This is in line with Blackburn (1980). It should also be remembered that the community-based interventions analyzed in Gottschalk et al. (1987) and the diversion programs in Gensheimer et al. (1986) showed similar low mean effect sizes to those in the study on socio-therapeutic prisons from Lösel et al. (1987). Furthermore, Garrett (1985) only analyzed programs located in an institutional or community residential (e.g., group home, halfway house) setting and found a relatively high overall effect. The picture becomes even more complicated if we take another look at the data from Andrews et al. (1990): Inappropriate treatments had the same negative effects in community as well as institutional settings. Obviously, if we do the wrong things it does not matter in what setting. Only appropriate treatment was more effective in community settings (mean effect size .35). However, even in institutional/residential settings, appropriate measures were relatively successful (mean .20) as compared to the overall effect.

These results suggest that psychosocial interventions can also be effective in institutional settings. However, relatively few controlled studies are available on treatment in prisons, and overall effects seem to be lower than in community settings. This may partially be due to differences in target groups (e.g., more antisocial or otherwise disturbed personalities in institutions). However, it is also plausible that treatment in institutions is less effective because punishment and security predominate, negative incarceration effects occur, there is a concentration of deviant role models, and the transfer of positive learning to the world outside is difficult (e.g., Feldman, 1989). Although some authors suggest clearly unfavourable effects of incarceration (e.g., Bondeson, 1989; Ortmann, 1992), others do not support the general criminogenic effects (e.g., Bonta & Gendreau, 1990; Murray & Cox, 1979; for aggregate data, see Farrington

90

& Langan, 1992; Moitra, 1987). Rather often, discussions on prisonisation and other negative incarceration effects are too undifferentiated. First of all, even "total institutions" are not totally the same in many aspects. Organisational and educational climate plays an important role (e.g., Lösel, in press; Moos, 1975). Furthermore, people react differently to objectively identical situations. For example, reconviction rates between 18 % and 55 % for discharged special hospital patients (Bailey & MacCulloch, 1992) or severe recidivism of about 50 % of those released from Germany's socio-therapeutic prisons (Dünkel & Geng, 1991; Egg, 1990) suggest that institutions are not generally "schools of crime."

Design control in studies on directly assessed incarceration effects is often insufficient, for example, when comparisons are made with the normal population regarding violence, suicidal tendencies, depression, and so forth. Negative effects of incarceration seem to depend on numerous moderator variables such as duration, the age of the inmate, the activation of coping mechanisms, offender personality, objective and subjective crowding, the stability of group relationships, the extent of control and repression, features of the subculture, the institutional climate, the degree of isolation from external reality, and so forth (see Bonta & Gendreau, 1990, 1992; Farrington & Nuttall, 1980; Hürlimann, 1992; Kette, 1991; Porporino & Dudley, 1984; Wormith, 1984). In view of the previous self- and other-endangering life-style of some inmates, the protective function of institutions should not be interpreted as only one-sided (e.g., Ruback & Innes, 1988). If applied as early as possible, treatment can help in reducing the impact of negative institutional effects (e.g., Zamble & Porporino, 1990).

Doubtless, when justified by normative and empirical reasons (e.g., public security, compensation of guilt), incarceration should be avoided as far as possible. This is not only more humane but also more cost-effective (e.g., Dünkel, 1987). However, the claim that treatment measures cannot be effective in prisons and similar institutional settings is not proven (see, also, Blackburn, 1980; Eysenck & Gudjonsson, 1989). There is a lack of research on the combination or interplay between potentially negative and positive effects in institutional contexts, and this applies particularly to the theoretically most suitable person-by-situation approach. It also seems worthwhile to apply the perspective of risk and protective factors from developmental psychopathology to the evaluation of correctional institutions (Lösel, in press).

Criteria of Effectiveness

The meta-analyses have shown that there are very different effect criteria. For example, recidivism, self-reported delinquency, attitude and personality measures, indicators of community or institutional adjustment, academic performance, or vocational accomplishment have been used in primary studies. While some meta-analyses included only studies on recidivism, others clearly indicated differential effects depending on the kind of criteria. Garrett (1985) and Gottschalk et al. (1987) have found much lower effect sizes for recidivism versus various adjustment or attitude measures. Gensheimer et al. (1986) have reported a similar tendency. In Lipsey's (1992) analysis, psychological measures showed larger effects than delinquency criteria and,

91

for example, school or vocational criteria. A large number of delinquency outcome measures, long follow-up intervals, as well as weak reliability and validity of effect criteria were associated with smaller effect sizes.

These and other results suggest that treatment effects are normally smaller in terms of recidivism than in other measures (see, also, Basta & Davidson, 1988; Feldman, 1989). That Lösel et al. (1987) did not find a difference may be due to the often not very valid personality variables used in evaluations of socio-therapeutic prisons. Although effect sizes in recidivism are relatively low in several research integrations, they do not indicate a zero effect. Furthermore, the effects of particularly successful programs are indicated in meta-analyses based on recidivism criteria (Andrews et al., 1990; Antanowicz & Ross, in press).

The problems in using only official recidivism as outcome measure have been discussed repeatedly (e.g., Lösel et al., 1987; Waldo & Griswold, 1979). However, for scientific as well as political reasons, this criterion should in no way be disregarded (see, also, Palmer, 1992). In using recidivism, adequate follow-up intervals as well as differentiated and comparable degrees of severity should regularly be taken into account. Even in otherwise sound evaluations, every reconviction for minor offenses is counted as a failure and follow-up periods of more than two years are rare. Not looking at the "survival rates" in long-term evaluations may lead to rather contradictory conclusions. For example, Egg (1990) found much lower recidivism rates for socio-therapy after two years, whereas, after four and more years, figures were similar to normal prisons. Such a delay of relapse is very common in offender treatment evaluation. It indicates the overlap between intervention and developmental effects (e.g., Loeber & Farrington, in press). Realistically, it should not just be interpreted as failure. More constructively, those developmental data can be seen as a basis for evaluating and improving aftercare and supervision, which are very important for relapse prevention.

It is also necessary to take a closer look at other criteria used in evaluation. In many studies, improvements are restricted to attitudes and skills in artificial situations rather than to antisocial behaviour or adjustment in everyday life (Kazdin, 1987). Direct criteria of delinquent behaviour or theoretically based behavioural criteria from other fields should be applied more often. Various studies use institutional behaviours or personality criteria that are not sufficiently valid in criminological terms (Blackburn, 1980; Feldman, 1989). Although poor institutional adjustment may be a moderate predictor of later recidivism (e.g., Monahan, 1989), good adjustment is not a sufficient precondition of stabilisation outside. In particular, it should be considered that treatment effects may not be reflected consistently across different criteria. For example, Lipsey (1992) found that studies with an impact on personality variables were not necessarily the same as those that showed an effect on recidivism. Measures of school participation, however, correlated strongly with delinquency criteria. Results like these indicate problems in determining valid intermediate goals and underline the importance of theory in planning not only treatment but also outcome criteria (e.g., Chen, 1989).

Most studies target effects in the offender. From a more comprehensive institutional perspective, change in the offender is only one of many possible goals. Particularly in the work with very difficult or mentally disordered clients, "success" of psychosocial measures may also be indicated in reducing institutional violence or suicide, improving organisational climate, enhancing staff satisfaction, shortening incarceration time, and so forth (e.g., Taylor & Gunn, 1984). In community programs, saving costs, positive experiences for the offenders, or services to the public and to disadvantaged people may be relevant criteria (e.g., McIvor, 1992). This does not mean that relapse prevention should not be the ultimate goal. However, it reminds us that "effectiveness" is always a question of multi-attributive utility.

Methodological Design

According to some meta-analyses, findings on effectiveness also vary on design quality. Not surprisingly, pretest- post-test designs without control showed higher effects on psychological variables (e.g., Gottschalk et al., 1987; Mayer et al., 1986). In most analyses, however, only controlled quasi-experimental studies were included. In Garrett (1985), and as a trend in Whitehead and Lab (1989), weaker or non-randomised designs had higher effects, while in Mayer et al. (1986) there was no, and in Gottschalk et al. (1987) even an opposing trend. Lipsey (1992) found that studies with larger samples, higher attrition rates, and control groups receiving some "treatment" contact showed lower effects. Lack of control group equivalence resulted in lower or higher effect sizes. Random versus non-random assignment, however, was not associated with outcome. In Andrews et al. (1990) there was no difference between "weaker" and "stronger" research designs. Lösel et al. (1987) applied a comprehensive category system for threats to validity (Cook and Campbell, 1979) and found that not internal validity but construct validity was negatively related to effect sizes. Analysing only methodologically rigorous studies, Antanowicz and Ross (in press) confirmed substantial differences between successful and unsuccessful programs.

These "mixed" results suggest that it is not only design weaknesses that lead to positive effects. However, there are still many methodological problems. Consequently, some authors argue that lack of randomisation or not in every sense comparable control groups invalidates evaluation totally (e.g., Ortmann, 1992). Such positions are neither fully right nor fully wrong. They categorise research according to a simple structure that neglects the intensive methodological discussion during the last 20 years on evaluation research. Accordingly, the idea that there exists the one powerful study without any threat to validity even in complex field situations seems to be hardly plausible (see, e.g., Cronbach et al., 1980). Of course, the ideal of the true experiment is desirable (Farrington, 1983), and many studies on offender treatment are already based on randomised designs or at least on some relevant matching procedures. However, as Cook and Campbell (1979) have shown, even experimental designs are not immune to a great number of threats to validity, while most quasi-experimental designs are in no way uninterpretable (see, also, Lösel & Nowack, 1987). For juridical, ethical, and practical reasons, experiments also may be inappropriate or impossible in specific settings (e.g., Genevie, Margolies, & Muhlin, 1986; Gunn & Robertson, 1982). In addition, experimentally planned studies often change into a quasi-experimental design through dropouts and other problems. When for example, dropouts perform particularly poorly (Lösel et al., 1987), this is an indication of the significance of client motivation (see Steller, 1977), which is not only an input variable but may change due to treatment conditions. Merely assigning dropouts to the treatment group in data analysis is no sufficient solution. They have often received only a low dosage of treatment and may have been demoralised or reinforced to a deviant identity after being discharged. Rigorously controlled and differentiated evaluations are necessary here.

Sweeping categorisations into "good" versus "bad" designs cannot replace the careful analysis of possible threats to validity in any study. Some threats are more relevant in offender treatment evaluation than others (Lösel et al., 1987). Their effects are also not unidirectional: Some may result in a smaller, others in a larger effect (Bliesener, 1993). Up to now, issues of external and construct validity have received insufficient attention as compared to internal validity (see Lösel et al., 1987). Again, the relationship to a sound theory is particularly important. Although true experiments should still play a central role in treatment evaluation, other strategies also need to be followed in the sense of Cook's (1985) critical multiplism. One particularly promising approach is to combine longitudinal research and experimental designs (Farrington, Ohlin, & Wilson, 1986; Loeber & Farrington, in press; Tonry, Ohlin, & Farrington, 1991).

Offender Characteristics

Early work on offender treatment has already suggested that measures have to be adjusted to the individual characteristics of the offender (e.g., Hood, 1967; Palmer, 1968; Sparks, 1968). More recent reviews also emphasise the importance of client variables (e.g., Gendreau & Ross, 1987; Sherman, 1988). However, meta-analytic results on this topic are still rather limited. In Andrews et al. (1990), high risk of offenders was one aspect of appropriate programs that showed larger effects. There was also a small positive effect of higher risk in Lipsey's (1992) study. In contrast, Antanowicz and Ross (in press) did not confirm this differential effect. Both Andrews et al. and Antanowicz and Ross found strong support for the need and the responsivity principle. However, the constructs subsumed under this category are seen as being generally important and do not reflect a real matching of program and individual offender's characteristics.

According to Lipsey (1992), age, prior offence history, and gender had no substantial impact on effect size. Due to a lack of studies on the latter variables, Whitehead and Lab (1989) hesitated to make any generalisations. Whereas Gensheimer et al. (1986) reported a negative correlation between age and magnitude of effect, Gottschalk et al. (1987), Lösel et al. (1987), and Mayer et al. (1986) found no significant relationship. Similarly, the distinction between programs in the adult versus juvenile justice system was not a moderator (Andrews et al., 1990). In Gottschalk et al. (1987), studies with higher proportions of males and non-adjudicated samples showed somewhat better results. Unexpectedly, indicators of particularly motivated clients' and offenders involvement in treatment planning were not significantly associated with successful programs (Antanowicz & Ross, in press).

94

The lack of consistent differential results on offender characteristics is not primarily a shortcoming of the meta-analyses. Often detailed information on this aspect is already missing in the primary studies. However, measures to which a neurotic offender may respond successfully can be totally inappropriate for an offender with an antisocial personality disorder. Offenders classified as psychopathically disordered also are generally more at risk for reconviction (e.g., Bailey & MacCulloch, 1992). Likewise, dangerous sex offenders may need not only more specific kinds of treatment as compared to "ordinary" criminals but also related forms of relapse prevention (Laws, 1989). Another example of the great importance of offender assessment is the very poor outcome for dropouts in German social therapy (Egg, 1990; Lösel et al., 1987). With respect to the offender's needs and rights, it is problematic to correct placement errors by sending "untreatables" too readily back to normal prison.

Research and practice need to identify those client characteristics that are most predictive of treatment response (Bornstein, Hamilton, & McFall, 1981). An adequate offender assessment not only includes static indicators of risk (see Gendreau & Ross, 1987; Monahan, 1989) but should comprehensively cover the major personal and situational issues that are relevant for the individual case (developmental characteristics, life-style, offense situation, related cognitions and feelings, the social contexts, etc.; e.g., Blackburn, 1992; Monahan, 1981; Mulvey & Lidz, 1993). When, for example, offenders reveal a predominance of external causal attributions in explaining their problems (e.g., Averbeck & Lösel, 1992; Goldstein, 1990) or when their problematic behaviour is based less on skill deficits and more on subcultural value orientations (Renwick, Ridley, & Ramm, 1993), an otherwise appropriate social skills training will probably not have the desired impact on criminal behaviour (see, also, Corrigan, 1991). According to Palmer (1992) it is necessary to assess (and target in the program) not only skill/capacity deficits, but also external pressures/disadvantages and internal difficulties of the offenders.

Furthermore, the assessment should not be limited to deficits and risks but also include protective factors. Resilience research has shown that even with high risk exposure (e.g., persons from multi-problem milieus), "natural" personal and social resources can lead to positive development. Protective factors may be, for example, a positive relationship to a reference person, social support, experiences of self-efficacy, or active coping style (e.g., Lösel & Bliesener, 1990; Rutter, 1990). To build on risk as well as protective factors is a very promising path for psychosocial interventions in deviant behaviour (e.g., Hawkins et al., 1992).

Organisational and Staff Characteristics

The majority of outcome evaluations examine relatively isolated, specific treatment programs. However, the specific organisational context, staff competences and cooperation, the social environment of the institution, government support, and so forth may have an impact on daily activities and effectiveness (e.g., Feldman, 1989; Lösel & Bliesener, 1989; McGuire, 1992; Palmer, 1992; Roberts, 1992). This does not just apply to residential settings but also, for example, to measures in schools or families (e.g.,

Guerra, 1991). In their meta-analyses, Lipsey (1992), Gottschalk et al. (1987), and Gensheimer et al. (1986) found that influences of the investigator on the treatment implementation were associated with larger effect sizes. This may be an indicator of staff motivation, however, it also could be a methodological artifact. Antanowicz and Ross (in press) analyzed variables like staff experience, motivation, training, supervision, or unified team and did not find any difference between successful and unsuccessful programs. Only in two variables (training and supervision) did a substantial number of studies report on these characteristics. Lösel et al. (1987) analysed personnel-prisoner ratio, size of institution, crisis periods, and other organisational characteristics as moderators. However, the number of studies was too small to make consistent conclusions.

Obviously, the meta-analyses tell us little about the impact of these characteristics. Organisational variables that may be relevant for treatment outcome overlap with those that have been addressed already in the treatment setting. Organisational structure, climate, and so forth can have a different influence in other-wise comparable institutions (e.g., Akers, Hayner, & Gruninger, 1977; Moos, 1975). For example, adolescents in residential homes were found to develop more positively when they experienced both a positive socio-emotional climate and a norm-oriented climate in the institution (Lösel, in press). Such context features probably depend essentially on characteristics of the staff. Therefore, it seems to be very important for an effective treatment to select or train staff who are suitably motivated and competent (see Ross, 1992). If there are already major differences between the various groups of staff regarding, for example, subjective theories of crime and attitudes to rehabilitation (see Averbeck & Lösel, 1992, 1993; Lösel, Bliesener, & Molitor, 1988), there is a risk of a low integrity of measures and, in part, contradictory actions. Staff even may counteract a program (Feldman, 1989). Similar problems are present not only within the specific organisation but also in the cooperation with other institutions involved (Mair, 1990). This particularly applies to the relationship between treatment and aftercare. If, for example, probation officers have very negative attitudes toward imprisonment (Averbeck & Lösel, 1993), the interventions of both institutions may be inconsistent. There is a great lack of empirical data on how far organisational factors influence the success or failure of offender treatment programs.

Process Characteristics

Some of the above-mentioned problems can be reduced when there is sufficient information on the actual course of offender treatment. However, careful process evaluations are still rare (e.g., Lösel et al., 1987; Sechrest & Rosenblatt, 1987). The judgment of measures (as well as their assignment to specific categories) is mostly performed with more or less explicit concepts or summary labels. Whether these actually are implemented adequately, that is, what is the integrity and intensity of the intervention, often cannot be estimated, although this is very important for the effect (e.g., Lösel & Wittmann, 1989). It has been shown repeatedly that treatment concepts have been implemented so poorly that their ineffectiveness is not surprising (see Quay, 1977; Rezmovic, 1984). In contrast, programs that have been implemented with a high level of integrity and intensity may reveal better effects (see Gendreau & Ross, 1987;

Palmer, 1992; Sechrest et al., 1979). This topic is also indicated by results on diversion: Although there is some empirical support for the philosophy of "doing less" (e.g., Heinz & Storz, 1992), successful measures require a substantial impact of psychosocial interventions (e.g., Gendreau & Ross, 1987).

The meta-analyses contain only few data on the factual intervention process. Lipsey (1992) found slightly larger effects in programs with good integrity. Gensheimer et al. (1986) and Gottschalk et al. (1987) reported larger effects for programs with higher intensity (hours of contact between service deliverers and offenders). Antanowicz and Ross (in press) dealt with several specific characteristics of treatment integrity and intensity, however, mainly due to a lack of data, there were no consistent findings.

From the perspective of process evaluation, offender treatment research is still in its infancy. While in general research on psychotherapy, the factual characteristics of the process are investigated in detail (e.g., therapeutic contract, bond, interventions; Orlinsky & Howard, 1986), most evaluations of offender treatment still rely on differentiations between concepts or "schools" (e.g., cognitive-behavioural versus psychodynamic). Accordingly, reports on the treatment implementation are rare or, for example, only used as an explanation for failure (e.g., Gottschalk et al., 1987). If the intervention process is clearly structured and analyzed, it is possible to work out, for example, the central elements of multi-modal approaches. Not only from the clinical but also from the methodological standpoint, it is necessary to pay attention to process characteristics. This is because effectivity depends on the reliability of the dependent variables (the criterion measures) as well as that of the independent variables (the treatment features; Lösel & Wittmann, 1989). Process data should also not be restricted to the experimental group. Transfer of treatment, experimental rivalry, demotivation, and so forth are methodological reasons for a closer look at the control conditions. Furthermore, in the justice system, control groups normally do not get "nothing" but different forms of intervention (e.g., regular sanctions). If we know more about the factual differences between both "treatments," smaller or larger effects may be more plausible.

As a detailed process evaluation requires much effort, it is admittedly easier to propose than to achieve. However, one starting point may be to pay more attention to descriptive validity in evaluation studies and reports (see Lösel et al., 1987). An economical instrument to improve at least the documentation in treatment programs is, for example, the Correctional Program Inventory of Gendreau and Andrews (1991).

Conclusions

Recent meta-analyses and other reviews of the outcome of offender treatment cover a very broad database of more than 500 studies. Overall, they repudiate the doctrine that "nothing works." Nowadays it is becoming clearer which interventions provide a meaningful response to antisocial behaviour and which do not. For example, there are encouraging effects for some types of program (e.g., theoretically sound, cognitive-behavioural, multi-modal, need-, and responsivity-oriented approaches). Other interventions seem to have substantially smaller or even negative effects. Effects in institutional settings, in "harder" criteria, and in stronger designs are tendentially lower than in the community, in "softer" criteria, and weaker designs. Most main and differential effects are small to medium but seem to be relevant even under aspects of cost-benefit.

However, the following restrictions should be taken into account: (a) The programs, offender groups, effect criteria, and settings analyzed in the primary studies are extremely heterogeneous. (b) With only one exception, published meta-analyses refer exclusively to the English-language and, above all, American field. (c) Up to now, the majority of evaluated treatment programs have addressed adolescents. (d) There is a lack of studies on adult offenders in institutional settings. (e) Some meta-analyses have also subsumed studies that deal with behaviour problems in at-risk groups (and not correctional treatment). (f) The methodological standards for the selected primary studies vary across meta-analyses. (g) Many primary studies are described so briefly in journal articles that coding of contents can be ambiguous. (h) Program concept and actual implementation may vary greatly. (i) Follow-up intervals are very different and often short. (j) Each meta-analysis exhibits specific integration techniques and differences in method. (k) The underlying primary studies in various meta-analyses are, to some extent, identical. (l) Also, within each meta-analysis, there is some overlap between studies due to multiple comparisons. (m) Effect sizes from different meta-analyses are not fully comparable, because different coefficients are used. (n) For many plausible moderators there is a substantial lack of primary studies.

Insofar, it is not surprising that various differential effects of meta-analyses are not yet consistent. Furthermore, detailed information on program, setting, client, and staff characteristics is often missing. That is why important aspects of successful treatment like integrity and intensity, staff competence and motivation, offender assessment, institutional climate, and so forth, are only partially confirmed. Although there are rather promising results, we are still far from a conclusive answer with respect to the question what works best with whom and under what conditions. More theoretically derived, well-controlled, sufficiently documented, and replicated evaluations are needed to address this topic. Qualitative forms of evaluations remain important as well, and they should also include complex interventions that are less amenable to experimental designs (Lösel et al., 1987). Furthermore, systematic approaches for integrating case studies are needed (e.g., McGuire, 1992b).

We should also bear in mind that complex interventions, which often include a broad spectrum of psychological, educational, social, ecological, and other measures, which address individual behaviours in a specific context, which are carried out by different persons under varying institutional and social conditions, and so forth, can only be conceived as generalisable social technologies to a limited extent. However, the recent findings encourage research and practice to address the existing problems in a more constructive manner as widespread scepticism in offender treatment suggest. These perspectives include:

1. International intensification of controlled evaluation research on psycho-social interventions;

2. Theoretically sound conceptualisation of kinds of treatment and their implementation;

3. Precise definition and assessment of target groups (e.g., risk, motivation, dropout problem);

4. Explication of theoretically meaningful and concrete goals of treatment (including criteria that are not just related to the individual offender);

5. Evaluation of specific treatment components as separate parts of complex interventions;

6. Differentiation and standardisation of multiple, graduated recidivism and crime-related behavioural criteria;

7. Systematic testing of intermediate effects (including negative effects like prisonisation) and their relation to long-term outcome;

8. Consideration of protective factors and their interplay with risks and intervention;

9. Combination of longitudinal and experimental treatment research;

10. Realisation and process evaluation of treatment integrity and intensity;

11. In cases of institutional treatment, evaluation of transition, release, aftercare, and relapse prevention;

12. Assessment of organisational and staff characteristics and their influence on treatment process and outcome;

13. Detailed documentation of treatment contents and outcomes (also for purposes of meta-evaluation);

14. Development of adequate evaluations of cost-effectiveness and cost-benefit;

15. Information to the public and policy makers with respect to adequate evaluations (e.g., effect size problem).

These and other developments will improve psychosocial interventions as a central component of differentiated reactions to criminality. As long as we do not repeat the mistake of overloading the concept with unrealistic expectations, "revivicated" rehabilitation may outlive more fashionable crime policies.

Appendix: A Brief Introduction to the Method of Meta-Analysis

Meta-analysis has become one of the most widely discussed and applied methods in recent evaluation research. Its goal is to integrate the state of knowledge in one field as representatively, systematically, and objectively as possible by using statistical methods. For this reason, it is particularly important in evaluating social interventions, as the findings in this field are often heterogeneous, inconsistent, controversial, and closely linked to questions of value.

Meta-analysis aims to overcome shortcomings in the traditional, qualitative literature review. These are, for example, sampling errors in the selection of relevant primary studies (file drawer problem), the neglect of important information (e.g., the size of effects), low sensitivity for differential effects, and the insufficient transparency of decision and evaluation processes (see Jackson, 1980). The dichotomy of meta-analysis versus qualitative literature review is nevertheless sometimes overstressed. Instead of just two alternatives, we have to consider a range of variants of research integration. They extend from the qualitative review, across compilations in tabular form, the listing of significances, counting of significant results (vote counting), and sign tests to modern forms of meta-analysis.

Meta-analysis is not a single method but a perspective that uses many techniques (Glass et al., 1981). A typical meta-analysis includes techniques that (a) integrate the single findings; (b) ascertain a mean size of the effects or relations involved; (c) estimate the reliability of the findings; and (d) identify factors that determine the differences between the results of the studies (Strube & Hartmann, 1983). However, different variants of meta-analysis do not pay equal attention to all four domains.

It is not possible to describe the various forms of meta-analysis here (see, e.g., Bangert-Drowns, 1986; Cooper, 1989; Glass, McGaw, & Smith, 1981; Hunter, Schmidt, & Jackson, 1982; Rosenthal, 1991). Only the most important practical steps can be sketched:

(1) Precise definition of the problem. The topic to be covered by a summary of research should be defined as unequivocally as possible. For example, it should be specified what is understood by the term of offender treatment, and that the integration will be restricted to outcomes in controlled studies with at least one treatment group and a control group. It is also specified that, for example, only studies on the treatment of juvenile delinquents or only studies performed during a set period will be included.

(2) Systematic selection of studies. The precisely defined problem definition is used to select relevant empirical primary studies according to explicit procedures. In order to avoid bias, it is necessary, for example, to define which types of publication will be considered (journal articles, articles in edited books, monographs), and whether unpublished work (doctoral dissertations, institutional research reports) should be included. The procedures used to perform the literature search (e.g., computer databases,

100

reviews) should also be specified. It is also necessary to set a minimum level of reported statistics in the primary studies and decide how to deal with multiple publications of the same data.

(3) Coding the studies according to content categories. In this step, all primary studies included have to be coded according to a standardised category system. In offender treatment, these categories refer to, for example, client features, types of treatment, duration of treatment, institutional context, type of outcome criteria, and follow-up intervals. As such categorisations are not always unequivocal (partly due to insufficient documentation in the primary studies), it is also necessary to test intercoder agreement.

(4) Assessing the methodological quality of studies. This step is mostly performed together with the content coding. It can involve ratings of single aspects of the methods used (e.g., randomisation vs. non-randomisation) or the performance of more comprehensive judgments on statistical validity, internal validity, construct validity, and external validity (see Cook & Campbell, 1979).

(5) Computation of effect sizes. Meta-analysis does not simply add up the number of statistically significant outcomes, but computes effect sizes for each study. Most meta-analysis apply d coefficients (Cohen, 1988) or the correlation coefficient r (Friedman, 1968). Each measure can be transformed into the other (see Footnote 1). The d coefficient is particularly suitable for quantitative outcome criteria (e.g., personality tests, behaviour ratings). This coefficient is based on dividing the difference between the means of the treatment and the control group by the standard deviation of the control group or the average standard deviation. The r index is more adequate for illustrating the results of qualitative outcome criteria. According to the Binomial Effect Size Display of Rosenthal and Rubin (1982), the magnitude of r is equivalent to the difference in success rates between treatment and control group. For example, an effect size of r = .10 indicates an increase in the success rate from .45 to .55; an r of .20, an increase from .40 to .60; an r of .30, an increase from .35 to .65; and so forth. If primary studies do not just apply one single outcome criterion, several effect sizes result (e.g., recidivism criteria, personality variables). Even when only one type of criterion is applied, various effect sizes can be derived (e.g., according to the severity of recidivism, with or without consideration of dropouts). To prevent too much weight being assigned to studies with several criteria, often only a mean effect size per study is used in further analysis. Then, an overall mean effect size is computed for all primary studies combined. In this procedure, individual studies are weighted according to sample size or other parameters (see Hedges & Olkin, 1985). The variance between individual studies can be tested to see whether they differ significantly in any way, or whether the different outcomes can be explained by sampling error alone. In addition, confidence intervals are estimated for the overall mean effect.

(6) Analysis of relations between study features and effect sizes. The next step is to examine the relations between the features described in Steps 3, 4, and 5. The procedure corresponds to traditional correlational analysis, except that the "units" are

not persons but the evaluated primary studies or their characteristics and effect sizes. Particular attention is focused on testing which moderating factors the outcomes depend upon (differential effects). In the field of offender treatment, this involves the investigation of, for example, which forms of intervention produce the largest and the smallest effect sizes; how outcomes differ according to effect criteria, follow-up intervals, or setting; whether there is a relation between methodological quality and outcomes; and so forth. Alongside correlations or comparisons of means, analysis of variance or regression analysis are also computed in order to estimate the relative contribution of the individual factors to the variation in the outcomes of the primary studies.

Meta-analysis also contains many problems. Some of them are: (a) biases in the selection of primary studies; (b) differences in the quality of the selected studies; (c) lack of independence in the data; (d) integration of non-comparable studies; (e) lack of theoretical foundation; (f) problems in practical coding; (g) deficits in the explication of decision rules; and (h) lack of uniformity in the results on similar topics. However, most of these criticisms apply to any type of research integration, and it is particularly meta-analysis that attempts to deal with the problems through systematic procedures and techniques (e.g., Cooper, 1991; Lösel, 1991; Rosenthal, 1991). Nowadays, there is hardly any doubt that meta-analysis represents a major advance in research integration. However, like any method, it should be seen as an aid to thought, not a substitute (Green & Hall, 1984). On a higher level, it requires similar quality standards and replications as the primary studies themselves (Bliesener, 1993; Matt & Cook, in press).

BIBLIOGRAPHY

Akers, R.L., Hayner, N.S., & Gruninger, W. (1977). Prisonisation in five countries: Types of prison and inmate characteristics. *Criminology, 14*, 527-554.

Andrews, D.A., Zinger, I., Hoge, R.D., Bonta, J., Gendreau, P., & Cullen, F.T. (1990). Does correctional treatment work? A clinically relevant and psychologically informed meta-analysis. *Criminology, 28*, 369-404.

Antanowicz, D., & Ross, R.R. (in press). *Essential components of successful rehabilitation programs for offenders.* Department of Criminology, University of Ottawa.

Averbeck, M., & Lösel, F. (1992). Subjective crime theories of young offenders and criminal justice officials. *International Journal of Psychology, 27*, 446.

Averbeck, M., & Lösel, F. (1993). Subjektive Theorien über Jugendkriminalität Eine Interview-Studie im Justizsystem. In M. Steller, K.-P. Dahle, & M. Basqué (Eds.), *Straftäterbehandlung: Argumente für eine Revitalisierung in Forschung und Praxis.* Pfaffenweiler: Centaurus.

Bailey, W.C. (1966). Correctional outcome: An evaluation of 100 reports. *Journal of Criminal Law, Criminology and Police Science, 57*, 153-160.

Bailey, J., & MacCulloch, M.J. (1992). Characteristics of 112 cases discharged directly to the community from a new Special Hospital and some comparisons of performance. *Journal of Forensic Psychiatry, 3*, 91-112.

Bangert-Drowns, R.L. (1986). Review of developments in meta-analytic method. *Psychological Bulletin, 99*, 388-399.

Basta, J.M., & Davidson II, W.S. (1988). Treatment of juvenile offenders: Study outcomes since 1980. *Behavioural Sciences & the Law, 6*, 353-384.

Beelmann, A., Pfingsten, U., & Lösel, F. (1992). *The effects of training social competence in children: A meta-analysis of recent evaluation studies.* Research report. Bielefeld: Research Centre "Prevention and Intervention in Childhood and Adolescence" of the German Research Association.

Blackburn, R. (1980). *Still not working? A look at recent outcomes in offender rehabilitation.* Paper presented at the Scottish Branch of the British Psychological Society Conference on Deviance, February 1980, Sterling, UK.

Blackburn, R. (1992). *The psychology of criminal conduct.* Chichester: Wiley.

Bliesener, T. (1993). *Der Einfluß der Forschungsqualität auf das Forschungsergebnis: Zur Evaluation der Validierung biographischer Daten in der Eignungsdiagnostik.* Habilitationsschrift. Universität Erlangen-Nürnberg.

Bondeson, U.V. (1989). *Prisoners in prison societies*. New Brunswick, NJ: Transaction Books.

Bonta, J., & Gendreau, P. (1990). Reexamining the cruel and unusual punishment of prison life. *Law and Human Behaviour, 14*, 347-372.

Bonta, J., & Gendreau, P. (1992). Coping with prison. In P. Suedfeld, & P.E. Tetlock (Eds.), *Psychology and social policy* (pp. 343-354). New York: Hemisphere.

Bornstein, P.H., Hamilton, S.B., & McFall, M.E. (1981). Modification of adult aggression: A critical review of theory, research, and practice. *Progress in Behaviour Modification, 12*, 299-350.

Brennan, P.A., & Mednick, S.A. (in press). Evidence for the adaption of a learning theory approach to criminal deterrence: A preliminary study. In E. Weitekamp, & H.-J. Kerner (Eds.), *Cross-national longitudinal research on human development and criminal behaviour*. Dordrecht, NL: Kluwer.

Brody, S.R. (1976). *The effectiveness of sentencing*. London: Her Majesty's Stationery Office.

Bullock, J.R., & Svyantek, D.J. (1985). Analyzing meta-analysis: Potential problems, an unsuccessful replication, and evaluation criteria. *Journal of Applied Psychology, 70*, 108-115.

Casey, R.J., & Berman, J.S. (1985). The outcome of psychotherapy with children. *Psychological Bulletin, 98*, 388-400.

Chen, H.T. (1989). *Theory-driven evaluations*. Newbury Park, CA: Sage.

Christie, N. (1986). Scandinavian criminology: Some perspectives. In H. Kury (Ed.), *Entwicklungstendenzen kriminologischer Forschung: Interdisziplinäre Wissenschaft zwischen Politik und Praxis* (pp. 109-118). Köln: Heymanns.

Cohen, J. (1988). *Statistical power analysis for the behavioural sciences*, 2nd ed. New York: Academic Press.

Cook, T.D. (1985). Post-positivist critical multiplism. In L. Shotland, & M.M. Mark (Eds.), *Social sciences and social policy* (pp. 21-62). Beverly Hills, CA: Sage.

Cook, T.D., & Campbell, D.T. (1979). *Quasi-experimentation. Design and analysis issues for field settings*. Chicago: Rand-McNally.

Cooper, H.M. (1989). *Integrating research: A guide for doing literature reviews*, 2nd ed. Newbury Park, CA: Sage.

Cooper, H.M. (1991). An introduction to meta-analysis and the integrative research review. In G. Albrecht, & H.-U. Otto (Eds.), *Social prevention and the social sciences* (pp. 288-304). Berlin, New York: de Gruyter.

Corrigan, P.W. (1991). Social skills training in adult psychiatric populations: A meta-analysis. *Journal of Behaviour Therapy and Experimental Psychiatry*, 22, 203-210.

Cronbach, L.J., Ambron, S.R., Dornbusch, S.M., Hess, R.D., Hornik, R.C., Philips, D.C., Walker, D.F., & Weiner, S.S. (1980). *Toward reform of program evaluation*. San Francisco: Jossey Bass.

Dünkel, F. (1987). *Die Herausforderung der geburtenschwachen Jahrgänge*. Freiburg i.Br.: Max-Planck-Institut für ausländisches und internationales Strafrecht.

Dünkel, F., & Geng, B. (1991). *Zur Rückfälligkeit von Karrieretätern nach unterschiedlichen Strafvollzugs- und Entlassungsformen*. Forschungsbericht. Freiburg i.Br.: Max-Planck-Institut für ausländisches und internationales Strafrecht.

Egg, R. (1984). *Straffälligkeit und Sozialtherapie*. Köln: Heymanns.

Egg, R. (1990). Sozialtherapeutische Behandlung und Rückfälligkeit im längerfristigen Vergleich. *Monatsschrift für Kriminologie und Strafrechtsreform*, 73, 358-368.

Egg, R. (Ed.) (1993). Sozialtherapie in den 90er Jahren. Wiesbaden: Kriminologische Zentralstelle.

Eysenck, H.J., & Gudjonsson, G. (1989). *The causes and cures of criminality*. New York: Plenum Press.

Farrington, D.P. (1983). Randomised experiments on crime and justice. In M. Tonry, & N. Morris (Eds.), *Crime and Justice*, vol. 4 (pp. 257-308). Chicago: University of Chicago Press.

Farrington, D.P. (1992). Psychological contributions to the explanation, prevention, and treatment of offending. In F. Lösel, D. Bender, & T. Bliesener (Eds.), *Psychology and Law. International perspectives* (pp. 35-51). Berlin, New York: de Gruyter

Farrington, D.P., & Langan, P.A. (1992). Changes in crime and punishment in England and America in the 1980s. *Justice Quarterly*, 9, 5-46.

Farrington, D.P., & Nuttall, C.P. (1980). Prison size, overcrowding, prison violence, and recidivism. *Journal of Criminal Justice*, 8, 221-231.

Farrington, D.P., Ohlin, L.E., & Wilson, J.Q. (1986). *Understanding and controlling crime*. New York: Springer.

Feldman, P. (1989). Applying psychology to the reduction of juvenile offending and offences: Methods and results. *Issues in Criminological and Legal Psychology*, 14, 3-32.

Friedman, H. (1968). Magnitude of experimental effect and a table for its rapid estimation. *Psychological Bulletin*, 70, 245-251.

Garrett, P. (1985). Effects of residential treatment of adjucated delinquents: A meta-analysis. *Journal of Research in Crime and Delinquency, 22*, 287-308.

Gendreau, P., & Andrews, D.A. (1990). Tertiary prevention: What the meta-analyses of the offender treatment literature tell us about "What works". *Canadian Journal of Criminology, 32*, 173-184.

Gendreau, P., & Andrews, D.A. (1991). *Correctional Program Intervention Inventory (CPEI)*, 2nd ed. New Brunswick, Ottawa, CAN.

Gendreau, P., & Ross, R.R. (1979). Effective correctional treatment: Bibliotherapy for cynics. *Crime and Delinquency, 25*, 463-489.

Gendreau, P., & Ross, R.R. (1987). Revivication of rehabilitation: Evidence from the 1980s. *Justice Quarterly, 4*, 349-407.

Genevie, L., Margolies, E., & Muhlin, G.L. (1986). How effective is correctional intervention? *Social Policy, 17*, 52-57.

Gensheimer, L.K., Mayer, J.P., Gottschalk, R., & Davidson II, W.S. (1986). Diverting youth from the juvenile justice system: A meta-analysis of intervention efficacy. In S.J. Apter, & A. Goldstein (Eds.), *Youth violence: Programs and prospects* (pp. 39-57). Elmsford, NY: Pergamon Press.

Glass, G.V., McGaw, B., & Smith, M.L. (1981). *Meta-analysis in social research.* Beverly Hills, CA: Sage.

Goldstein, A.P. (1990). *Delinquents on delinquency.* Campaign, IL: Research Press.

Gottfredson, M., & Hirschi, T.M. (1990). *A general theory of crime.* Stanford, CA: Stanford University Press.

Gottschalk, R., Davidson II, W.S., Gensheimer, L.K., & Mayer, J.P. (1987). Community-based interventions. In H.C. Quay (Ed.), *Handbook of juvenile delinquency* (pp. 266-289). New York: Wiley.

Green, S.B., & Hall, J.A. (1984). Quantitative methods for literature reviews. *Annual Review of Psychology, 35*, 37-53.

Greenberg, P.F. (1977). The correctional effects of corrections: A survey of evaluations. In D.F. Greenberg (Ed.), *Corrections and punishment* (pp. 111-148). Beverly Hills, CA: Sage.

Greenwood, P.W., & Turner, S. (1985). *The Vision Quest Program: An evaluation.* Santa Monica, CA: Rand Corporation.

Guerra, N. (1991). *Social cognitive factors in the prevention of antisocial behaviour.* Paper presented at the 11th Biennial Meetings of the International Society for the Study of Behavioural Development, July 1991, Minneapolis, MN.

Gunn, J., & Robertson, G. (1982). An evaluation of Grendon Prison. In J. Gunn, & D.P. Farrington (Eds.), *Abnormal offenders, delinquency and the criminal justice system.* London: Wiley.

Hawkins, J.D., Catalino, R.F., & Miller, J.Y. (1992). Risk and protective factors for alcohol and other drug problems in adolescence and early adulthood: Implications for substance abuse prevention. *Psychological Bulletin, 112,* 64-105.

Hedges, L.V., & Olkin, I. (1985). *Statistical methods for meta-analysis.* Orlando: Academic Press.

Heinz, W., & Storz, R. (1992). *Diversion im Jugendstrafverfahren der Bundesrepublik Deutschland.* Bonn: Forum Verlag.

Hollin, C.R. (1990). *Cognitive-behavioural interventions with young offenders.* Elmsford, NY: Pergamon Press.

Hood, R. (1967). Research on the effectiveness of punishments and treatments. In European Committee on Crime Problems (Ed.), *Collected studies in criminological research,* vol. I. (pp. 73-113). Strasbourg: Council of Europe.

Hürlimann, M. (1992). *Führer und Einflußfaktoren in der Subkultur des Strafvollzugs.* Phil. Dissertation. Universität Erlangen-Nürnberg.

Hunter, J.E., Schmidt, F.L., & Jackson, G.B. (1982). *Meta-analysis: Cumulating research findings across studies.* Beverly Hills, CA: Sage.

Izzo, R.L., & Ross, R.R. (1990). Meta-analysis of rehabilitation programs for juvenile delinquents. A brief report. *Criminal Justice and Behaviour, 17,* 134-142.

Jackson, N.S. (1980). Methods for integrative reviews. *Review of Educational Research, 50,* 438-460.

Jeffery, C.R. (1979). *Punishment and deterrence: A psychological statement.* In C.R. Jeffery (Ed.), Biology and crime (pp. 100-121). Beverly Hills, CA: Sage.

Jessor, R. (1987). Problem-Behaviour Theory, psychosocial development, and adolescent problem drinking. *British Journal of Addiction, 82,* 435-446.

Kaiser, G., Dünkel, F., & Ortmann, R. (1982). Die sozialtherapeutische Anstalt- Das Ende einer Reform? *Zeitschrift für Rechtspolitik, 15,* 198-207.

Kaiser, G., Kerner, H.-J., & Schöch, H. (1991) *Strafvollzug*, 4. Aufl. Heidelberg: C.F. Müller.

Karstedt-Henke, S. (1991). Diversion - Ein Freibrief für Straftaten? *DVVJ-Journal, 2*, 108-113.

Kazdin, A. (1987). Treatment of antisocial behaviour in children: Current status and future directions. *Psychological Bulletin, 102*, 187-203.

Kette, G. (1991). *Haft. Eine sozialpsychologische Analyse*. Göttingen: Hogrefe.

Killias, M. (Ed.) (1992). *Rückfall und Bewährung/Récidive et Réhabilitation*. Chur, CH: Rüegger.

Laws, D.R. (Ed.) (1989). *Relapse prevention with sex offenders*. New York: Guilford Press.

Lipsey, M.W. (1992a). Juvenile delinquency treatment: A meta-analytic inquiry into variability of effects. In T.D. Cook, H. Cooper, D.S. Cordray, H. Hartmann, L.V. Hedges, R.L. Light, T.A. Louis, & F. Mosteller (Eds.), *Meta-analysis for explanation* (pp. 83-127). New York: Russell Sage Foundation.

Lipsey, M.W. (1992b). The effect of treatment on juvenile delinquents: Results from meta-analysis. In F. Lösel, D. Bender, & T. Bliesener (Eds.), *Psychology and law. International perspectives* (131-143). Berlin, New York: de Gruyter.

Lipton, D., Martinson, R., & Wilks, J. (1975). *The effectiveness of correctional treatment*. New York: Praeger.

Loeber, R. (1990). Disruptive and antisocial behaviour in childhood and adolescence: Development and risk factors. In K. Hurrelmann, & F. Lösel (Eds.), *Health hasards in adolescence* (pp. 223-257). Berlin, New York: De Gruyter.

Loeber, R., & Farrington, D.P. (in press). Problems and solutions in longitudinal and experimental treatment studies of child psychopathology and delinquency. *Journal of Consulting and Clinical Psychology*.

Lösel, F. (1975). *Handlungskontrolle und Jugenddelinquenz*. Stuttgart: Enke.

Lösel, F. (1991). Meta-analysis and social prevention: Evaluation and a study on the family-hypothesis in developmental psychopathology. In G. Albrecht, & H.-U. Otto (Eds.), *Social prevention and the social sciences* (pp. 305-332). Berlin, New York: de Gruyter.

Lösel, F. (1992). Sprechen Evaluationsergebnisse von Meta-Analysen für einen frischen Wind in der Straftäterbehandlung? In M. Killias (Ed.), *Rückfall und Bewährung/Récidive et Réhabilitation* (pp. 335-353). Chur, CH: Rüegger.

Lösel, F. (1993). Meta-analytische Beiträge zur wiederbelebten Diskussion des Behandlungsgedankens. In M. Steller, K.-P. Dahle, & M. Basqué (Eds.) (1993), *Straftäterbehandlung. Argumente für eine Revitalisierung in Forschung und Praxis.* Pfaffenweiler: Centaurus.

Lösel, F. (in press). Protective effects of social resources in adolescents at high risk for antisocial behaviour. In E. Weitekamp, & H.-J. Kerner (Eds.), *Cross-national longitudinal research on human development and criminal behaviour.* Dordrecht, NL: Kluwer (in press).

Lösel, F., & Bliesener, T. (1989). Psychology in prison: Role assessment and testing of an organisational model. In H. Wegener, F. Lösel, & J. Haisch (Eds.), *Criminal behaviour and the justice system: Psychological perspectives* (pp. 419-439). New York: Springer.

Lösel, F., & Bliesener, T. (1990). Resilience in adolescence: A study on the generalisability of protective factors. In K. Hurrelmann, & F. Lösel (Eds.), *Health hasards in adolescence* (pp. 299-320). Berlin, New York: de Gruyter.

Lösel, F., Bliesener, T., & Molitor, A. (1988). Social psychology in the criminal justice system: A study on role perceptions and stereotypes of prison personnel. In P.J. van Koppen, D.J. Hessing, & G. van den Heuvel (Eds.), *Lawyers on psychology and psychologists on law* (pp. 167-184). Amsterdam: Swets & Zeitlinger.

Lösel, F., & Köferl, P.(1989). Evaluation research on correctional treatment in West Germany: A meta-analysis. In H. Wegener, F. Lösel, & J. Haisch (Eds.), *Criminal behaviour and the justice system: Psychological perspectives* (pp. 334-355). New York: Springer.

Lösel, F., Köferl, P., & Weber, F. (1987). *Meta-Evaluation der Sozialtherapie.* Stuttgart: Enke.

Lösel, F., & Nowack, W. (1987). Evaluationsforschung. In J. Schultz-Gambard (Ed.), *Angewandte Sozialpsychologie* (pp.57-87). Weinheim: Psychologie Verlags Union.

Lösel, F., & Wittmann, W.W. (1989) The relationship of treatment integrity and intensity to outcome criteria. In R.F. Conner, & M. Hendricks (Eds.), *International innovations in evaluation methodology. New Directions for Program Evaluation, No. 42* (pp. 97-108). San Francisco: Jossey-Bass.

Logan, C. (1972). Evaluation research in crime and delinquency: A reappraisal. *Journal of Criminal Law, Criminology and Police Science, 63,* 378-387.

Mair, G. (1990). Evaluating the effects of diversion strategies on the attitudes and practices of agents of the criminal justice system. *Report for the 19th Criminological Research Conference: New social strategies and the criminal justice system.* Strasbourg: Council of Europe.

Martinson, R. (1974). What works? Questions and answers about prison reform. *Public Interest, 10*, 22-54.

Martinson, R. (1979). New findings, new views: A note of caution regarding sentencing reform. *Hofstra Law Review, 7*, 242-258.

Matt, G.E. (1989). Decision, rules for selecting effect sizes in meta-analysis: A review and reanalysis of psychotherapy outcome studies. *Psychological Bulletin, 105*, 106-115.

Matt, G.E., & Cook, T. (in press). Threats to the validity of research synthesis. In H.M. Cooper & L.V. Hedges (Eds.), *Handbook of research synthesis*.

Mayer, J.P., Gensheimer L.K., Davidson II, W.S., & Gottschalk, R. (1986). Social learning treatment within juvenile justice: A meta-analysis of impact in the natural environment. In S.J. Apter, & A. Goldstein (Eds.), *Youth violence: Programs and prospects* (pp. 24-38). Elmsford, NY: Pergamon Press.

McCord, J. (1978). A thirty-year follow-up of treatment effects. *American Psychologist, 33*, 284-289.

McGuire, J. (1992). Things to do to make your programme work. In B. Rowson, & J. McGuire (Eds.), *What works: Effective methods to reduce re-offending* (pp. 48 - 51). Conference Proceedings, Manchester.

McGuire, J. (1992b). Interpreting treatment-outcome studies of anti-social behaviour: Combining meta-analyses and single case designs. *International Journal of Psychology, 27*, 446.

McGuire, J., & Priestley, P. (1992). Some things do work: Psychological interventions with offenders and the effectiveness debate. In F. Lösel, D. Bender, & T. Bliesener (Eds.), *Psychology and law: International perspectives* (pp. 163-174). Berlin, New York: de Gruyter.

McIvor, G. (1992). *Reconviction among offenders sentenced to community service. Research report.* Stirling, Scotland: University of Stirling, Social Work Research Centre.

Meltzoff, J., & Kornreich, M. (1970). *Research in psychotherapy.* Chicago: Atherton.

Moffitt, T.E., & Silva, P.A. (1988). IQ and delinquency: A direct test of the differential detection hypthesis. *Journal of Abnormal Psychology, 97*, 330-333.

Moitra, S.D. (1987). *Crimes and punishments. A comparison study of temporal variations.*

Freiburg i.Br.: Max-Planck-Institut für ausländisches und internationales Strafrecht.

Monahan, J. (1981). *Predicting violent behaviour: An assessment of clinical techniques.* Beverly Hills, CA: Sage.

Monahan, J. (1989). Prediction of criminal behaviour: Recent developments in research and policy in the United States. In H. Wegener, F. Lösel, & J. Haisch (Eds.), *Criminal behaviour and the justice system: Psychological perspectives* (pp. 40-52). New York: Springer.

Moos, R. (1975). *Evaluating correctional and community settings.* New York: Wiley.

Morris, E.K., & Braukman, C.J. (Eds.). *Behavioural approaches to crime and delinquency: A handbook of applications, research, and concepts.* New York: Plenum Press.

Mulvey, E.P., & Lidz, C.W. (1993). Measuring patient violence in dangerousness research. *Law and Human Behaviour, 17,* 277-288.

Murray, C.A., & Cox, L.A. (1979). *Beyond probation: Juvenile corrections and the chronic delinquent.* Beverly Hills, CA: Sage.

Novaco, R.N. (1975). *Anger control: The development and evaluation of an experimental treatment.* Lexington: Lexington Books.

Orlinsky, D.E., & Howard, K.I. (1986). Process and outcome in psychotherapy. In S.L. Garfield, & A.E. Bergin (Eds.), *Handbook of psychotherapy and behaviour change,* 3rd ed. (pp. 311-381). New York: Wiley.

Ortmann, R. (1992). Die Nettobilanz einer Resozialisierung im Strafvollzug: Negativ? In H. Kury (Ed.), *Gesellschaftliche Umwälzung: Kriminalitätserfahrungen, Straffälligkeit und soziale Kontrolle* (pp. 375-451). Freiburg i.Br.: Max-Planck-Institut für ausländisches und internationales Strafrecht.

Palmer, T. (1968). Types of treaters and types of juvenile offenders. *Youth Authority Quarterly, 18,* 14-23.

Palmer, T. (1975). Martinson revisited. *Journal of Research in Crime and Delinquency, 12,* 133-152.

Palmer, T. (1992). *The re-emergence of correctional intervention.* Newbury Park, CA: Sage.
Porporino, F.J., & Dudley, K. (1984). *Analysis of the effects of overcrowding in Canadian penitentiaries.* Ottawa: Solicitor General Canada.

Prentice, D.A., & Miller, D.T. (1992). When small effects are impressive. *Psychological Bulletin, 112,* 160-164.

Prentky, R., & Burgess, A.W. (1992). Rehabilition of child molesters: A cost-benefit analysis. In A.W. Burgess (Ed.), *Child trauma I: Issues and research* (pp.417-442). New York: Garland.

Quay, H.C. (1977). The three faces of evaluation: What can be expected to work? *Criminal Justice and Behaviour*, *4*, 341 - 354.

Renwick, S.J.D., Ridley, A., & Ramm, M.C. (1993). *Deficits and disfunctions*: *Old assumptions revisited*. Paper presented at the European Conference: Clinical Psychology and Offenders, April 1993, Royal Holloway and Bedford New College, Surrey, England.

Rezmovic, E.L. (1984). Assessing treatment implementation amid the slings and arrows of reality. *Evaluation Review*, *2*, 187-204.

Roberts, C. (1992). Effective practice and service delivery. Paper presented at What Works 1992, Conference on progress in effective work with offenders. September 1992, Salford, UK.

Romig, A.D. (1978). *Justice for our children. An examination of juvenile delinquent rehabilitation programs*. Lexington, MA: Lexington Books.

Rosenthal, R. (1991). *Meta-analytic procedures for social research*, 2nd. ed. Newbury Park, CA: Sage.

Rosenthal, R., & Rubin, D.B. (1982). A simple general purpose display of magnitude of experimental effect. *Journal of Educational Psychology*, *74*, 166-169.

Ross, R.R. (1992). Reasoning and rehabilitation of offenders. In B. Rowson, & J. McGuire (Eds.), *What works: Effective methods to reduce re-offending* (pp. 21-26). Conference Proceedings, Manchester.

Ross, R.R., Fabiano, E., & Ross, R.D. (1986). *Reasoning and rehabilitation: A handbook for teaching cognitive skills*. Ottawa: Cognitive Center.

Rowson, B., & McGuire, J. (Eds.) (1992). *What works: Effective methods to reduce re-offending*. Conference Proceedings, Manchester.

Ruback, R.B., & Innes, C.A. (1988). The relevance and irrelevance of psychological research: The example of prison crowding. *American Psychologist*, *43*, 683-693.

Rutter, M. (1990). Psychosocial resilience and protective mechanisms. In J. Rolf, A. Masten, D. Cicchetti, K. Nuechterlein, & S. Weintraub (Eds.), *Risk and protective factors in the development of psychopathology* (pp. 181-214). New York: Cambridge University Press.

Schüler-Springorum, H. (1986). Die sozialtherapeutischen Anstalten - ein kriminalpolitisches Lehrstück. In H.J. Hirsch, G. Kaiser, & H. Marquardt (Eds.), *Gedächtnisschrift für Hilde Kaufmann* (pp. 167-188). Berlin: De Gruyter.

Sechrest, L., & Rosenblatt, A. (1987). Research methods. In H.C. Quay (Ed.), *Handbook of juvenile delinquency* (pp. 417-450). New York: Wiley.

Sechrest, L. B., White, S.O., & Brown, E.D. (Eds.) (1979). *The rehabilitation of criminal offenders: Problems and prospects.* Washington, D.C.: National Academy of Sciences.

Shapiro, D. A., & Shapiro, D. (1983). Meta-analysis of comparative therapy outcome studies: A replication and refinement. *Psychological Bulletin, 92,* 581-604.

Sherman, L.W. (1988). Randomised experiments in criminal sanctions. In H.S. Bloom, D.S. Cordray, & R.J. Light (Eds.), *Lessons from selected program and policy areas* (pp. 85-98). New Directions for Program Evaluation, no. 37. San Francisco Jossey-Bass.

Sparks, R.F. (1968). Types of treatment for types of offenders. In European Committee on Crime Problems (Ed.), *Collected studies in criminological research,* vol. 3. Strasbourg: Council of Europe.

Smith, M.L., Glass, G.V., & Miller, T.I. (1980). *The benefits of psychotherapy.* Baltimore: Johns Hopkins University Press.

Steller, M. (1977). *Sozialtherapie statt Strafvollzug.* Köln: Kiepenheuer.

Strube, M.J., & Hartmann, D.P. (1983). Meta-analysis: Techniques, applications, and functions. *Journal of Consulting and Clinical Psychology, 51,* 14-27.

Taylor, P., & Gunn, J. (1984. Violence and psychologists. *British Medical Journal, 289,* 9-12.

Thornton, D.M. (1987). Treatment effects on recidivism: A reappraisal of the "nothing works" doctrine. In B.J. McGurk, D.M. Thornton, & M. Williams (Eds.), *Applying psychology to imprisonment* (pp. 181-189). London: H.M.S.O.

Tittle, C.R., Villemez, W.J., & Smith, D.A. (1978. The myth of social class and criminality: An empirical assessment of the empirical evidence. *American Sociological Review, 43,* 643-656.

Tonry, M., Ohlin, L.E., & Farrington, D.P. (1991). *Human development and criminal behaviour.* New York: Springer.

Waldo, G., & Griswold, D. (1979). Issues in the measurement of recidivism. In L.B. Sechrest, S.O. White, & E.D. Brown (Eds.), *The rehabilitation of criminal offenders: Problems and prospects* (pp. 225-250). Washington, D.C.: National Academy Sciences.

Weisz, J.R., Weiss, B., Alicke, M.D., & Klotz, M.L. (1987). Effectiveness of psychotherapy with children and adolescents: A meta-analysis for clinicians. *Journal of Consulting and Clinical Psychology, 55,* 542-549.

Whitehead, J.T., & Lab, S.P. (1989). A meta-analysis of juvenile correctional treatment. *Journal of Research in Crime and Delinquency, 26,* 276-295.

Wilson, J.Q., & Herrnstein, R.J. (1985). *Crime and human nature.* New York: Simon & Schuster.

Winterdyk, J., & Roesch, R. (1981). A wilderness experimental program as an alternative for probationers: An evaluation. *Canadian Journal of Criminology, 23,* 39-49.

Wormith, J.S. (1984). The controversy over the effects of long-term imprisonment. *Canadian Journal of Criminology, 26,* 423-437.

Wright, E.W., & Dixon, M.C. (1977). Community prevention and treatment of juvenile delinquency. A review of evaluations. *Journal of Research in Crime and Delinquency, 14,* 35-67.

Yochelson, S., & Samenow, S.E. (1976). *The criminal personality, vol. I: A profile for change.* New York: Aronson.

Zamble, E., & Porporino, F.J. (1990). Coping, imprisonment, and rehabilitation: Some data and their implications. *Criminal Justice and Behaviour, 17,* 53-70.

PSYCHOSOCIAL INTERVENTIONS IN THE CRIMINAL JUSTICE SYSTEM

20th Criminological Research
Conference
(1993)

IMPLEMENTING PSYCHOSOCIAL INTERVENTIONS LINKED TO COMMUNITY SANCTIONS

by
Mrs J. ROBERTS
Hereford and Worcester Probation Service
(United Kingdom)

CONTENTS

1. Introduction

1.1 The purpose of this paper is not simply to describe how psychosocial interventions can be applied through community sanctions, and specifically through probation order supervision methods; but also to examine those practical constraints and diverse influences upon the work of the probation service in England and Wales, which may determine whether successful methods can be applied. I will offer with some definitions of effectiveness, and the corresponding aspects of evaluation. My perspective is not that of the independent researcher, but of a probation service manager, with a responsibility to ensure effective service delivery, by establishing those conditions which support it, and limiting adverse influences which undermine it.

2. Background

2.1 The theme of holding a balance within an array of divergent interests can immediately be identified from a very brief examination of the legal, historical and structural position of probation services. I shall be describing arrangements in England and Wales, but practical aspects of probation work are very similar throughout the United Kingdom — it is the legal, historical and structural arrangements which vary in Scotland, and in Northern Ireland.

2.2 Probation originated in volunteer help to offenders facing draconian punishments in the 19th century, and was in wide use before legislative provision in 1907. Probation officers were originally employed by local courts, and the local base of today's probation services retains strong links to courts. Service boundaries follow those of local authorities, but there has been little local political influence (except indirectly upon resourcing levels). The nature of probation work requires close partnership with a wide range of local services, (although because probation officers are trained alongside social workers, they have traditionally had stronger affinity with them than with other criminal justice agencies). One result of this localised structure was a very varied pattern of service delivery, in which innovation and flexibility were prominent features. This together with other factors led the judiciary (whose working arrangements require them to adjudicate in different areas of the country) to complain of the inconsistency (in both type and quality) of probation service provision.

2.3 Since 1967, criminal justice legislation has progressively enlarged the contribution of the probation service to the criminal justice system, while over the past ten years the policies of central government have increasingly determined the shape and direction of probation practice. Key examples of the latter are centrally determined resource levels; the Statement of Purpose and Three Year Plan (1992), to which the equivalent policies of local probation committees must now be subordinated; and (also 1992). National Standards for the Supervision of Offenders in the Community, which lay down minimum levels and frequencies of contact with offenders who are under supervision in the community, after custodial sentences, or the subject of pre-sentence reports. Examples of our developing role in the wider criminal justice system include responsibility for voluntary after-care of prisoners (1966) and parole (1968), community service (1972), advice in cautioning (early 1970s), advice to Crown prosecutors on bail

119

and discontinuance (late 1980s),contributions to successful crime prevention programmes; post-custodial supervision of all prisoners sentenced to 12 months or longer (1991 Criminal Justice Act).

2.4 The Audit Commission identified that the probation services in England and Wales contribute from their experience of working with offenders to most of the key decision stages in the criminal justice process (Figure 1). The workload of the probation service reflects this, (Table 1) with about twice the number of offenders under supervision in the community as are in prison (on remand or serving a sentence). Following the 1991 Act, the numbers of prisoners who will be supervised after release will increase.

3.   Aims and effectiveness

3.1 It follows from the complex context in which probation services operate, that definitions of aims, methods and effectiveness are similarly complex and potentially contradictory. (Indeed, it will emerge that there is an absence of concensus about aims, about the translation of aims into methods and that nonetheless evidence of effectiveness is required to pass the tests of both scientific rigour and public credibility!). Four definitions of effectiveness have dominated thinking about the work of the probation service, and although their relative prominence has changed over recent decades, no single definition has prevailed to the exclusion of the rest.

3.2   Effectiveness in carrying out the decisions of the courts

3.2.1   This could be said to be a perennial expectation, although not often tested or demonstrated by sufficiently scientific means. This is unfortunate, since community sentences are in fact remarkably effective in this respect, and could be more highly valued. Unfortunately, community sentences cannot emulate the greater certainty of custodial measures, and the demands they make, as well as their general cost-effectiveness, are less readily recognised, and therefore not weighed in the balance.

3.2.2   Judges and magistrates (lay unpaid sentencers who deal with the majority of criminal court cases) in England and Wales are given little background training in the overall effectiveness of different means of dealing with offenders. They may therefore be susceptible to the influence of their own experience (in dealing with offenders who have not responded to measures previously imposed) and to the influence of public opinion and the mass media. Assumptions about effectiveness in carrying out the decisions of the court consequently tend to favour the custodial sentence, which is seen by many as the only real punishment, and the benchmark against which all others are measured.

3.3   Effectiveness in helping people

3.3.1   Probation undoubtedly has the edge, however, when effectiveness is weighed in terms of meeting offenders' needs. David Thomas (1979) profoundly influenced sentencing practice with his account of an offence/offender dichotomy, which required judges and magistrates to consider the offender's needs only where they outweighed the gravity of the offence. Perhaps this is how the term "soft option" as applied to probation was coined. Because such use of probation implies indulgence on the part of sentencers, they and we have been remarkably uninterested in the subject of effectiveness in meeting offenders' needs, especially as perceived by the offenders themselves. If there is subsequent reoffending, the effectiveness of probation help is not examined, although blame may be attached to the offender for failing to take full advantage of the indulgence and help that has been offered. The offers are less likely to be repeated, even if the needs remain as great as before — which seems to assume a perceived link between social need and offending.

3.3.2   I will deal later with the concentration of social disadvantage among offender populations. This undoubtedly lends moral weight to the idea that dealing with social needs is appropriate, and may foster the assumption that it will reduce reoffending. From a traditional social casework approach to recent developments in "What Works" (to reduce reoffending) it is clear that methods which seek to mitigate social disadvantage are important, but demonstrations of the link between meeting social needs and reduced offending at the individual level are rare.

3.4   Effectiveness in diverting from custody

3.4.1   The steady increase in the prison population after the Second World War eventually led to a new test of effectiveness for probation — its capacity to provide credible alternatives to custody. Not surprisingly, in a culture where imprisonment (or worse) is seen as the only true punishment, probation efforts in this direction have not proved very successful. Where rates of use of custody have been influenced, the cause is more likely to have been formal restrictions upon sentencers than the attractions of measures such as community service orders or offending behaviour programmes. (This can be illustrated by examining use of custody and alternatives for young adult offenders 1969-1990 (Table 2)). This does not imply that such measures are not popular — community service orders are very widely used — but that simply extending restrictions on the liberty of offenders in the community is not accepted by courts as equivalent to custody.

3.4.2   Probation officers certainly succeeded in persuading courts to use community sanctions like the community service order and the probation order for more serious offenders (Table 3). As a result, probation officers now work with recidivists to an extent that was unimaginable when I began to work with probationers 25 years ago. Increased use of forms of diversion for minor and younger offenders have contributed to this trend.

3.4.3   The introduction of such measures as day centres and programmes was originally intended to encourage diversion from custody, by partially restricting liberty and influencing behaviour. It was assumed that courts would be reluctant to use standard probation orders with more serious or recidivist offenders, because the standard probation order is perceived as offering help. Probation officers had been discouraged by the fashionable view that "nothing works" (Martinson; Brody) from examining the potential effects of these new probation methods on further offending. Indeed, until the 1980s, research staff were employed by only a handful of (mainly larger) probation services. It was assumed that all necessary research would be commissioned by the Home Office. Yet four experimental day training centres, established in 1974 by the Home Office, were funded relatively generously but never evaluated before they were legally abolished via the 1982 Criminal Justice Act.

3.5   Effectiveness in reducing offending

3.5.1   This has long been an implicit justification for the work of probation officers, but until recently it has not been seen by them as other than an indirect effect (via social needs) or a comparative one — "less damaging" than custody. Very broad comparisons between use of different sentences for offenders with different criminal histories tended to show that probation was less effective with first offenders than other measures, but more effective with recidivists (Walker). Such findings supported arguments for custodial alternatives and the move away from working with less heavily convicted offenders typical of the probation caseload until the 1980s (Table 4). Home Office research (the IMPACT studies) tested in some detail the effectiveness of probation work with different groups of offenders. The probation methods used would today be regarded as broadly of a helping nature, with experimental officers using a wider range of interventions and sharper focus on the offender's environment. The results were deemed inconclusive, although in fact where accurately directed at offenders with lower criminal tendencies and many personal social problems, both problems and reoffending were reduced.

4.   Practical constraints upon the provision of community sanctions

4.1   Current legal framework

4.1.1   Use of different community sanctions has fluctuated with these varying expectations of probation service effectiveness. Currently, the 1991 Criminal Justice Act favours community sentences as providing restriction of liberty commensurate with the seriousness of the offence, except where offences are minor, or so serious that only a custodial sentence will suffice. The probation service is expected to convince courts and the public of the credibility of community sentences in this respect (restriction of liberty) and hence as a punishment. Nevertheless, the Act identifies the purposes of probation (for the first time in the history of the probation order) as aimed at

> "(...) securing the rehabilitation of the offender; or (...) protecting the public from harm by him or preventing the commission by him of further offences (...)" (sec.7.2(1)).

4.1.2   One immediate reaction from sentencers has been to deplore the loss of a helping response to minor offenders with social problems. In order to discourage use of expensive community sentences for such offenders, we have organised voluntary provision to meet such need (although it is not at all clear that this provision will be much used — it may be that the underlying complaint was about loss of discretion, not loss of provision). Probation officers are able, through their key role in the criminal courts and knowledge of community resources, to identify and refer suitable defendants for voluntary help, leaving courts to deal with the offence on its merits, usually via discharge or a fine.

4.1.3   Where offenders whose offences are "serious enough" to attract a community sentence are concerned, the provision of reports to courts enables probation officers to identify the suitability of individual offenders for specific community sanctions. Originally the provisions of the Act did not permit courts to take previous criminal history into account when sentencing (except in strictly limited circumstances). Following highly publicised judicial criticism of these and other restrictions, amendments to the Act were introduced in August 1993. Probation officers were however always able to consider the record of previous convictions when identifying suitability. Probation officers must — having identified a suitable proposal for sentence — explain to the court how the proposed sentence will deprive the offender of his or her liberty. Meeting offenders' needs may still be the objective of both courts and the probation service, but it must remain subordinate to the "just deserts" framework of the Act. In the training for magistrates and probation officers received prior to the introduction of the Act (with national standardised training materials) the main emphasis was on establishing the new framework. It would seem, given the picture now emerging of increased use of community service orders at the expense of probation orders, that there is a need to increase understanding of how the purposes of probation defined in the Act (see 4.1.1) fit within such a framework.

4.1.4   The apparent loss of confidence in proposing probation methods which have a psycho-social objective may have occurred because the restrictive aspects of probation are not easy to present as "punishment". The combination order, newly available under the 1991 Criminal Justice Act, appears to be proving popular because it combines probation with community service — help with punishment. At the same time, courts — also unconvinced about the comparability of restriction of liberty with imprisonment — are often very ready to apply programmes which deal with particular forms of offending without sufficient regard for the principle of proportionality which underpins the new Act. There may also be confusion because in their qualifying training probation officers have been taught about "just deserts" and rehabilitative methods as opposites and incompatible; rather than as capable of interacting in the way which the Act provides.

4.1.5   I have suggested that the historical and legal context of probation service work has involved a complex and sometimes contradictory set of expectations for work with offenders. There are many further sources of competing and sometimes conflicting demand affecting practitioners in the probation service, and their capacity to carry out their duties under legislation such as the 1991 Criminal Justice Act.

4.2   Social circumstances of offenders

4.2.1   The social circumstances of offenders remain an important dimension, even if meeting offenders' needs is a less prominent or acceptable objective. In 1969, Martin Davies described the links between offending and such adverse social circumstances as home circumstances, unemployment, and the influence of peers, for a group of young men aged 17 to 20. He suggested that "(...) because such problems show a statistical association with the likelihood of reconviction, it is impossible for the probation officer to ignore them in determining his treatment aim" (Davies, p.121).

4.2.2   If that is the case, how much more so would it be true today? Earlier this year, a team from Lancaster University published descriptive research commissioned by the Association of Chief Officers of Probation, which paints a markedly bleaker picture than Davies. Of the 1400 young people aged 17, 20 and 23 under all forms of supervision including parole and prison after-care:

—   two thirds were unemployed;

—   two-thirds had income below £40 per week;

—   two thirds of 17 year olds had no income at all;

—   one quarter had been in the care of local authority;

—   nearly half of those with convictions had previously served a custodial sentence (Stewart and Stewart).

4.2.3   Davies' group were seemingly so unlikely to have served a custodial sentence that it was not included in his questionnaire. Over half his sample were still living with both parents in the family home, whereas only 17 % of the Lancaster sample were still living with at least one parent (although up to 46 % were recognised as having a mobile lifestyle which included living in the parental home for at least part of the time). More telling is the fact that a third of the Lancaster sample had left home before the age of 16, although income support is not provided before the age of 18 except in special circumstances.

4.2.4   The two samples were not absolutely comparable, and it is not my purpose to identify whether this comparative deterioration in the social circumstances of those under probation service supervision is due to wider social changes, changes in the selection of the caseload, or specific links between social problems and offending. My guess would be that all three processes are involved. What seems to me important is the scale of the change, which has taken place during my own career as a probation officer; and the level of disadvantage which now provides the context for our attempts to provide community punishments or to reduce offending behaviour or to assist offenders. If there is an increasing gap between the advantaged and disadvantaged, helping offenders to move across the gap and find a positive role in society is increasingly difficult.

4.2.5   The incidence of substance abuse among offenders has probably always been high — the temperance movement features strongly in the history of the probation service. But today drug abuse vies with alcohol as a trigger for offending — both as a motive for theft, robbery and burglary and as illegal behaviour in its own right. Other forms of disadvantage seem to have become prominent as a result of social policy changes. It is estimated (Pritchard) that around 20 % of people on probation caseloads feature mental disorder or abnormality, and a recent study (Mendelson) suggests that forensic psychiatrists regard probation officers as reliable and informed in this area of work.

4.2.6   The concentration of disadvantage in inner city areas, where minority ethnic groups often feature disproportionately, means that probation officers in those areas are faced with levels of social deprivation quite unlike those which occur in more suburban or rural areas. In the latter cases, disadvantage and deprivation can still occur, but at the same time choice and opportunity may be less remote. The over-representation of African Caribbean men and women in the prison population may derive directly from discrimination and concentration of disadvantage, combined with the types of offence (drugs, violence) for which they are more frequently convicted (Ashworth; Cavadino and Dignan).

4.3   Support systems in the community

4.3.1   The main implication of the increasing concentration of disadvantage among offenders under the supervision of the probation service is the corresponding need for access to resources and services in the community. This is in the context of overall reduction in some services (e.g. public housing). Twenty-five years ago, the probation officer supervising those described by Martin Davies would have maintained his or her own local network of friendly employers and providers of accommodation. The limited level of need could be met by use of such personal networks, an approach which would be inadequate today. A national network of probation homes and hostels provided for those whom courts felt should be accommodated away from their home to receive more intensive help or control.

4.4   Public and political opinion

4.4.1   The criminal justice system has been under constant attack in recent years, for failing to satisfy public demand for tough sentencing. Yet England and Wales has one of the highest proportionate prison populations in Europe. In such a climate, probation officers — while admired for working in such an unattractive profession — are regarded by many as frankly misguided and unreliable in their views about offenders. Those who draw their knowledge about crime and offenders from the tabloid Press tend to believe the opposite of the facts about — for example — the effectiveness of imprisonment, the value of resettling offenders in their own communities, the levels of risk which particular types of offender present to the public, and the proportion of known crime processed through the criminal justice system. Probation officers are occasionally confronted with extreme expressions of hostility — for example over the location of a probation hostel — but more insidious is the increasing gap between their knowledge base and public opinion. Dialogue is often difficult to establish, and the public remains stubbornly uninformed about the realities of probation officers' work and in particular their effectiveness in managing risk via non-custodial methods. In such a hostile climate, it is of little comfort that several government research surveys of the opinions of victims show that they do not share vengeful attitudes. Government research is dismissed as less valid than instinctive responses to fear of crime whipped up by the mass-circulation newspapers.

4.4.2   It is also relevant here that while the policies of government are by no means hostile to the probation service, which has been relatively well funded compared with certain other public services, and which occupies a "centre stage" position in the current legislative provision, there is a similar preoccupation with "toughness on crime" among the members of the majority Conservative party. Probation officers experience the way government expresses its policies — for example depicting car thieves not as people but as predatory hyenas — as antithetical to their own respect for individuals and constructive methods of working with offenders. The Prime Minister's somewhat blander comment about offenders as needing "a little more condemnation, a little less understanding" nevertheless makes the same point.

4.5   Enforcement and enforceability

4.5.1   It seems likely that with the changes in the probation caseload and the social circumstances of offenders described above, enforcement of the new legislative provisions will be a far more demanding matter than it was with the probationers described by Martin Davies. Today's offenders will have failed in many respects, particularly in education, employment and relationships; and they will be remote from incentives and positive opportunities for achievement. Traditionally, theoretical teaching about the social casework relationship has emphasised the importance of developing motivation through positive influence and support. Probation officers remain concerned to support the capacity of individual offenders for positive choice and personal growth. Many would refer to the concept of contract-setting, to describe how they approach the identification of goals for supervision.

4.5.2   Ironically, it is such concerns and concepts which contribute to lack of judicial and political confidence in probation methods. The introduction of National Standards for Supervision of Offenders is designed to ensure consistent (minimum) levels of contact and to limit discretion about dealing with failures to comply. Achieving success with more unpromising material and within tighter constraints becomes correspondingly more difficult.

4.5.3   Most probation officers would however probably agree that "care and control" are inextricably linked; and would for this reason endorse the importance of respecting the offender's right to consent and choice (self-determination). In practice, studies by Hardiker and Webb; Day; Fielding; all involving analysis of probation officers' accounts of their work and its moral or theoretical base, all demonstrate the variety of balances that are achieved in the care/control dynamic. Laurence Singer found it helpful to differentiate "care and control" (as the ideological basis) from "support-surveillance" (as the practical application).

4.6 Staff and training

4.6.1   Recruitment of probation officers is now restricted to those holding a specific social work qualification (2 year diploma or 4 year combined degree/diploma), and about 60 % of newly appointed probation officers hold it at postgraduate level. In theory they should have pursued specialised studies, but recruitment needs may dictate that a proportion of new probation officers are recruited from other social work backgrounds (local authority social work, mental health etc).

4.6.2   The focus of training has shifted markedly over recent years, influenced in turn by social work theory, briefly by sociology (Bean) and then taking a more penological focus, with more explicit acceptance of a social control element. In spite of this, probation officers are a close-knit group of staff, with a strong occupational culture, highly adaptive to be point of being over-ready to abandon or change existing methods. This characteristic is important, but the reasons for it are not clear. It may be that in working with high levels of failure, constant renewal or change of method is a means of maintaining optimism. It may help practitioners to maintain "professional autonomy". Unfortunately, it leads to an absence of investment in professional expertise (and a collusion with "nothing works") which may seriously limit effectiveness.

5.   Community sanctions; the scope for psychosocial intervention

5.1   The probation order with standard conditions

5.1.1   This order has a long and fairly consistent history since its informal existence as a lenient response was affirmed by legislation in 1907. Its historical purpose of enabling courts to respond leniently to the offender's circumstances is persistent, and as a consequence, its implementation can also feature ambiguity, as to whether it is the offending or the circumstances which are the primary focus of attention.

5.1.2   Technically it is possible to include conditions to suit the circumstances of the individual case, but practitioners tend to believe that enforcement is difficult without motivation, and limited use is made of such additions. Standard conditions (which are not prescribed by law) are to

—   be under the supervision of a probation officer for a specified period;

—   report to the probation officer as required (and to receive home visits if required);

—   keep the officer informed of any changes of address.

5.1.3   Until the 1991 Act, the status of the probation order was that of an alternative to a sentence, and it included a requirement to be of good behaviour and lead an honest (and industrious) life. The effect of this was that further conviction would allow courts to deal with the original offence for which the offender had been placed on probation (instead of sentencing him or her). Given the level of demands which some types of probation order had already begun to make upon defendants, the acknowledgment of the probation order as a sentence was overdue, and the 1991 Act formally acknowledges the role of the probation order as a restriction of liberty.

5.1.4   It should be noted that it remains possible to make a probation order without a pre-sentence report having been prepared — although this is not regarded as good practice, because it does not allow consent and motivation to be fully tested away from the pressures of the courtroom. However, where such a report is prepared, it does not invariably contain a plan for supervision, and such deficiencies seem to undermine the argument about the need to test motivation. It seems likely that the present loss of confidence in the probation order since the introduction of the 1991 Criminal Justice Act could be significantly reversed if such written plans were provided to the courts, so that they could have a view of the likely content of supervision and of its potential impact upon offending and the offender's circumstances.

5.1.5   Probation orders can be for any length from six months to three years. Six month orders have a slightly specialised application with which I will deal separately. The average length of orders has reduced steadily, and in practice the average probationer remains on the caseload for just over a year. Orders can be discharged early for good progress as well as revoked on further conviction.

5.1.6   Describing how supervision is undertaken presents a problem about classification of methods. Probation officers use a very wide and eclectic range of approaches to the supervision of probationers, probably depending on their original training, length of experience, personality, and the characteristics of the area and team in which they work. The size and composition of workload is likely to be an important factor in determining method, with urgent deadlines (particularly for court reports) taking priority. Individual officers will use different approaches with different offenders — in fact the probation order is by definition highly individualised. Singer (1989) identifies a process he calls "personalisation", where the probation officer derives from the range of theories and approaches at his or her disposal, an approach tailored to the circumstances of the individual case. Apart from research projects such as IMPACT, there have been few attempts to examine the effectiveness of these different repertoires (but see also Trotter for an example from Australia of an examination of the effectiveness of pro-social modelling). Indeed, far more research and policy interest has focussed on the processes which lead to the making of probation orders and other community sentences, than on their subsequent implementation or effectiveness. In turn probation officers may have measured their own effectiveness in terms of getting orders made (pulling the chestnuts out of the fire was the traditional term), — and similarly on getting orders completed — the result of the supervisory process.

5.1.7   It is worth noting that under the 1991 Criminal Justice Act, pre-sentence reports are required to have a narrower focus than earlier reports. They are "offence-centred", containing information about the detail of the offence, aggravating and mitigating factors and a discussion of the seriousness of the matter. The report writer then moves on to discuss the availability of community sentences which are

128

appropriate for the offender and provide a suitable restriction of liberty. It is possible that the move away from providing detailed information about the offender's family and social history will subtly influence the content of supervision which follows.

5.1.8   Probation officers are required to record their work with offenders in some detail, including regular summaries of intervention and of progress with plans. Some form of objective-setting is therefore part of normal practice. This requirement has been included in National Standards for Supervision of Offenders. The varied circumstances of offenders under supervision and the largely social work training base of the probation service leads to a wide range of possible objectives for intervention, with varying relevance to offending behaviour. Although reoffending is regarded as failure by the supervisor, direct attention to offending behaviour was less common, until the last ten years or so, than attention to the social conditions assumed to encourage it; and to establishing a law-abiding and responsible lifestyle where pressures to offend would be reduced. Such indirect approaches are nonetheless sensible, and may indeed be an essential preliminary to a direct focus on offending behaviour. Someone with employment, a steady income, moderate habits, rewarding family or social relationships is far more likely to stay out of trouble than an unemployed, homeless alcoholic.

5.1.9   There are likely to be two consistent and basic components in the supervision of offenders on probation, whatever other methods or objectives are chosen. Probation involves regular reporting in person at an office (usually), at a frequency which can be varied by the officer. Reporting can itself establish a limited structure in chaotic lives, and give a sense of purpose and limited achievement. The second element is the relationship between offender and supervisor(s) — in reality an offender may have several supervisors during an order. The meaning of the relationship will vary, but it is bound to have some sort of meaning, and at best can be a very powerful influence (the basis of social casework).

5.1.10   Although Fielding (1984) found many officers minimised the value of practical support, the provision of support and encouragement to solve practical problems is likely to be an almost universal component of supervision. Martin Davies (1981) argued the importance of the less glamorous "maintenance" role; and studies of the effectiveness of brief, task-centred work confirm this (Goldberg and Stanley). This is surely logical, if only because probation officers are expected to be helpful, and people with problems of a practical nature (such as those described by Stewart and Stewart) are likely to see them as knowledgeable, for example about income maintenance issues, or the payment of fines, and influential with others in authority. Such interactions will usually establish a relationship capable of positive influence. Some practitioners will seek to build on this fairly practical and low-key use of relationship, to establish a basis for working with the offender on more intimate and personal issues, and especially on the offender's relationships with others. Such probation officers would recognise and seek to develop the core components of effective counselling relationships, identified by Truax and Carkhoff (1967) in their analysis of a range of counselling methods, — accurate empathy, genuineness and non-possessive warmth — but it would probably be unrealistic to expect to find such skilled levels of counselling being undertaken in all cases.

5.1.11   Supervision will very often involve linking the offender to other resources which can provide help/advice, either within the probation service or outside. This may take the form of intercession with another agency, explaining or renegotiating the offender's standing, or seeking resources or opportunities to improve his or her situation. Income maintenance and accommodation are likely to be the most common objectives of such liaison, but the full range of objectives may include such creative examples as educational, sporting, leisure and voluntary work opportunities.

5.1.12   Probation officers draw less frequently on more formal and specialised methods of intervention, including a long-standing tradition of groupwork with a psychodynamic emphasis. These are often the methods which attract status and recognition in the expert literature. Use of methods borrowed from the field of education is becoming widespread, under the general title of "social skills". This approach, (Priestley, P., McGuire, J., et al) uses structured methods and materials to teach the acquisition of a range of skills, and which can be applied with individuals as well as in group settings. A number of probation services have compiled useful collections of material designed specifically for work on a one-to-one basis, to deal with offending generally, social functioning and life skills, or for use with special groups such as problem drinkers (Nottinghamshire Probation Service; Gloucestershire Probation Service). Much of this type of material which I shall later describe in connection with group programmes can be adapted for use in individual supervision.

5.1.13   Social casework is a somewhat elastic term used to describe the range of methods which involve the deliberate establishment and use of relationship to influence behaviour through the development of insight. As a definition of method, it is capable of accommodating quite minimal levels of contact and intervention, and a result is somewhat discredited and no longer fashionable. Nevertheless, it still exerts a strong influence, especially on the practice of more experienced practitioners. Concepts which have their origins in psychoanalysis, such as historically based assessment, and "transference", would still be understood and correctly applied by such practitioners. More open support is still accorded to the value base of social casework, with the emphasis on respect for individual choice, capacity for personal responsibility and growth, and the professional standards of behaviour implicit in these values.

5.1.14   One of the methods which evolved from social casework was the task-centred approach (Goldberg and Stanley) The objective is to equip offenders with skills and experience in problem solving, and may involve correcting faulty approaches in order to replace them. An essential feature is the reduction of seemingly insuperable problems to small and achievable steps, and the origins of this method in behavioural psychology are evident. There is also an overlap with social skills techniques, and more broadly with methods which favour brief and intensive intervention (Reid and Epstein). When the six month probation order was introduced in 1978, it was specifically proposed as a means of assisting offenders to achieve designated limited objectives, such as sorting out debts or a family problem.

5.1.15   Family-centred methods attract much respect, although they are less widely practised than might be supposed. Family therapy consists of relatively structured and often time-limited techniques for engaging the whole family in understanding and modifying the dynamics of family relationships, and is particularly valuable with the families of adolescent offenders.

5.1.16   Relatively small groups of practitioners have elected to acquire qualifications in such specialised techniques as Heimler social functioning methods, transactional analysis (and also in family therapy referred to above). Such opportunities are rarer than they were, but practitioners qualified in this way still use these methods or derivatives of them.

5.1.17   These examples of supervision method illustrate clearly the difficulty of evaluating the effectiveness of such diverse approaches. Diversity of approach is combined with (and possible causally linked with) practitioner resistance to evaluative methods. At present effectiveness is still approached only at the individual case level (which can nevertheless be a valuable source of learning). There is an urgent need to gain some intellectual control over this situation, so that more may be learned about "what works" at the collective as well as the individual level. An examination of 95 published studies of effectiveness of a wide range of social work methods by Macdonald, Sheldon and Gillespie shows that positive results were reported in at least three quarters of the studies. The implications for the practice of individuals who adapt and match methods to individual cases are important. It would not be practical to demand that a repertoire of methods, which have accreted and interacted over decades, be standardised; but we need to explore and clarify this process of selecting methods, and the integrity of their application. What is needed is the development of some frameworks which will enable individual practice to be described, communicated and evaluated. I will describe two such possibilities (which are not mutually exclusive). The first I owe to Colin Roberts (1992), who developed a description of a hierarchy of interventions which practitioners find helpful, and which is also designed to inform organisational priorities in recruiting external resources to support work with offenders (Figure 2). Such a model invites agreement among practitioners to classify their own work within a framework which can be adapted to local needs and circumstances.

5.1.18   The second system provides a complementary rather than alternative approach. Called "case management", it is being introduced in my own area, in association with the further development of a computerised information system. Its purpose is to allow practitioners to choose their identified approach to supervising offenders, and to record and evaluate its progress and effectiveness in conjunction with the offender. Outcomes and reconvictions will be examined, in relation to particular aspects. The key features of the system are:

—   identification of factors which have contributed to offending;

—   identification of objectives for supervision;

—   identification of methods to be used;

— identification of resources to be used;

— regular review of progress with objectives at pre-determined intervals, and resetting of objectives if appropriate;

— final evaluation, including identification of most and least helpful interventions.

5.1.19   The participation of the offender in all these stages is regarded as important, and it is especially important to identify and describe the offender's evaluation independently from that of the supervisor. Coding of the main elements at each stage will permit detailed questions about practice to be answered — for example, whether attention to specific types of social disadvantage is connected with reduced reoffending; whether some practitioners or methods are more effective with some types of offender than others. Such an approach is expected to encourage individual as well as collective learning, but will obviously take some time to produce useful findings.

5.2   The probation order with additional (individual) conditions

5.2.1   Since 1948 the conditions of a probation order have not been prescribed by law. It is theoretically possible for a court to attach any conditions to an order it considers appropriate (subject to legal definitions of reasonableness, etc., and to the consent of the offender). In practice the court's reason for wishing to impose such conditions probably points to a likely difficulty of enforcement. Consent given in such circumstances is often not a reliable indicator of future behaviour.

5.2.2   Two forms of additional requirement are common: to receive medical treatment, and to reside only where approved by the probation officer. In practice, medical practitioners will not be associated with court action against patients who refuse treatment in such circumstances, and this form of condition therefore has been regarded as having limited value, except possibly of a presentational kind. The number of such court orders has declined steadily over the past ten years. However, since the development of regional forensic psychiatric and psychological services, a stronger partnership has developed between probation officers and these services, and Mendelson has reported positively on the association between conditions for treatment in probation orders and the completion of treatment plans (Mendelson).

5.2.3   Approved residence conditions are more enforceable, but are not popular with many probation officers who believe they are unlikely to have lasting influence through such means. Under the 1991 Criminal Justice Act, powers have been introduced to require probationers to attend specialised treatment facilities for drug or alcohol abuse, on a residential or non-residential basis. At present, it is not clear whether sufficient resources will be provided to support this new power.

5.3   Condition of a probation order to attend an approved hostel

5.3.1   Probation hostels (and previously homes for juveniles) have a very long history, which has probably been much affected by changing fashions in penal policy. With a few exceptions, they have not been resourced to provide consistent psychosocial intervention; only this year, the Home Office has agreed to improve funding to allow for at least two people to be on duty at any one time. Few of the staff are qualified for this work, and the emphasis is generally on providing a supportive environment, with realistic rules about behaviour including night curfew. Hostels accommodate around 25 offenders on average, many of who will be on bail rather than on probation. A few may be on parole or home leave. Orders for residence as part of a probation order have declined from over 1300 annually in the early 1980s to 878 in 1991.

5.3.2   There has been little research into probation hostels. Sinclair (1971) found that success in relation to reoffending was associated with the style of the person in charge — friendly but firm regimes seemed to work best. Fisher and Wilson studied two contrasting regimes, one with a democratic regime with few formal rules,designed to encourage constructive use of freedom and learning from mistakes; the other requiring progress to be understood as conformity with a strict regime. The rate of absconding from the latter hostel was about 50 % higher, but the levels of reconvictions from both hostels were similar.

5.3.3   The key Home Office performance indicators of the success of hostels are occupancy and absconding rates. Home Office attempts to expand the provision of such hostels (primarily for those on bail to reduce the remand population) have been limited by vociferous and well-organised public opposition from local residents.

5.4   Probation orders with Schedule 11 requirements

5.4.1   The framing of schedule 11 to the 1982 Criminal Justice Act illustrates the flexible nature of the legislation within which the probation service operates. Section 4A of the schedule requires the probationer (as a special requirement of the order) to present himself or herself to a specified person at place specified in the order, and to participate (or refrain from participating) in specified activities, for a specified period of up to sixty days. Section 4B requires an offender to attend a probation centre, again for up to sixty days. Neither requirement can involve compulsory residential attendance.

5.4.2   Probation centres (with different nomenclature) had existed since the 1970s, providing facilities ranging from a type of sanctuary for vagrant petty recidivists, to club-type facilities for ex-prisoners, to a supportive activity-based programme for a broad range of offenders, to a highly-structured regime for serious and high-risk offenders (especially at the four day training centres established experimentally under the 1972 Criminal Justice Act). Apart from these four centres, the legal propriety of requiring probationers to attend such centres as a condition of a probation order was dubious, and eventually successfully challenged (Cullen v. Rogers). The 1982 Schedule was a means of legitimating the continuation of this range of provision.

5.4.3   At least one of the day training centres combined the structured programme with therapeutic groupwork. Various forms of groupwork based on group therapy were being used with offenders subject to probation orders from at least the late 1960s. For a time ideological commitment to the method was strong, but now appears to have waned, apart from specialised work for example with paedophiles, where group dynamics are an essential element of confrontational approaches. The shift to educational (e.g. social skills) and cognitive/behavioural approaches in individual practice was probably accelerated by these developments in group work practice.

5.4.4 The 1982 legislation was backed with funding for probation centres, and a diverse and expanding level of provision gradually standardised around two main types — those centres which offered programmes designed to deal with specific types of offenders, and those which offered a range of activities — educational, training, creative, sport, leisure — designed to occupy the offender, and improve his or her capabilities.

5.4.5 George Mair described the operation of probation day centres in 1988 (Home Office study 100), commenting on the wide differences to be found in the range of centres, and he contrasted the unplanned evolution of some centres, with the careful planning and monitoring seen at others. At that time there were over 80 centres or projects designated as centres in the 56 probation areas. A number of areas had none, one area (Lancashire) had eleven — one in each main centre of population. He concluded that while centres seemed successful in providing regimes suitable for offenders who might otherwise have gone to custody, there was little attempt to monitor effectiveness in reducing offending.

6. Developing effective offending behaviour programmes

6.1 The impact of "nothing works"

6.1.1 It is important to connect the provisions of the 1982 Criminal Justice Act, with the impact of the "nothing works" findings (Martinson, Brody). George Mair's report on probation day centres illustrates the preference for providing buildings as locations to which offenders could be directed to occupy their time with useful activities. This seemed to have become a more prominent objective than seeking to influence offending (and one that apparently appealed to judges and magistrates who could visit such buildings). Some of us resisted this, and in this section I will describe how in my own area, while not expecting to have much impact on reconvictions, we developed programmes which did so.

6.1.2 When the 1982 Act was introduced, it contained provisions which might (and did) encourage greater use of (youth) custody for young adults by magistrates. The provision we developed, as an alternative, was designed specifically to meet the needs of this group. In practical terms, the difference in content compared with day centre programmes can be quite narrow. Our intention was that the programme should be seen as providing a solution to a difficult sentencing problem — persistent young offenders who had already served a short period of detention, who had committed a further serious offence. We reasoned that sentencers might feel able to justify use of a non-custodial provision for such groups, if it were specifically designed to focus on their offending behaviour. (The willingness of courts to use this first programme designed for 17-20 year old men at risk of custody, led us later to develop programmes for paedophiles, persistent drink drivers and violent offenders, all of which are well supported by courts).

6.1.3   Not surprisingly in view of the prevailing climate of pessimism (this was in 1983) we did not expect to have much impact on reoffending, but we undertook to evaluate our success in this respect, in order to demonstrate to courts that (hopefully) our approach involved no greater risk to the community than use of custody.

6.2   Programme content

6.2.1   The first programme (the Young Offender Project) was therefore designed to meet the assumed needs of young men, aged 17 to 20 and at risk of receiving the new sentence of youth custody because they had committed serious offences and already served a short custodial sentence (detention centre). We assumed that because many of them would have dropped out of school early, they would lack social and educational skills; through serving a custodial sentence, they would have limited access to community resources; and as persistent young property offenders (a significant target group) they would need alternative sources of achievement and status to replace burgling houses and stealing cars. (We designed the programme for young men only because very few young women were sent to custody from the area). The programme therefore contained a mix of social skills, information about and practice in gaining access to legitimate community resources, and challenging activities (motorbike racing, climbing, canoeing, etc). The duration of the programme was 25 days, spread over seven weeks, as a condition of a probation order, and including a five day residential programme at an adventure centre. It therefore involved less than half the maximum 60 day duration possible under the provision of Schedule 11 of the 1982 Criminal Justice Act, plus normal probation order supervision for up to a total of three years.

6.2.2   In order to give sentencers a clear picture of what would happen to offenders on the programme, we published its contents, and circulated it widely to courts. In addition, every report which recommended that the offender attend the programme included a detailed plan of the arrangements for the offender, the date the programme would start, and the offender's (informed) consent. An important feature was that programmes were available at four week intervals, offering sentencers an element of immediacy in the impact of their sentence. Sentencers were promised (and provided with) progress reports on each offender after he had attended the programme.

6.2.3   The team which ran the programme were expected to keep to the outline format, but could vary the individual sessions appropriately, and a particularly useful element was a session in which a burglary victim talked about his or her experience — followed by exercises to encourage the offenders to discuss and understand the impact of burglary. Staff from community agencies (from benefits agencies to public libraries) made contributions, and offenders would then visit the community agencies to learn to use the facilities themselves.

6.2.4   Participation in the programme involved some offenders in lengthy and complicated travel arrangements, but attendance was not a problem. Staff did however find themselves faced with a more sophisticated and unpredictable group of offenders than they had ever handled before, and developed new skills in managing such groups. Drugtaking and stealing from local shops, and hostility from young people living near the adventure centre proved the most problematic. Use of commercial adventure centres taught us that only the best resourced (and most expensive) were likely to be able to cope with our group.

6.3   Evaluation of the Young Offender Project

6.3.1   After five years, it was time to fulfil our promise to courts that we would evaluate the risk to the community of using the programme instead of a custodial sentence. Running the programme had involved such a succession of practical crises and known failures, that we approached this without optimism. The results of the evaluation were therefore very unexpected.

6.3.2   The evaluation compared all those who had been sentenced to participate in the project (including some who reoffended so quickly that they did not complete, or even start, the programme); with all those who were recommended for the project but sent to custody. The evaluation involved 109 young offenders sentenced during the first two years of the project, 1984-1985. Over this period, no offender recommended to the courts to attend the Project was sentenced to any other outcome, although in later years very small numbers of offenders received other community sentences instead. The project sample was comparable (in terms of key characteristics) with a randomly drawn group of young offenders sent to youth custody from courts in the area in the same period (Table 5).

6.3.3   Initial reconviction rates for the groups within two years of being sentenced/released from custody (Table 6) gave an immediate if limited account of the success of the project. More telling was an examination of the cumulative proportions reconvicted (Table 7 and Figure 3). These show that within two years, the custody sample A had accumulated about half as many convictions again as the project group; and that custody effectively provided the community with only one month more "protection" than the project, even allowing for the fact that the project group was at liberty "during sentence".

6.3.4   More detailed analysis of subgroups (Table 8) showed that the project achieved the highest success rates (compared with the custody samples) with property offenders (burglars and car thieves); and more generally with the more persistent offenders (six or more previous convictions) and those who had served a custodial sentence before the project or comparison sentence. We had evidently been less successful with those convicted of violent offences, and this has led us to establish a different programme for that group.

6.3.5   At present a six year follow up of these initial project and custody A samples is being undertaken, as well as a two year follow up on all those who undertook the programme over a five year period. The differences found in the initial comparison of those sentenced in the first two years of the Project have persisted (Table 9). There are also indications that these outcomes cannot be attributed to the enthusiastic impact of innovators, since a similar two year reconviction rate for project subjects (67 %) has now been recorded for the whole five years of the project's existence, from 1984 to

1989, although the staff group changed completely over the same period. There are other possible explanations, for example that the selection process involved in sentencing also identified some independent characteristic associated with success or failure; young men who appeared to "deserve" a further chance might also be less likely to be reconvicted, regardless of the sentence imposed. If so, it remains important that a sufficiently credible alternative was offered, and underlines the importance of evaluating all work with offenders in like terms.

6.4   Characteristics of successful offending behaviour programmes

6.4.1   Our initial analysis was completed at a time when only one other (very comparable) Welsh study had just reported similar results (Raynor, 1988). News of Gendreau and Ross's meta-analysis (1987) had not yet filtered through to those involved in probation work or research in this country. (Some people dismissed our project results as the product of flawed methodology — it could not be true because nothing works!).

6.4.2   Findings from a range of sources have helped to identify the common characteristics of successful programmes of this kind, which current understanding suggests should include the following:

—   a multi-modal, well integrated programme of intervention, which combines attention to each offender's individual needs, with group process and facilities;

—   primary focus on offending behaviour, the acquisition of skills and reasoning capacity, and improved access to community resources;

—   programme integrity — delivering the planned programme consistently (with the consistent presence of trained staff);

—   time-limited, contractual intervention;

—   care in selecting offenders for intervention;

—   staff with relevant skills, including advocacy and brokerage;

—   staff able to engage openly and enthusiastically with offenders and cope flexibly with problems;

—   provision of tasks for offenders to undertake at home between programme sessions, for example completion of (drinking or expenditure) diaries;

—   a commitment to evaluation during as well as after the programme.

6.5   The impact on probation service aims and objectives

6.5.1   When the Project was established in 1984, our work with offenders on probation orders had featured mainly counselling or social work approaches, with offenders with limited records of offending, and whose needs were seen as primarily social. When we reviewed the long term plan for our service in Hereford and Worcester, the findings from the Project and other related studies guided our thinking to the extent that we set the following main objectives for our work over the ensuing five years (1989-1994):

To concentrate resources and intervention on more serious offenders and more persistent offenders, who present courts with difficult sentencing problems and who are therefore at risk of a custodial sentence;

To reduce the reoffending of those offenders, without increasing risk to the community;

To work in partnership with other services and organisations and with volunteers and community groups, to ensure offenders' access to positive opportunities for achievement and recognition;

To promote and maintain the confidence of courts and the public in community sentences.

6.5.2   This strategic statement is translated into more detailed plans, and annual objectives are derived from the plans, and pursued at all levels in the organisation; with constant attention to the reconciliation of the aims of our own organisation with the demands and expectations being made on it by the outside world.

7.   Managing the implementation of effective community sanctions

7.1   Probation services in England and Wales are at the beginning of a new learning curve, now that we understand the possibility of real influence on offending behaviour. Clearly we have not understood the exact scope or limits of that influence, and practice and evaluation methods will need much development and refinement. Much can be learned by dialogue and co-operation between disciplines as well as within them. However, it is also critically important to ensure that the organisation of the service is supportive of effective practice, and I have described earlier some aspects of probation service culture and organisation that do not conduce to, for example, programme integrity.

7.1.2   In this section, therefore, I will describe the range of management initiatives and techniques which can support and encourage effective practice; that is practice, the effectiveness of which can be identified and developed. Effectiveness in reducing reoffending is now the priority for my local service, but other objectives — helping offenders, ensuring that sentences are carried out — remain important.

7.1.3   These ideas have evolved in a small management group which has necessarily been influenced by contemporary ideas, by the experience of its members, and to an extent by exposure to formal theory about the management of such organisations. However, the latter influence has not been very formally acquired; what probation service managers know about management theory is often derived as much from their own experience,as from formal training. It could be argued that there is a need to equip service managers more formally to develop the potential of the organisation to support effective practice.

7.1.4   Although I have already referred to some elements of this management strategy in earlier sections, for the sake of completeness further references are included here.

7.2   Organisational style

7.2.1   The organisation needs to be open and receptive to the outside world — which can provide resources, comment on its effectiveness, support its influence. Community resources are needed for offenders, the courts must be satisfied as customers, the academic world and other professions are a source of knowledge and expertise, other criminal justice agencies can share experience and skills (and indeed in some instances, for example prisons and psychiatric services, can contribute directly to effective work with offenders). If probation officers are to feel confident in drawing on these external resources, the organisation has to be managed and structured in ways which encourage this (e.g. wide and reciprocal participation in management and advisory structures, receptiveness to research initiatives, and — particularly important — formalising and structuring links with community resources).

7.2.2   The service's "products" must be presented properly to the outside world, and in particular "marketed" to customers and explained to the public. Courts, prisons and offenders must be actively provided with clear accounts of service provision, and be able to challenge non-delivery of promised provision or quality. At the same time, courts must be discouraged from indiscriminate use of provision for offenders who are unsuitable. Success is not measured in terms of high levels of referral by courts — this will inevitably increase the risk of failure, for us and for offenders. This is particularly important because experience so far suggests that it is the most persistent offenders — potentially the least popular with courts — who benefit most from such programmes. Accurate targeting therefore depends to a considerable extent on courts' confidence in our work with high risk offenders.

7.2.3   Courts' confidence depends on public confidence. Every single member of staff must regard it as their responsibility to promote good public understanding of the work of the service, on the basis that to anyone who knows they are a probation employee, they are de facto an ambassador for the service (in and out of working hours). The interest of the press media must be actively responded to, and proactively sought.

7.2.4   Minority groups, especially any which may expect to be systematically discriminated against, should receive special attention, to establish trust in the capacity of the organisation to deal with them fairly and provide relevant services.

7.3 The structure of the organisation

7.3.1 This should promote a cohesive sense of joint purpose and mutual accountability. Employing a few enthusiastic expert practitioners is not enough — the whole organisation must be part of the quest for effectiveness. Although "vertical" hierarchies are important for delivering accountable and cost-effective services, they can impede processes which encourage sharing of resources and improvement of practice. The "line" management structure should therefore be balanced by functional structures and strong lateral links, and the hierarchy should be as "flat" as possible, with ample opportunities for staff at levels to work closely with those in other grades and other settings. It is important that decisions taken close to the user (courts, offenders) are consistent with the objectives of the organisation as a whole, and structures can promote or impede this, as can processes. Consultation about change is important, and it should be undertaken in the spirit that everyone can contribute a useful perspective on proposed changes; and that practitioners in particular have knowledge, experience and skills which complement the political and structural perspectives of managers. Consultation and dialogue within the organisation (as well as with key external groups) should be understood as a systematic means of reconciling political expectations with professional norms.

7.4 Determining priorities

7.4.1 In a service like probation, with a very wide range of responsibilities and external relationships, the setting of priorities should not mean neglect of less central responsibilities. The relationship of all relevant work to the priorities needs to be determined, and clearly identified and explained for the benefit of staff who may otherwise feel their work is less valued. (Conversely, if some responsibilities are so separate that it is difficult to achieve this, separate status may need to be accorded to that work).

7.4.2 The establishment of such inclusive priorities for the organisation should be translated into and then govern all key aspects of its operation — the distribution of resources, including training and staff development; the setting of shorter-term objectives; the processes and structures for planning and delivering shorter and longer term policy advice and practice change; the designated responsibilities of staff including senior managers; evaluation systems and processes. People in the organisation should be held to account, through policies, job descriptions, personal appraisal systems, etc., for the part they play in the achievement of service objectives.

7.5 Securing staff commitment

7.5.1 The commitment of all staff (including support staff) to the strategic aim, purposes and objectives of the organisation must be deliberately secured and maintained. This starts with recruitment, and should also underpin promotion procedures. Those seeking posts should be fully informed about the work of the organisation, and their commitment as well as their capacity for the work involved thoroughly tested in the selection procedure. Although it is better to avoid only recruiting "stars" (assuming that is possible) it is essential to ensure that all recruits are capable of and enthusiastic about the demands of intensive work with high-risk offenders. It is better to have staff vacancies, and to repeat recruitment procedures, than to be forced to avoid using some staff for key duties. Staff commitment is increased if they can volunteer themselves for particular types of practice, and can elect regular changes of practice setting.

7.5.2   Induction, especially of newly qualified probation officers, should be thorough, and aimed at further familiarisation with policies, procedures, structures, to equip staff as quickly as possible to feel fully involved in and contributing to the organisation. The period between qualifying training/recruitment, and being considered ready to tackle any specialist type of practice should be reduced to the minimum, and there should be no ritual order of progress through different types of specialist work (or as qualification for promotion). At the same time it should be clearly established that all staff will be expected take their turn at all tasks if required, and especially unpopular ones. The aim is not to defeat the powerful practice culture in the probation service, but to harness it to the strategic purposes of the organisation.

7.5.3   Good ideas and initiatives which help to develop effectiveness need to be publicised and promoted, within the organisation and outside it. Practitioners can be trusted to initiate new approaches, but these must be evaluated, and "captured" within the service strategy if they are to be resourced and developed. Practitioners' disenchantment with existing provision should be rigorously tested and challenged; the only acceptable criteria for abandoning established provision should be that it is not effective, or that there is no customer requirement for it (i.e.not that the customer is reluctant to use it, but that the need has disappeared — for example that the demography of the offender population has changed).

7.5.4   Relationships with organisations which represent staff need to be carefully maintained, in a climate of mutual respect for the concerns of each side. It should be assumed that all interests can be satisfactorily reconciled within the overall aims and purposes of the organisation, and that the welfare and support of staff is important in that respect.

7.5.5   The value accorded to support staff will be repaid by the contribution they make to the organisation. If they feel marginal, their potential will not be realised — a serious waste of resources.

7.6   Supporting staff and developing their skills

7.6.1   The processes and structures needed to support staff who work in a hostile and unrewarding context must be active and vigorous. All probation staff need to receive regular formal supervision, designed to provide support and to develop good practice; and in addition need access to means of consultation about practice (including external sources where no internal source is available). Programme staff in particular may need internal supervisors and external consultants. The extent of failure and disappointment involved in working with high-risk groups can quickly erode staff commitment and confidence, if support and development mechanisms are not built in and be given high priority by supervisors and managers, as well as staff.

7.6.2   Supervision and consultancy can also support other important processes (accountability, appraisal, monitoring of standards), which will be acceptable if set in the overall context of supporting and developing staff in their practice. Other elements of this overall context include staff career planning/development, the provision of inservice training, and opportunities to acquire post-qualifying awards.

7.6.3   The potential of in-service training to change long-established service cultures is in general under-exploited in the probation service (although provision for such training is often quite generous). Mid-Glamorgan Probation Service is noteworthy for having committed itself to a cognitive/behavioural programme called STOP, under the guidance of Robert Ross whose approach they had adopted, to the extent of training three-quarters of their probation officers (and relevant supervisors) to use the method from the outset. Other staff were subsequently also given training, against their future deployment in these duties. Raynor and Vanstone report very positively on the impact of this approach upon staff:

> "(...) 62 % reported that they had become more optimistic about the potential effectiveness of work with offenders and 79 % had developed more positive views about the effectiveness and function of probation orders and the probation service as a result of involvement in STOP. Many also reported an increased confidence in the capacity of probationers to bring about positive changes in their own lives (...)" (in press, 1993).

7.6.4   In my own area, we have initiated an in-service programme to assist practitioners and their supervisors to adjust to a range of new expectations — including external ones such as National Standards and race and ethnic monitoring — but particularly focussing on applying knowledge about "what works" and promoting commitment to effectiveness. We have recognised that some staff cannot absorb new learning until established cultures have been "unfrozen" and revised or discarded. Professional confidence and responsibility need to be maintained, at a time when government policies are somewhat focussed on measures of efficiency, economy, and customer satisfaction and other evidence of "managerialism" which although important, may tend to produce mechanistic responses.

7.7   A culture of learning

7.7.1   Not least, the organisation needs to adopt a culture of learning about effectiveness, described by Raynor and Vanstone as "a culture of curiosity — a culture in which managers and practitioners alike are interested in whether or not their work with people has the intended effect" (in press). I have already referred above to the staff development aspects of this; traditionally it was assumed that these, plus regular exhortation would lead inexorably to appropriate adjustments to practice. In reality, sustained use of a wide repertoire of measures is needed to produce what Philip Priestley describes as the "experimental" approach:

"(...) all work undertaken with offenders should have clearly stated aims, should have outcomes that can be measured with some precision,and should be written up and shared with others who work in the same field (...) And it requires the conscious construction of an information community (...)" (1991).

7.7.2   The first step in the construction of Priestley's "information community" should be the immediate organisation — the team, the service in which the practitioner is employed. An anti-management culture in which such information is only shared among practitioners loses much potential for effectiveness; and vice versa.

7.7.3   A consumer focus is very important, and can illustrate the value of learning from both praise and criticism. Offenders themselves are in some respects the only reliable source of information about whether what is being delivered is meeting the objectives. On the whole, they are remarkably positive and appreciative of non-custodial methods, and very tolerant of mediocre practice if they believe that they have escaped a prison sentence. Good practice can enhance their capacity to choose to participate, understand their rights and exercise responsible choices. This means that the feedback provided by consumers increases in value with the quality of the practice.

7.7.4   This is illustrated by Andrew Willis (1992), who also shows how the consumer perspective must be built in to service delivery — trying to contact offenders after they have completed a period of supervision is an exercise in futility. His paper describes a survey of young men participating in an offending behaviour programme, and their views clearly resolved the dilemma of probation officers about the tensions between care and control. The offenders did not see this demanding programme as punishment, but as helping them to stop offending (the formal aim of the programme):

"(...) when clients were asked to assess the programme on a 'care' versus 'control' dichotomy, over 80 % responded in non-control, reductivist terms (...)" (p.19).

7.7.5   Perhaps the most difficult issue in establishing a learning and information culture is that of practice integrity, especially for programmes: how to ensure that planned provision is delivered as planned, and sufficiently consistently to test its effectiveness over a period of several years. Many of the elements of "good management" already referred to in this section provide a necessary foundation for consistency of practice, while others will provide a culture which thrives on evaluation:

—   frameworks which help manage practitioner discretion over choice of method (see 5.1.7 and 5.1.9 above);

—   establishing accountability for practitioner decisions, in the way Priestley describes (see 6.7.1 above);

—   the research and information capability to handle the quantities of information involved in long term evaluations, and the necessary statistical analysis;

—   routine monitoring and feedback which maintains commitment to programme integrity;

—   auditing and inspecting practice regularly, to ensure that service delivery does appear to the observer to meet the description which practitioners are recording, and to examine the broad pattern of approach being taken, to locate overall standards and promote improvements (see e.g. Raynor and Vanstone, in press).

7.7.8   Developing good quality practice also depends on people, and some key roles require special personal qualities:

—   "product champions" — people inside and outside the organisation who command the respect of practitioners, and whose support for particular methods can be influential;

—   "mixers and fixers", who have the responsibility to locate problems and promote improvements by mixing with practitioners, observing their practice, but at the same time being widely informed about effectiveness;

—   and above all, supervisors and managers with commitment to effectiveness, and credibility with the practitioners for whom they are responsible.

7.7.9   It has been particularly encouraging that positive findings about probation practice in England and Wales have been supported and confirmed by similar results in other countries. This underlines the importance of willingness to learn from other sources, and particularly other disciplines, for example using a range of assessment methods, or drawing on the assessment skills of other disciplines. At the same time there is a reciprocal responsibility, to ensure transfer of learning between agencies and disciplines.

TABLES AND FIGURES

Table 1: Composition of Probation Service Workload, England and Wales, 1991

PERSONS SUPERVISED BY THE PROBATION SERVICE ON 31 DECEMBER 1991	
TYPES OF SUPERVISION	**NO. OF PERSONS**
TYPE OF SUPERVISION	
Court orders Probation	51 827
Suspended sentence supervision	3 106
Money payment supervision	8 422
Community service order	30 409
TOTAL COURT ORDERS	**89 318**
AFTER-CARE	
Detention in a young offender institution	10 443
Parole	8 237
Life	3 382
Detention under section 53(2) of the C & Y P act 1933	269
Extended sentence	44
Psychiatric hospital conditional discharge	147
Total statutory after-care	**22 459**
Voluntary after-care	30 651
Total after-care	**52 947**
TOTAL CRIMINAL SUPERVISION	**139 453**
DOMESTIC SUPERVISION	
Matrimonial proceedings	1 817
Wardship supervision	65
Guardianship supervision	106
Children Act 1975 supervision	7
TOTAL DOMESTIC SUPERVISION	**2 027**
TOTAL	**141 475**

Table 1:   Continuation

SOCIAL INQUIRY REPORTS PREPARED DURING 1991	
TYPE OF COURT FOR WHICH REPORTS PREPARED	**NO. OF REPORTS**
Magistrates' Courts: Adult	127 994
Juvenile: Aged 13 and under	162
Juvenile: Aged 14 and over	7 673
Crown Court	63 115
On appearance for sentence after deferment	2 194
TOTAL	**201 138**
OTHER REPORTS OF INQUIRIES	
CRIMINAL INQUIRIES:	
Bail information	7 263
Means Inquiries	7 586
Local Review Committee or People Board	19 285
Inquiries for institutions	7 376
TOTAL	**41 510**
DOMESTIC INQUIRIES:	
Inquiries concerning custody of and access to children:	
Magistrates' Courts	7 984
High and County Courts	17 870
Satisfaction reports	398
Guardian *ad litem* inquiries:	
Adoption proceedings	399
Other proceedings	110
Welfare reports under Children Act 1989	855
Other civil reports	1 406
TOTAL	**29 022**

HOME OFFICE: Probation statistics England and Wales 1991

Table 2: Proportionate use of sentences in England and Wales: 1969-1990

YEARS	69	70	71	72	73	74	75	76	77	78	79	80	81	82	83	84	85	86	87	88	89	90
Other non-cust	61	62	62	63	67	67	66	65	65	65	60	60	56	56	55	55	53	53	52	52	56	57
Probation	14	12	12	12	11	10	9	8	7	6	8	8	9	9	9	10	11	12	12	12	12	13
C S	0	0	0	0	0	1	2	4	5	6	7	9	11	11	13	13	13	14	13	13	13	13
Susp Cust	4	3	3	4	3	3	4	4	4	5	5	4	4	5	2	0	0	0	0	0	0	0
Custody	19	20	19	19	16	16	17	18	17	19	18	18	19	18	19	20	20	21	21	20	17	14

17-20 Year old males, indictable offences

HOME OFFICE: Criminal Statistics

Table 3:   Persons commencing Probation by previous most serious sentence

PREVIOUS MOST SERIOUS SENTENCE (in %)	1980	1985	1990
Custody	29	37	38
Suspended custody	-	-	2
Community service order	3	8	9
Supervision	15	13	13
Fine	18	17	13
Other	3	4	5
Not recorded	13	10	7
Number of previous convictions	19	13	12

HOME OFFICE: Probation Statistics England and Wales 1980, 1985, 1990

Table 4:   Actual reconvictions of adult men shown as % of those "expected" (T.I.C. offence types) — 6 year follow-up

PREVIOUS STANDARD LIST CONVICTIONS			
Sentence	None %	One %	Two-Four %	Five + %
Fine, etc	96	93	92	97
Probation	188	94	85	100
Imprisonment	69	102	104	102

Note: percentages below 100 mean better than expected results; above 100 mean worse than expected.

Walker, N: The Effectiveness of Probation. Probation Journal, September 1983, pp.99-103

Table 5:   **Young Offender Project Evaluation**
Characteristics of the Project Group and Custody Groups (see note 1)

	PROJECT n = 53		CUSTODY A n = 56		CUSTODY B n = 51	
Sentenced at Crown Court (See note 2)	20	38 %	38	68 %	32	63 %
Average number of previous convictions	5,9		5,4		4,3	
No previous convictions %	0		4		14	
Six or more previous convictions%	51		51		37	
Previous custody or care order %	75		68		57	
Two or more previous custody/ % care orders	36		34		25	
Previous community sentence %	83		75		61	
Principal criminal offence:						
Burglary %	68		68		41	
Violence %	2		3		27	
Robbery %	0		5		12	
Theft %	28		22		12	
Most serious previous offence:						
Burglary %	74		73		49	
Violence, robbery %	8		10		12	
Arson %	2		2		6	
Theft, receiving %	11		4		4	
Taking cars %	6		7		8	
Forgery, deception %	0		2		6	

Note 1: The three samples were:
1. **Project sample: all those young men sentenced to attend the project from Frebuary 1984 to December 1985 (including four who did not complete due to breach/further convictions).**
2. **Custody A sample: all those young men recommended for the project, but sentenced to youth custody over the same period. There were no other outcomes. Average sentence length 10.5 months.**
3. **Custody B sample: a random 60 % sample of 85 young men sentenced to youth custody in the same area over the same period, not recommended for the project. Average sentence length 12.5 months.**

Note 2: The lower proportion sentenced at crown court to attend the project may be due to the fact that the lower (magistrates) court had the first opportunity to take up the recommendation for the project.

C.H. Roberts, Oxford, 1988

Table 6:   **Young Offender Project Evaluation**

Reconvictions and Subsequent Custodial Disposals

	YOP SAMPLE		CUSTODY A		CUSTODY B	
	n	%	n	%	n	%
Reconvicted:						
in less than 12 months	29	55	43	77	30	59
in 12 months to 2 years	7	13	7	12	5	10
Subsequent cust. sentence	22	41	36	64	16	31
Not reconvicted	17	32	6	11	16	31

C.H. Roberts, Oxford, 1988

Table 7:   **Young Offender Project Evaluation**

Cumulative Proportions Reconvicted
Time elapsed from date of original sentence to reconviction

	YOP SAMPLE (n = 53)			CUSTODY A SAMPLE (n = 56)		
	Reconvictions			Reconvictions		
	First	Subseq	Total	First	Subseq	Total
Time from original conviction:						
0 - 3 months	0	0	0	0	0	0
4 - 6 months	13	0	13	3	0	3
7 - 9 months	10	2	25	15	3	21
10 - 12 months	6	4	35	11	9	41
13 - 18 months	7	9	51	12	17	70
19 - 24 months	0	11	62	7	15	92
Total	**36**	**26**	**62**	**48**	**44**	**92**

C.H. Roberts, Oxford, 1988

Table 8: **Young Offender Project**

Reconvictions of Project Group and Custody Group
after six years from date of sentence

	PROJECT GROUP n = 53	CUSTODY A GROUP n = 56
Number not reconvicted	7	3
Not subsequently sentenced to custody	27	18
Total number of further convictions	164	289
Total number of further custodial sentences	56	101
Total length of custodial sentences imposed in months	930	1 812

C.H. Roberts, Oxford, 1993

Figure 1   Probation Service Contribution to Criminal Justice

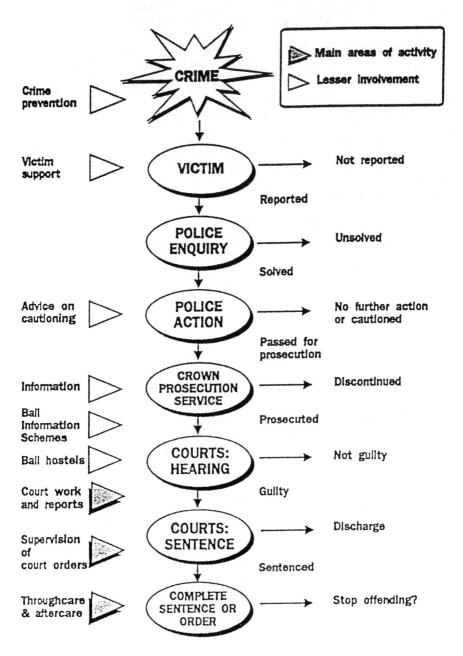

Audit Commission, 1989

Figure 2   Individual Offender Focus

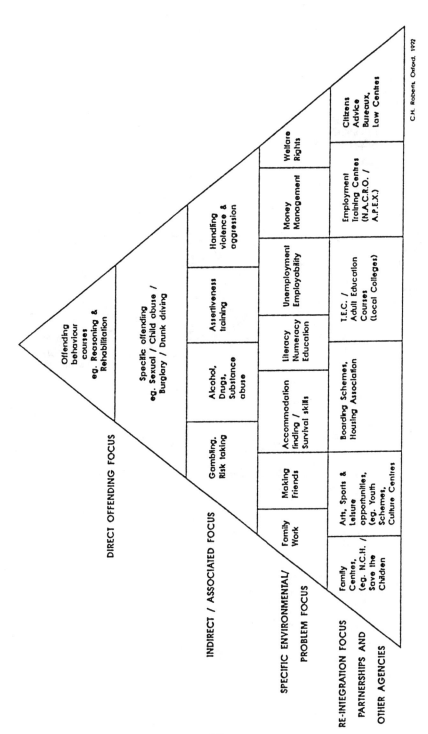

C.H. Roberts, Oxford, 1992

Figure 3   **Young Offender Project**

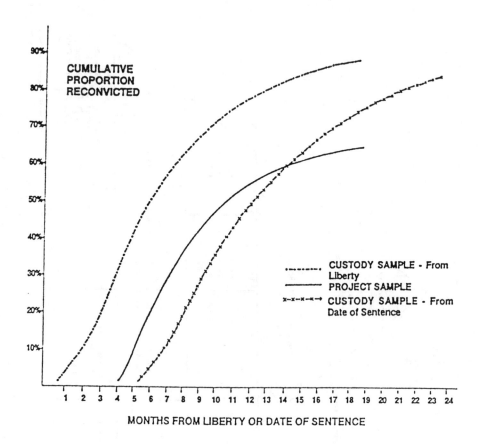

MONTHS FROM LIBERTY OR DATE OF SENTENCE

C.H. Roberts, Oxford, 1988

BIBLIOGRAPHY

Ashworth, A. *Sentencing and criminal Justice.* Weidenfeld and Nicolson, London, 1992.

Bean, P. *Rehabilitation and Deviance.* RKP London, 1976.

Brody, S. *The effectiveness of sentencing: a review of the literature.* Home Office Research Study n° 35, 1976.

Cavadino, M. and Dignan, J. *The Penal System: an Introduction.* Sage, London, 1992.

Davies, M. *Probationers in their Social Environment.* H.M.S.O. London, 1969.

Davies, M. *The Essentiel Social Worker.* Heinemann, London, 1981.

Day, P. *Social Work and Social Control.* Tavistock, London, 1981.

Fielding, N. *Probation Pratice: Client Support under Social Control.* Gower, 1984.

Fisher, R. and Wilson, C. *Authority or Freedom? Probation Hostels for Adults.* Gower, Aldershot, 1982.

Gendreau, P. and Ross, R. *Revivification of rehabilitation: Evidence from the 1980s.* Justice Quarterly, 4, 349-407, 1987.

Goldberg, M. and Stanley, S. *A Task Centred Approach to Probation.* in King, J. (ed.) Pressures and Changes in the Probation Service. Cambridge University Press, 1979.

Hardiker, P. and Webb, D. *Explaining deviant behaviour: the social context of "action" and "infraction" accounts in the probation service.* Sociology, 13, n.1, 1979, p.1.

Home Office. *National Standards for Supervision of Offenders.* 1992.

Macdonald, G., Sheldon B. and Gillespie, J. *Contemporary studies of the effectiveness of social work.* In British Journal of Social Work, 1992, pp 615-643.

Mair, G. *Probation Day Centres.* Home Office Research Study n° 100, 1988.

Martinson, R. *What works? — Questions and answers about prison reform.* The Public Interest, 23, 22-54, 1974.

Mendelson, E. *A survey of practice at a regional forensic service: what do forensic psychiatrists do?* British Journal of Psychiatry, 160, 769-776, 1992.

Nottinghamshire Probation Service. *Targets for change.* 1991.

Priestley, P. Rational Corrections. In proceedings of 1991 Salford "What works" conference. Greater Manchester Probation Service, 1992.

Priestley, P., MacGuire, J., Flegg, D., Hemsley, D and Welham, D. *Social Skills and Personal Problem solving: a Handbook of Methods*. London, Tavistock, 1978.

Pritchard, C., Cotton, A., Godson, D., Cox, M. and Weeks, S. *Mental Illness, Drug and Alcohol Abuse and HIV Risk Behaviour in 214 Young Adult Probation Clients*. In Social Work and Social Sciences Review, 3, (2), pp 150-162, 1992.

Raynor, P. *Probation as an Alternative to Custody*. Avebury, Aldershot, 1988.

Raynor, P. and Vanstone, M. *Evaluating Straight Thinking on Probation: Process and Outcome*. In press, 1993.

Reid, J. and Epstein, L. *Task Centred Casework*. Columbia, New York, 1972.

Roberts, C. *Effective practice and service delivery*. Unpublished paper contributed to the 1992 What Works Conference, Salford University, 1992.

Sinclair, I. *Hostels for Probationers*. Home Office Research Unit, 1971.

Singer, L. *Adult Probation and Juvenile Supervision: Beyond the Care-Control Dilemma*. Avebury, 1989.

Stewart, G. and Stewart, J., *Social Circumstances of Younger Offenders under Supervision*. Association of Chief Officers of Probation, London, 1993.

Thomas, D. *Principles of sentencing*. Heinemann 1979.

Trotter, C. *The supervision of Offenders — What Works?* Australian Criminology Research Council, 1993.*

Truax, C. and Carkhuff, R. *Towards Effective Counseling and Psychotherapy: Training and practice*. Aldine, Chicago, 1967.

Walker, N. *The effectiveness of probation*. Probation Journal, September 1983.

Willis, A. *Talking tough to offenders: Letting the client speak and its implications for effective supervision*. Unpublished paper given to Salford "What Works?" conference, 1992.

PSYCHOSOCIAL INTERVENTIONS
IN THE
CRIMINAL JUSTICE SYSTEM

20th Criminological Research
Conference
(1993)

PROBLEMS OF THERAPEUTIC INTERVENTIONS REGARDING
CERTAIN CATEGORIES OF OFFENDERS,
FOR EXAMPLE IN THE FIELDS OF SEXUAL OFFENCES,
VIOLENCE IN THE FAMILY AND DRUG ADDICTION

by
Mr J.M. ELCHARDUS
A. Lacassagne Institute, Lyons
(France)

Introduction

There was a time when medical science was expected to "cure" criminal forms of behaviour by giving them a nosographic classification in the same way and on the same broad lines as the major categories of human diseases. A "therapeutic model" was seen as one aspect of the treatment of criminals, and it was hoped that clinical methods applied systematically to offenders or deviants would in the long run appreciably reduce the incidence of these socially harmful behaviour patterns.

In fact, attempts to treat a subject for delinquency, regarded as an illness, did not produce the hoped-for results. Pathology did not adequately reflect criminal forms of behaviour, and treatment yielded no entirely satisfactory solution. It had to be recognised that criminal and clinical categories did not correspond. The clinical approach was in particular severely criticised for having raised the hope that it held the scientific solution to crime. At worst, this severe disillusionment resulted in a retreat to the reduced field of "medical-legal illnesses" in the hypothetical search for one single crime-producing cause. At best, the clinician was led to redefine his field of competence in the light of the prison context in which he worked, giving up any idea of spearheading research in the treatment of criminals.

To those disappointed by the total failure of psychosocial intervention, the clinician can say no more than that the prison population needs him because of its high rate of psychiatric morbidity, and because of the terrible disturbances caused by identity problems as revealed by certain behavioural disorders having criminal implications.

All developed countries have prison psychiatric facilities capable of providing the necessary treatment for a large number of prisoners deemed responsible for their acts but who may, perhaps because of being in prison, show signs of psychological disorders varying in form and severity. The work of the psychiatrist in the criminal system has become a reality which can no longer be regarded as a mere palliative or a pretence at offsetting the harmful effects of custody. The prison psychiatric service is required to treat all such prisoners, except where their condition exceeds the capacity of the treatment available, in which case they are referred to a psychiatric hospital (see in France, Article D. 398 of the Criminal Procedure Code). Irrespective of the measures taken by each country, the convenient traditional distinction between subjects to be classified as criminals and mental patients who are solely of concern to a psychiatrist has largely become obsolete, and the trend is increasingly to consider that offenders suffering from psychological disorders should both be punished and given medical treatment. To quote Garapon (1993): "As between offender **or** mentally ill, and offender **and** mentally ill, the problem is wrongly stated. In both cases the patient is considered as a whole, in the same way as if he were only an offender or only mentally ill. The offender/mentally ill alternative has no room for a third category which would avoid the stigma of madness or crime... It is no accident that so much concern is shown today for violence in the family, with renewed attention paid to conjugal rape, incest and child abuse, i.e. all problems involving people who are never third parties".

Here we also have a trend away from specialised psychiatric prisons back towards organised treatment during custody, followed by arrangements for treatment as part of the probation order (COLIN 1993).

As a clinical activity, therapeutic intervention should not however be confused with the wider idea of "treatment of the criminal" in the sense of all the measures applied to prisoners as a whole so as to help them benefit as far as possible from detention and to reduce their criminal propensities.

Strictly speaking, therapy can only apply to an illness. In this case, by contrast with other forms of psychosocial action, we are concerned not with adaptation but with health. As regards mental health, the adaptation of the subject to his environment is obviously important, but the first aim of treatment is nevertheless to achieve a cure, or at least to relieve suffering. It is thus difficult to talk of treatment when the sole aim is to modify a behaviour pattern described as socially harmful. It is not necessary to dwell on this point, bearing in mind the possibilities for collusion between psychiatrists and a totalitarian regime on the pretext of the scientific detection of antisocial behaviour at the first sign of dissidence.

Admittedly, in western countries clinicians in prisons do not find their role perverted in this way, but the clinician's art is subject to a range of contradictions liable to dilute its basic principles. We should therefore examine in greater detail the relationship between pathology and certain categories of offenders, and then consider how treatment should be given.

1.   Categories and categorisation methods

The question of special treatment for specific categories of offenders arises in terms somewhat different from the question of the general organisation of psychiatric treatment in a penal context. In the same way as psychiatric treatment is a matter for the most traditional approach, even when conducted in a very special context, so the aim of offering specific treatment to persons depending on their offence presupposes a selection of those due to receive treatment, the means to be employed and the expected results; all these go beyond the usual context of the practice of psychiatric medicine, whether in prison or elsewhere. This first problem, which gives rise to a whole series of other questions, is so to speak a problem of definition. There is no doubt that the requirements of convenience and the optimum use of complex and expensive resources militate in favour of categorising the criminal population in the light of the harmful behaviour perpetrated, so as to develop highly specialised resources in order to reach the designated target. This would mean that alongside general psychiatry there would be a form of "special psychiatry" having very specific objectives and holding out hopes of greater efficiency. Before proceeding on these lines, we should look more closely at the justification for a definition of categories.

1.1 Categories used in the prison system

For criminal justice practitioners it is useful to have categories based on their experience of the prison population: it can rightly be considered that, for example, sex offenders pose specific problems due to the type of offence, the reactions it provokes in prison, and the risk of recidivism. The same is true for drug addicts, violent young offenders and those guilty of violence in the family. These categories are penal in the sense of a type of crime, but can also be grouped under other criteria such as age, addictive forms of behaviour, recidivism, resistance to probation, the context of the violence and the subject's reactions to the micro- or macro-social environment.

The categories are therefore drawn up by tradition and are completely empirical, without any common denominator other than the fact that they take account of different types of custody. They thus permeate the entire penal microcosm; and the clinician, like everyone else, accepts this sociological approach, and will have to get rid of this fairly natural tendency to take a part for the whole, the symptom for the disease, and the label for the individual.

1.2 Criminological categories

Another way of categorising those who are dealt with by the criminal justice system is to define their status in terms of the legal texts which govern their appearance in court and their sentencing

1.2.1 The first category consists of those deemed unfit on account of their psychological disorders to take part in criminal procedures. All criminal justice systems have at some point a selection process operating on principles not always necessarily the same, but which result in withdrawing from normal criminal proceedings those whose psychological disorders are such that they cannot be held wholly or partially responsible for their acts, or who appear to be temporarily or permanently unfit to attend court, or who are in a state of health incompatible with a form of punishment mainly consisting of detention. Based on expert advice, this selection process then commits the seriously mentally ill, depending on the country concerned, either to specialised prison hospitals or to the public psychiatric hospital system, in which some hospitals have special units.

In France, selection quite simply withdraws "lunatics" from the action of the law. The present trend among law psychiatrists is to avoid categorising the mentally ill offender as irresponsible, since they consider that however disturbed the individual, the refusal to take account of his act, regarded as if it had in fact never taken place, is tantamount to "psychological death" (Demay Report, quoted by Ayme 1990).

In the United Kingdom (Heginbotham, 1990), by contrast with the vague generic concept of "insanity" in French legislation, mental disease is defined and classified. The measures taken vary depending on whether the subject suffers from "mental disorder", "severe mental impairment", "mental impairment" or "psychopathic disorder". The placement orders by courts include consideration of the benefits expected from treatment (treatability tests).

In Spain (Garcia Carbajosa, 1990), the High Court issued in May 1985 a classification of mental diseases in relation to crime. It distinguished between several categories based on major psychiatric nosographic classes, with specific recommendations as to the evaluation of responsibility.

In Italy (Molinaro 1990), despite radical reforms in the organisation of public psychiatric care, the positivist criminological tradition has maintained a dual system : on the one hand, punishment as such, retributive in nature, with specific sentences for fixed periods, and on the other (not necessarily exclusively) "security measures" designed to protect society, determined solely as regards their minimum duration and commensurate not with the offence but with the dangerousness of the offender. Recent statistics show that in the last few years, as a result of the 1978 law to de-institutionalise psychiatric treatment, the population of prison psychiatric hospitals has declined both as a percentage and in absolute figures.

1.2.2.   Whatever the country, the drug addict comes under a somewhat special criminal category, being regarded by the law as both an offender and mentally ill (French law of 31 December 1970). In cases where he is only a user, his legal status lies somewhere between that of liable for punishment and requiring a treatment order. The magistrate is then in a position to give an order for specific treatment in the case of those on trial who are designated to him as falling within a certain legal category.

1.2.3   This criminological approach leads each country to define, at least negatively, the limits of insanity and fitness to stand trial. From this point of view it seems clearly necessary to identify as accurately as possible the categories of individuals to be dealt with under specific measures, so as to find the right form of "punishment" suited to each case. The diversity of the criteria currently enforced shows that this is neither self-evident nor universally applied. We have here an interface between the respect for equality required by true justice, involving a degree of abstraction and generalisation, and consideration of the individual case in relation to major social institutions. In all countries this interface has been worn down by national practices, so much so that it is difficult in some areas to find a clear borderline between action by the courts and action by the social services.

1.3   Clinical categories

Since we are here concerned with illness and its treatment, we must refer to clinicians to see how they classify the patients entrusted to them.

1.3.1   Traditional action of law psychiatry

As regards offenders considered as at least partly responsible for their acts, psychiatrists apply the nosographic classification used in general psychiatry. Studies on the dangerously mentally ill (Benezech 1981) show that overall, the mentally ill population is not significantly more dangerous than the general population (Gunn 1977), and that the percentage of mentally ill accused persons recognised as irresponsible for their acts is low, around 15 per cent (LOO 1973). The psychiatric examination conducted by Gillies (1976) of 367 male murderers identified 302 normal subjects; of the other 65 the very great majority were psychopaths — a common finding — with a high proportion of psychotics requiring specially codified treatment.

While certain clinical forms of mental disease particularly predispose patients to crime (heboïdophrenia, delirious paranoia) there is nevertheless no need to classify them diagnostic problem.

1.3.2   The growing complexity of the diagnostic field.

In recent decades the clinical approach to offenders has made great diagnostic and therapeutic progress, with real developments in psychiatric care for the prison population and a growing awareness of the great incidence of psychiatric disorders in prisons. The present trend away from defining the offender as irresponsible has also been a factor in increasing the number of prisoners with psychological disorders whose offence can be linked with their specific disorder. It is estimated that one-third of those committed to prison reveal at the systematic medical examination psychological disorders, chiefly borderline cases described as states of psychological imbalance, alcoholism or drug addiction (Balier 1988). Bricout (1989) estimates that psychopaths represent 10 per cent of the prison population, 1 per cent of them being dangerous psychopaths. Canadian estimates are similar, with 22 per cent of the prison population manifesting an "antisocial personality disorder" (Hodgins 1993).

In addition, psychiatric typology today is spreading out in an attempt to find a multi-axial model representing the infinite complexity of individual pathological situations (DSM III R International Classification of Mental Disorders). If major categories such a schizophrenia, depression or psychopathy are no longer adequate to describe an individual pathological state, obviously any typology referring to features other than the mental disorder as such will be irrelevant, foremost among them the category of psychopaths.

1.3.2.1   Studies on psychopathy

In 1975 the Butler report stated: "Since its introduction more than 90 years ago, the term "psychopathic disorder" has been used in practice in various ways to cover a narrow or wide range of mental disorders, and to indicate causal or clinical differences from other mental disorders. The result is that we now have a great variety of opinions on the etiology, symptoms and treatment of "psychopathy", a term which is to be interpreted only with reference to the special sense in which it is employed by the individual psychiatrist (...) As a concept it is no longer useful or meaningful".

It has however remained in wide use, and is still open to the same criticism, to be found for example in the explanatory memorandum to the Council of Europe recommendation No. R(82) 17 on the custody and treatment of dangerous prisoners: "Psychopaths/sociopaths manifest a persistent disorder or disability of personality, manifesting itself in abnormally violent aggressive conduct, not regarded as mental disorder and not amenable to psychiatric treatment".

The development of prison psychiatry has nevertheless brought out a great variety of pathological situations and diagnoses within the psychopathic constellation. While we cannot here enter into the details of these clinical studies, it should be stressed from the outset that if the term "psychopath" continues to be used so frequently, it is no doubt because it reflects a need, and the lack of any other satisfying definition. It designates subjects on the borderline between insanity and crime, psychosis, neurosis or perversion, between an individual personality structure and the social reprobation of aspects of their behaviour (Gravier 1986). The latter standpoint is taken by Anglo-Saxon writers with their "anti-social personality" concept, which is used by DSM III R and emphasises behavioural and social adaptation disorders. The psychodynamic approach reveals the structural affinity of such personalities with borderline states, which Kernberg (1975) considers as encompassing all of them. In addition to a tentative classification of these states, as elusive as it is complex, these and many other studies show the importance of less noticeable symptoms, masked by repetitive outbreaks of violence. Clinical observation reveals that behind the acting out there is frequently an overwhelming, diffuse and uncontrollable anxiety, often not perceived as such by the individual, giving rise to major regressive movements which in some cases build up attitudes of total dependence (GRAVIER 1986). Such persons are very often afflicted by feelings of loneliness and emptiness perceived as boredom, driving them to seek perpetual change (Lemperiere 1977) and gratification through immediate pleasure (Bendjilali 1981). All these disorders are also observed in the narcissistic organisation of borderline cases, leading to the emptying of all relations of their affective content and attesting the proximity of the overwhelming inexpressible depression described by all the authors quoted by Scharbach (1983). Depression induces a feeling of emptiness, powerless and inhibition devoid of remorse or guilt. Among psychopaths this becomes self-pity and emotional demands or manipulation: at the borderline with depression all the functions of the ego are threatened with disorganisation (Kernberg 1975). Relations are dominated by emotional avidity, sometimes with tyrannical demands which are absolutely intolerant of any kind of frustration (Bendjilali 1981). On the neurotic plane there are frequent manifestations of hysteria and phobias, some physical, others more archaic, resembling the nocturnal terrors of childhood (Balier 1988) and all representations of a terrifyingly impulsive dynamic. Psychotic manifestations are also not infrequent, in the form of delirious outbursts, or more often states of temporary unsystemised depersonalisation which may constitute the bulk of "prison psychoses" (Balier 1993).

These personality structures provide an ideal terrain for addictive behaviour (drug abuse, alcoholism) and sexual deviation of all kinds. The main component is a chaotic and polymorphous sexuality, but Gravier (1986) also notes the close relation between these structures and forms of perversion, and the frequently genuinely perverse element in the acting out (sadism, masochism, cruelty, prostitution). Debray (1981) notes a pleasure in debasement and a desire to sully sex, often masking deeprooted fear and an identity disorder.

The traditional recognition of the poverty of these subjects' fantasies, like that of all borderline cases, includes this "sideration of the imagination and the resulting anxiety-creating link, without any intermediate element, between the real and the

164

symbolic" (Bergeret 1975). Yet while there is an absence of developed fantasies, these subjects nevertheless express themselves in a flow of images, sometimes taken from the cinema (Hochmann 1980), or terrifying nightmares exacerbated by the fact of their detention (Balier 1988). Thus a primitive life of the imagination is often buried away, denied by the subject, and cut off from any associative psychological link. Here we have one of the major therapeutic openings.

This clinical overview is obviously restricted and simplified, but it suffices to show that it would be erroneous to content oneself with the clinical approach to the sole categories established, in some cases by clinicians themselves, of the manifestations which are the most visible but also the most superficial. A precise psychopathological approach shows up the irrelevance of categories based solely on the offence committed. A given subject may in fact be rightly categorised as sex offender, violent criminal, drug addict or even a psychotic, depending on the circumstances and time of the offence.

The same conclusions might be drawn from the detailed approach to the categories of "drug addicts" (Vedrinne 1987) or "violent offenders" (Duncker 1992), but it is nevertheless in the case of sex offenders that work on typology has made the most specific progress, perhaps due in part to the varying forms of aggression involved.

1.3.2.2 Sex offenders

Many studies have explored the field of sex offences using epidemiological methods to establish classification models for sex offenders. All come up against the customary difficulties, namely uncertain diagnosis, the unreliability of different people's judgement, and the overlapping of subgroups. However, several typologies of rape concord sufficiently to identify four major themes: the desire for power, an excess of rage, sadism and antisocial behaviour, which account for the main types of aggression committed (McKibben 1993). Recent cluster analyses reveal the variables which most frequently come together: these result in the Knight and Prentky (1990) classification model of rapists, distinguishing between four typical profiles based on opportunity, undifferentiated rage, sexual motivation and revenge. Nine subgroups are related to social skills.

As regards paedophiles, classifications can be established on the basis of types of motivation, as in the model proposed by Groth (1982). Groth begins by separating violent from non-violent offenders and then uses the psychodynamic concepts of fixation and regression to establish subtypes in the category of non-violent seducers, and progressive tables of anger, power and sadism for rapists. While this typology can be criticised for its lack of operational diagnostic criteria, it is nevertheless useful to the clinician in providing diagnostic landmarks. Knight's model (1989), based on reliable methods and statistics, is much more specific with regard to epidemiological requirements. It introduces a multi-axial system of reference points (degrees of paedophilia fixation, and frequency of contacts with children) which leads on beyond a classification restricted to typical cases (McKibben 1993).

As regards psychodynamics, Van Gijseghem (1988) defines a number of perverse structures based on the specific form of relation to an object. Taking up MAC Dougall (1980), he notes the absence of any single perverse structure, and a continuum situating it between an extreme of archaic non-object-related sexuality and extreme Oedipal sexuality. Each offender is classified on this axis and also in the light of the way he relates to his environment, of counter-transfer elements and of the significance and nature of the sexual aggression (Aubut 1993).

Though useful, these categories should not be used in too literal or stereotyped a way if one is to remain sensitive to the distress perceptible even with the most serious offenders (Prins 1991).

1.4   Chapter conclusions

It is obvious that an act cannot be regarded as an illness, even if it is likely to reflect a pathological state, without thus epitomising it (as is the case, for example, with suicide). This means that categories based on the type of offence cannot, without causing terrible confusion, be regarded *a priori* as valid for basing a diagnosis or suggesting a form of treatment. Such categories entail choosing a one-dimensional characteristic which ignores a series of variables that are however vital for consideration of the situation. "This masking of the influence of variables has a specific orientation (...) the aim is almost always to appraise personality in terms of adaptability to the requirements of society" (Debuyst 1977). Clinical categories cannot be reduced to criminal ones (or for that matter any other category).

However, selection on the basis of the offence, despite its heterogeneity, in fact groups together a large number of people manifesting sufficiently serious psychological disorders to need treatment. Furthermore, a notable proportion of subjects classified in a given category of offenders have psychological disorders which, if not similar, are at least comparable: many perverts are found among sex offenders, and many borderline cases among drug addicts, etc. Thus there is a certain amount of overlapping between these categories and clinical categories which at first sight might be confused with them. In fact, clinical experience shows that serious behavioural disorders are often symptomatic of complex personality disorders, aside from resemblances suggestive of a "drug addiction personality" or the "psychological profile of the rapist". It can be seen that personality flaws, or the dead-end of impulsiveness, reveal major identity difficulties for which deviant behaviour is no more than a possible form of expression. Treatment should apply, directly or otherwise, to these faults in the make-up of the personality, whatever their ultimate symptomatic manifestation in acts of violence. Even where the techniques used are designed to modify behaviour towards a goal, treatment concerns more than behaviour; it also considers the possibly extremely dangerous survival methods adopted by the subject to preserve his feeling of identity and his impulsiveness. From this point of view, individual treatment will depend more on the type of pathology than that of the offence committed.

2   The major lines of specialised therapeutic intervention

If we are to throw any light on the field of psychiatric intervention applied to offenders, we must briefly digress to describe the major options of present-day psychiatry. The reason is that the approach to the psychologically ill is based on widely differing, not to say opposed, theoretical concepts which underly a great variety of therapeutic strategies and aims.

2.1   Current psychiatric orientations

While all psychiatrists agree that mental illness is a typically human phenomenon comprising simultaneously psychological suffering (the affective aspect), errors of judgement (the intellectual aspect) and behavioural disorder (the moral aspect), they rapidly diverge in their views as to the causes of these disorders (Geissmann 1993). Present-day psychiatry is divided on three major lines, depending on whether the emphasis is on the organic attribution, the mental or behavioural manifestation, or the subconscious dynamic of the psychological disorder.

2.1.1   Briefly, the current psychiatric scene shows three major groupings:

—   Neuro-science: biological psychiatry and chemical therapy;

—   Cognitive science: theory of behaviour, aims at rehabilitation;

—   Psychodynamics: psychological theories of psycho-affective maturation, applied in psychotherapies.

Biological psychiatry refers to a frankly medical model, in the classic meaning of the term: identification and evaluation of particularities regarded as symptoms — nosographic systemisation — then prescription of medication which should act on the nerve centres responsible — and finally, evaluation of the development of symptoms.

In this approach there is no hesitation in using scales of evaluation which categorise patients according to broad pathological types. There is a homogenisation and modelisation of disturbances. The patient can be passive.

The cognitive/behaviourist approach is based more on the observation of the inadequacy of the individual's relationship with his environment than on the idea of lesion or psychological notions.

The aim is to rehabilitate the individual by correcting his errors of management of his behaviour; he must therefore participate in a programme in which there is a high degree of self-evaluation. He is therefore active, but these techniques can result in a dependent relationship.

The psychodynamic approach is based on the search for the meaning of a patient's actions according to the state of the construction of his personality. It is a matter of bringing what is acted out impulsively and in ignorance of self and others into the domain of mental representations. In this approach, the therapists are involved not simply as operators but respond to the patient in his psycho-affective problematic. The treatment does not content itself with using the phenomena of transference, but seeks to elucidate them for the benefit of the subject, in a process of psychological maturation.

2.1.2   Cognitive-behaviourist approach and categorisation

The very idea of specific forms of treatment for categories of offenders means that if we abandon anatomical-biological theories of delinquency we find ourselves in the sphere of behavioural theory and a perception of the disorder which lays emphasis on the visible signs of behaviour or conduct diagnosed as pathological. It is therefore not surprising that most experiments in treating offenders are carried out from a behaviourist angle. Our references are naturally taken from countries in which the behaviourist school of thought predominates, i.e. mainly in North America.

2.2   An overview of cognitive-behaviourist techniques

We shall begin with this type of treatment, on which we have the most to say as regards techniques. These are the most selective, easy to evaluate and as it were the most criminological.

By definition, the diagnostic process in the cognitive-behaviourist approach is concerned with how the individual expresses himself in his conduct, particularly with reference to social skills. Here one concentrates on the subject's impulsiveness, lack of social adaptation, poverty of abstract reasoning, egocentrism, or inability to solve problems of interpersonal relations (Farrington 1993). The therapeutic programmes applied all aim at changing the subject's way of thinking, in particular getting him to reflect before acting, to envisage the consequences of his acts and to work out other solutions to these problems than acting out. The aim is also to make him aware of what other people feel when subjected to violence.

Specific programmes are proposed to this end, each with a specific objective and technique, for example training in social skills, learning the meaning of social values, recognising and understanding other people's feelings, and participating in role games with types of behaviour adapted to community life (Ross, quoted by Farrington). If necessary, specific programmes can be applied which match the classification models worked out from typological studies.

Programmes are subjected to continuing comparative evaluation studies to assess their validity and effectiveness as regards recidivism. They are adapted to each individual case, quite apart from the treatment of the offender as such. Thus we have behavioural training programmes for the offender's close circle (the parents of psychopathic children, a paedophile's family, violent young peer groups) all aimed at modifying the offender's reactions to his environment (Patterson, quoted by FARRINGTON). Systemic family therapy can be included in programmes with a view to modifying the way social exchanges take place within the family group.

In Europe, especially French-speaking Europe, there are only rare programmes for treating specific categories of offenders, whereas North America has more than 600 centres for sex offenders (Gazan 1991). Bornstein and Coutanceau (1993) note that in 1985 prison statistics showed that 12 per cent of the French prison population were sex offenders: "(...) In France, discussion continues on whether or not there is any advantage in systematically taking responsibility for sex offenders". Gazan (1993) suggests several explanations for this lack of therapeutic facilities: differences in the sex models used as paradigms, European backwardness as regards the latest "fashion in psychoanalysis" and also European reluctance to take the step of applying treatment to the aggressor.

2.2.1 Example of a typical sex offender programme

Gazan (1991) reviews progress in this type of treatment and gives details of application procedures. The aim is to provide guidance, freely accepted by the subject, aimed not at a cure but at preventing a relapse. A typical programme includes "identifying critical situations which lead to acting out (the "PIG"); developing action methods to enable the subject to resist his aggressiveness; using problem-oriented methods; and the remodelling, in greater depth, of the subject's experience of life". The subject attends a weekly "practical work group" along with other individuals unable to control their sexual behaviour, with harmful results to others. One of the first things the subject learns is to identify his own PIG, how to recognise it, how it behaves, what makes it aggressive, what it feeds on, what it is afraid of, what calms it, and how the subject can come to terms with it. A plethysmographic examination of the penis (objective measurement of sexual arousal by predetermined stimuli) may help the subject to understand himself better.

Using behavioural and cognitive methods the group participants work on their motivation and exercise of will power so as to "identify, refocus and increase their control over events to come" (Carey & McGrath, quoted by Gazan). Libido-inhibiting drugs are used "under strict, regular and prolonged medical supervision ... and represent as regards psychosexual disorders pharmacological instruments which have restored their joy in life to patients who were previously hopeless cases" (Servais, quoted by Gazan). In the longer term, the subject is monitored in a counselling group in which he learns to foresee the chain of events leading up to aggression, realise the harm inflicted on the victim, and to bring about a "cognitive restructuring" through awareness of his erroneous interpretation of reality. He will then be ready to use a "decision matrix" covering the short, medium and long term which will help him to envisage the consequences of his choices of action. Group therapy aims at influencing in depth the major narcissistic components of the subject's ego or of his low self-esteem; as necessary it is supplemented by individual interviews and the use of special problem-oriented techniques. The types of treatment involved are behavioural, designed to control an erection associated with a disagreeable smell ("punishment signal received"), produce masturbatory satiation so as to evacuate from a dangerous scenario its power to arouse, and progressive fading in which a non-deviant sex image is superimposed on the previous deviance-creating image. From the cognitive point of view, the subject is given sex education and learns social skills. These programmes are applied only after evaluation and tests of the subject's social abilities, characteristics and antecedents, and an analysis of risk situations.

2.2.2   For other categories of offender (violent subjects, young psychopaths, drug addicts) the treatment principle and programme applied are the same, in both prisons and the community. For drug addicts the question is often complicated by the legal provisions associating a custodial sentence with a treatment order, treatment being much the same whether required from "free" or prison consultants. Treatment frequently includes the codified use of specific "substitution product" programmes (methadone, Temgesic ...). Prison and health care policies vary from one country to another depending on the criminological classification of drug abuse and also on prevailing guidelines for therapeutic assistance. While obviously we cannot expect the large-scale distribution of a substitution product to restrict drug use or control the AIDS epidemic (Duncker 1990) opinions still vary widely as regards the application to the drug addict population of behavioural techniques associated with controlled use of substitution products. Here the problem goes beyond the field of psychosocial action.

2.2.3   Results and evaluation criteria

As noted above, the behavioural approaches applied in programmes comprise from the outset an evaluation component based on the compilation of data which can be processed statistically. They have thus a standing research function, and give rise to many publications, mostly in English, whose findings may differ somewhat but which always express results in figures in the light of a restricted number of criteria, headed by that of recidivism. More homogeneous, and probably more reliable results are obtained by the meta-analytical methods well described by Professor Lösel in his report. There is thus no need to revert in detail to them, but they must at least be mentioned, since they are part of this type of approach.

Proulx (1993) gives a detailed interpretation of the effectiveness of treatment with recidivist sex offenders. After stressing the methodological bias inherent in the virtual impossibility of establishing exactly equivalent groups, and the divergent views of authors on the duration of monitoring, the population under study and the definition of recividism, he returns to the meta-analytical study by Hanson (1989) of 25 investigations. For both groups (those given treatment and the others) the recidivism rate is the same, 15 per cent, which seems to indicate that treatment of sex offenders achieves no results; this coincides with Furby's (1989) conclusions. However, when examining results by the type of treatment applied, Hanson finds a recidivism rate of 10.2 per cent in the case of four cognitive and behavioural treatment programmes (sex education, social skills, modification of sexual preferences) an 11 per cent rate for programmes using only one or two of these methods, and a rise to 19 per cent or more for patients having undergone only unstructured group treatment. Yet even these results are liable to biased interpretation and should be regarded with caution. Whatever the case, it seems that the recividist rate for subjects at risk who are not treated is very high.

170

As regards the different techniques used, an evaluative comparative study of investigations into the treatment of young offenders (Mulvey 1993) shows that in institutions the behaviourist interventions (Andrews 1989), the cognitive approach focused on social skills (Serna 1986), and family therapies (Barton 1985) are more effective than peer groups or unstructured therapy groups (Gottfredson 1987). Mulvey also notes methodological differences creating uncertainty as to what is really being evaluated: the somewhat aleatory conditions which lead to placing a given offender in a treatment programme, the impossibility of determining which of the changes observed is precisely due to treatment, and the risk of focusing treatment on a medical type of model irrespective of environmental interreactions, which may lead to overestimating the favourable reactions observed during the programme, all of which will disappear once the subject has returned to his normal environment.

2.3   The biological approach

We have seen that in North America the use of anti-libido medication is part of complex cognitive and behavioural programmes as one of a number of aids. In Europe experiments with these products are relatively isolated, and the clinicians involved (Cordier 1991) agree that they should be prescribed with great care and closely monitored over a long period. No published findings definitely advocate or prescribe their use for the category of sex offenders as a whole; it seems that the best results can be expected from individuals suffering from a painful uncontrollable impulsiveness which urges them on to sexual assaults and is followed by an intense feeling of guilt. They should be used to supplement other forms of treatment (Gagne 1993).

With psychoactive medicines, neuroleptics and tranquillizers, we are on the more traditional ground of psychiatry for the treatment of acute or chronic mental illness. The more or less general use of these drugs by prison doctors will depend on their psychiatric training and their views of the role played by psychiatric disorders in the genesis of crime (Tardiff 1992). Thus the treatment of violent patients in prison hospitals may in some cases be based almost solely on the use of psychoactive drugs, though this practice is severely criticised (see for example recent reports by the Committee for the Prevention of Torture on the inspection of prison psychiatric services in several European countries).

2.4   The psychological approach

Here deviant forms of behaviour are referred to the subject's individual history. Neither the treatment programme nor the behavioural goal to be sought can be drawn up in advance. Objective evaluation by category of patients can be carried out only in part, due to the relative nature of the criteria attesting subjective maturation. The psychodynamic approach is therefore less suitable for establishing diagnostic categories, and even still less for therapeutic categories. While there are few epidemiological studies due to this lack of measurable data, the literature on the psycho-relational situation of these patients is plentiful and relevant, as indicated above in the discussion of psychopathy. Contrary to certain generally accepted views, psychological treatment is not confined to individual psychotherapy, and still less to a facile psychological classification of all types of human behaviour. All the institutional psychotherapeutic thinking underlying public psychiatric practice teaches therapists to recognise, and identify with their patients in, pathological relational interactions. This is why the clinicians concerned are very attentive to the problems of the environment, recognised as an area of rules and taboos, but which is also an area of trust and verbal communication in which one can venture to establish a therapeutic relationship.

2.5   The problem of the treatment context

These three approaches have different registers and cannot be combined. There is of course the risk that the clinician might allow himself to become enclosed in the single logic of one of these orientations, considering it the only scientifically valid one, to the detriment of the slightest opening to the other two. A preferential orientation is probably necessary, but it can benefit from a different perspective on the same subject. For example, what is obtained from a better psychological maturation will have behavioural consequences which are more easily evaluated. In addition, as treatment proceeds recourse may be had to one or another of these approaches, depending on the patient's abilities and ongoing development (Aubut 1993).

In fact, in addition to techniques, what is required is to set up a rigorous operational framework giving therapeutic interventions their place and significance. A good example is the practice of institutional socio-therapy in the Champ-Dollon Prison, Geneva (De Montmollin 1985, 1986, Bernheim, 1993). Here community treatment based on United Kingdom and Netherlands experience is offered to categories of prisoners who, without being mentally ill in the traditional sense of the term, manifest serious character disorders, whose psychological behaviour is rigid and maladjusted, and whose impulsiveness and blurred identity lead them to repetitive violent acts or sexual behaviour. Such individuals are admitted only on their own written request and after preliminary interviews. In the prison centre they are given no psychoactive medication. The programme includes carefully designed activities and discussion periods, so that "each individual, as he sees how the others behave, ends up by seeing himself". Gradually a feeling of belonging and responsibility may emerge, with reduced feelings of suffering, hatred and humiliation due to detention, and a significant improvement in clinical signs such as self-esteem, anguish, depression, critical sense and relations with reality, other people and those in authority. In this kind of centre there is no specially complex standard programme, only vigilant attention to links which can reestablish subjectivity where formerly there was only a desire to dominate.

Briefly, techniques are only useful when they fit into a coherent whole which is capable of modifying the distorted relations entertained by the subject in his vision of the world and other people. As with any change in a human being, a modification can be obtained by a whole range of interactions, from simple information to the most complex psychological treatment, including education, reeducation, cognitive/behaviourist techniques, socio-therapy, the therapeutic environment and transfer-based forms of psychotherapy.

It is very difficult to compare these therapeutic techniques without at the same time indicating their target, institutional framework and working methods. This organisational aspect is the essential backdrop against which technical procedures will be more or less eclectic in the ways they help to produce a change in the subject (AUBUT 1993).

The psychiatric organisation required to provide such treatment should therefore be large-scale, competent and diversified but sufficiently homogeneous to ensure a permanent and reliable therapeutic framework.

3. Specialised therapeutic interventions in prisons

It is thus only on the scale of a system of treatment that "specific therapy" can be envisaged, whether in the context of a typology based on acts or with special emphasis on the profound personality disorders approach. M. Colin repeatedly states that a psychiatrist in isolation can do nothing. High-quality treatment needs an institutional framework with established techniques and operating methods.

3.1 The major orientations of prison psychiatric treatment systems

Prison psychiatric facilities are developing in each country in the light of the social place and field of competence recognised to psychiatry for treating not only mental disorders as such but also their consequences for the behaviour and socialisation of subjects diagnosed as ill, deviants or socially dangerous. Thus the decision as to whether interventions with these subjects come under psychiatry or other social agencies may vary from one country to another: for example, in general psychiatry, the long-term management of stabilised psychotics will in Anglo-Saxon countries be more readily entrusted to social services, whereas in France and Italy it will remain the responsibility of a medical-social psychiatric team. In the one case the accent will be on the pathology to be treated, in the other the work of social rehabilitation.

Several factors affect the type of facility instituted: legal provisions placing the treatment institution administratively or otherwise under the authority of the law, more or less developed probation services, prison reform policy based on objectives and criminological categories. Also involved are medical traditions and the choice of health care policy, which depending on the country gives psychiatrists a back seat or on the contrary puts them in the first line of the major problems of social maladjustment, either working solely in their hospitals or included in the social fabric with responsibility for the mental health of the population as a whole.

This option of psychiatry integrated with the workings of society is the one adopted in France, with the institution of a general psychiatric sector, adapted to the prison population, in Regional Medical Psychological Services (SMPRs). In the case of specific treatment for categories of offenders, the option of setting up SMPRs deserves study, since the sector's policy principle aims at global effect. Rather than specialised institutions or procedures, SMPRs are public psychiatric services equipped like their counterparts in the same sector and financed like them from the public health budget, with the same schedule of conditions which, instead of applying to a geographical sector, concerns the population of the prison region in which they are located. Operating in fact as unified prison psychiatric services, independent of the prison administration, unlike probation or medical services, SMPRs are installed in remand centres for those awaiting trial or prisoners with short sentences. French prisons also have 16 "drug addiction units" set up in 1987 to provide specific treatment for drug addicts in prison, which work in association with SMPRs. There is currently a proposal to incorporate these units in SMPRs, thus confirming the unifying approach of this form of prison psychiatric organisation.

Two examples of treatment institutes, both recently the subject of publications, well illustrate the adoption of these prison psychiatric options applied to categories of offenders. The P. Pinel Institute in Montreal (Aubut et Coll. 1993) has set up a separate unit for sex offenders, and the Varces SMPR (Balier 1988) treats in a detention centre prisoners recognised as responsible for their acts but manifesting psychological disturbances causing violent behaviour.

3.2   The Philippe Pinel Institute

The treatment of sex offenders by J. Aubut's team in Quebec has for more than ten years been trying to bring together North American (cognitive or behaviourist) and European (psychoanalytical) concepts. It is with this eclectic view of the phenomenon of sex offences that the Institute offers consenting patients a programme of treatment based on two fundamental objectives: preventing re-offending, and improving the aggressor's quality of life. Therapeutic techniques are adapted to each client according to his needs, inadequacies and psychological abilities. The techniques are re-evaluated periodically according to the development.

With patients who recognise that they have deviant fantasies and impulses to act them out, behavioural (aversion), cognitive (management of relapse) or even biological (anti-androgens) techniques are used. When the subject has greater control over his actions, therapy can deal with psycho-relational problems (training in social skills, individual or group therapy). The choice of a cognitive or psychodynamic approach would depend on the client's verbal, symbolic and introspective abilities rather than the theoretical orientation of the therapist. All the treatment programmes, including institutional therapy, applied to the patient in the therapeutic environment "should be regarded not as a context in which the patient is plunged successively into different therapeutic baths ... but as a place for observing all the elements associated with a client's sex offence" (Aubut).

The authors stress two fundamental elements which, before any technique is employed, they regard as preconditions for their work:

—   work in a multidisciplinary team;

–   a programme of treatment extending over time: sex offenders manifest disturbances or chronic inadequacies in various areas, and it is impossible to treat them properly in a few months. The minimum duration of treatment is two years, which usually implies outside treatment; this also makes it possible to validate and generalise what is learnt in social life.

These strategies are based on conceptions inspired by the bio-psychosocial model (Engel), which takes account of all the variables there might be in the life of a subject: historical, contingent, psychological, social and biological. All these variables can contribute to the individual's offending and all can be used in treatment. It is therefore a multi-factor, dynamic conception rather than functional and lesion-oriented. When frustrated in a conflict situation, the subject is exposed to the return of unresolved primordial conflicts which are projected on those around him. The resulting unease can be perceptible to people around the subject while he himself is unable to identify or name it. It is then that deviant sexual fantasies come into force, which the sex offender will make more bearable by cognitive distortions. Thus a paedophile will claim that it is normal to have sexual contact with children, because it is a form of love and education. Similarly, a rapist will say that many women consciously or unconsciously want to be raped. These cognitive distortions are followed, on the path to re-offending, by slight changes of habit which are apparently anodyne but that those around him will be unable to decipher. For example, a paedophile will take a detour on his return from work and casually go by a school. The increased risk which precedes the act is not recognised by the subject himself.

The prevention of relapse as a therapeutic technique is aimed essentially at the client's self control. It is a cognitive, educational approach most often practised in a group. The signs of a possible relapse are discussed with the therapist, dedramatised and situated in their context as sources of learning and opportunities for avoiding a relapse. As with other pathologies, such as alcoholism and diabetes, there is no such thing as a cure, but there are remissions. From this point of view, the sex offender must never regard himself as free from the possibility of a relapse and must learn to manage his sexual pathology and improve his quality of life.

It can be seen through this example of an institution focused specifically on one category of offender that progress has been made in criminal psychiatry by:

–   taking account of the complexity of the many factors involved in deviant behaviour as much in their acknowledgement and understanding as in the techniques employed to help their resolution;

–   the recognition of the primordial therapeutic vector represented by the relationship. From the simple positive investment of the therapist in the cognitive group to the analysis of the transfer in the therapies based on psychoanalysis.

Thus the separation of diagnostic and therapeutic phases dear to classical clinicians loses its organising function: rather than a description of the premises followed by restoration, the clinical approach brings together a subject who cannot be reduced to his act and does not understand what comes over him, with a multidisciplinary group of clinicians able progressively to understand his psychological structure.

It is the subject who remains the centre of his therapists' attention, but the subject in his situation, that is, someone who has been formed by a particular historical, cultural and social environment, which has forged his identity and brought about his offending.

The criminological concern to prevent re-offending is here an integral part of the therapeutic programme which begins with an encounter with the criminal justice system.

3.3   Example of the Varces SMPR

Dr. BALIER is Head Physician of one of the 18 French SMPRs. He has developed a particularly rigorous and profound analysis of the psychological disturbances encountered in extremely violent individuals, whether their violence is murderous, sexual, expressed within the family, or even suicidal.

According to his observations, such individuals, faced with the threat of their impulses becoming uncontrollable and their psychological instability, have only been able to escape psychotic collapse by forming a very particular type of relation to the Other. This relation, "without love or hate" is very close to the relationship of dominance of the early years of life. When the Other is destroyed (by murder or rape, for example), he is violently signified in his alterity from the subject by the very act which destroys him, which is the only way left to safeguard the inside-outside boundaries in a movement close to delirious creation. It is psychic activity itself which is threatened with destruction and it is remarkable that many of these authors of destruction have no memory at all of what they have done, or at least until the therapeutic work of psychic development has enabled them to reappropriate the mental representations of this violence.

In the study of the psychic movements at work in such pathologies, it would be pointless to try to find a particular personality structure that could be described as a "psychopathic personality" or "antisocial" or as a "criminal personality". In this respect, the approach is opposed to common representations of pathological violence and also to classifying tendencies.

Beyond these behavioural disorders, or the masks of affective indifference, the framework of relationships offered by therapy can bring about the emergence — fragile, incomplete and conflictual — of a psychic activity of contact in subjects whom any internalisation would threaten with collapse. Here also, the clinical analysis of these subjects is part and parcel of the unfolding therapeutic relationship.

Balier (1993) sums up the therapy in four major processes:

— the restoration of narcissism in the course of individual talks, helping the subject to recognise its force through the reconstruction of his own history;

— the split in the subject's psyche disappears: he is referred back to reality and to his denial of all that troubles him. This means containing his resulting anguish, a development which can only really be brought about in prison;

— the work is done through talking with the subject and in spoken groups, and using mediation (drawing, psychodrama, relaxation);

— repairing the vacuum created by the trauma, working on therapist-patient identifications. This part of the therapy is highly mobilising and agonising for the therapist faced with annihilation. It is therefore essential that he should not work on his own: the team always comprises three therapists for each patient, who communicate with each other on everything said and felt. Only in this way can the patient integrate the therapist in his psyche as someone who will reorganise the vacuum.

The therapeutic objectives are the same as for any psychotherapy, that is, not the sedation of a symptom, and the ceasing of offending, but getting the subject to integrate psychically the elements which previously he has only been able to act out and evacuate through violence. One could speak of an access to internalisation, "with the cure in addition".

The means must correspond to this objective. They must be not only material but also above all methodological, organising the rigorously structured and developed intervention of a complete psychiatric team. This clinical work takes place within the prison where the SMPR is located.

Unlike many people, C. Balier says that for him the firm framework and reliability of the prison context is indispensable for the therapeutic context to be established, endure and differentiate itself. In his experience, the prison context is far from being an obstacle to treatment, despite the tensions.

This ten-year experience of the "psychoanalysis of violent behaviour" confirms the change of attitude that has already been noted in Quebec. The clinical attitude to the criminal loses its static, expert aspect and becomes oriented towards a diachronic knowledge of the subject observed within the dynamics of treatment. We find again here in another form M. Colin's statement that an appraisal can only cast light on the subject if it is an integral part of the treatment process.

The discourse on prison is changing: it is not regarded as a therapeutic method but as a context which can sometimes make it possible to organise treatment. It is presented as a living environment, very strict but very safe, in which the context of treatment can be established without any other interference than the necessity of permanent work on everyone's attitude. This differentiation of contexts is one way to end the alienation from the totalitarian nature of both prison and hospital on the part of subjects who have a totally arbitrary representation of the world.

The attitude is resolutely distinguished from the criminal justice process, in the "clarity of our position with regard to the judicial system which carries out its work, in which we do not involve ours (...) which enables us to maintain our therapeutic role ..." (Balier 1988).

In this distancing, technical independence and ethical rigour are jealously protected. The clinician lays down the conditions for his work within the broader context of the prison which imposes its constraints on him, but which does not try to extend its control over what happens between him and his patients.

4.   The problems of therapeutic interventions with specific categories of offenders

We have studied above some of the problems stemming from vague definitions of the terms "therapeutic intervention" and "categories of offenders". While not all the contradictions noted can be resolved, appropriate treatment does seem possible for very psychologically disturbed individuals, whatever their ultimate form of access to it. Nevertheless, even in the best-established therapeutic contexts, there persists a series of real questions as to the actual conditions governing treatment: the problems of consent and the obligation to treat, medical confidentiality, and the technical independence of the clinician. The ethical imperatives of psychiatry in the prison context have been clearly set out by Bernheim (1980), recommending that the practitioner refrain from taking part in judicial decisions or intervening in spheres within the competence of the prison administration; that he respect the prisoner's right not to be treated, and that he define the treatment programme with reference wherever possible to hospital practice.

4.1   Forcible treatment and consent

The requirement of free informed consent to treatment is a universal principle involving freedom of decision for the individual and a moral, professional commitment by the doctor to treat and if possible cure him (Guillod 1986). Technically, it is possible to treat a prisoner without his consent, with drugs or conditioning techniques, with a degree of success by making him dependent on and submissive to doctors. Such techniques can be employed to many ends other than therapy, such as inhumane and degrading treatment, and this is a particularly sensitive point of the infringement of human rights. Without going to this extreme, there is always the risk of treatment given to someone without his consent sliding into a relationship of dominance/submission, particularly if it concerns the psyche. It is furthermore not always easy to obtain the informed consent of someone whose faculty of understanding and analysing reality is impaired. In prison systems this principle is therefore rightly and jealously protected, and all prison treatment practice includes a clause on consent. Generally speaking, forcible treatment cannot take place in prison, and prisoners requiring such treatment are therefore referred to hospital authorities, who apply their own ethical and legal rules under their own responsibility.

Aside from treatment in prison, judges or prosecutors may make an order for treatment as an integral part of a range of probation measures. Whether or not the treatment is specific (drug addicts, sex offenders), some judges responsible for the execution of sentences regard these as backup measures taking their significance from probation measures as a whole, and not as an alternative to imprisonment (Passet 1993). Such forcible treatment can therefore be envisaged only in strictly individual cases, not as a generic measure applying to all offenders (for example, alcoholic drivers or drug addicts), particularly since in France the law provides for a therapeutic order for drug addicts as an alternative to a custodial sentence. Forcible treatment is both a measure prescribed and a term introducing a meaning and third dimension (Garapon 1993) giving the offender "a status which notifies him that he cannot evade responsibility as a human being for an act whose prohibition was suspended by him as the author of that act" (Legendre 1991).

Forcible treatment is thus recognised as a necessary restriction on freedom, without necessarily being the only one (Passet 1993).

While judges and clinicians agree that consent would have only relative value and that the treatment would fail if "negotiated" with a reduced sentence (Fogel 1977), other less glaringly obvious factors can also vitiate the "therapeutic contract". The question of consent is a very delicate one in relation to the criminal population and in particular the prison context. Economic and disciplinary considerations and the result expected of the interventions place both offender and clinician in a somewhat confused contractual situation where the subject's expressed needs and the judicial authority's desire to promote normalisation are inextricably mixed up with "the submission to authority" of the various protagonists (François 1979).

The problem of this vitiated consent in the prison environment is greater than the absolute refusal of treatment. In the latter case, it could be said that there is at least the advantage of clarity, people know where they stand and, if a conflict arises, its terms will be clear to those involved.

In some cases therefore the clinician must be able to take responsibility for interpreting his patient's consent. With seriously disturbed patients who have little hold on reality and whose psychological functioning is psychotic, we will be closer to the idea of "assistance to a person in danger", faced with the absolute necessity of restoring what can be potentiated of the subject, before hoping that therapy might result in changed behaviour. This would mean various stages of consent.

It must be stressed that it is not a question here of formal consent with, for example, the patient signing protocols or contracts. Nor is it a question of the "acceptability" of treatment, a notion basic to a statistical method for evaluating the commitment and assiduity of patients in cognitive-behaviourist programmes (Chaffin 1992), which shows that the most highly mentally structured subjects are most likely to be amenable to treatment. Neither the type of the punishment (Lundervold 1992) nor pathological characteristics (Wierson 1992) yield valid correlations with acceptability. It can be deduced that consent cannot be regarded as one in a list of items, but that it always concerns the subject's sphere of freedom. This is a recurring problem for practising psychiatrists, obliging them when providing treatment to be specially vigilant about the requirements of professional ethics. In the most difficult cases in which the relationship cannot be based on a sufficiently stable identity, obtaining formal consent would be to give a subject with identity problems a capacity to contract which he cannot sustain.

In conclusion, it may be worth noting that consent presupposes something that can be consented to. In France, the lack of psychiatric facilities in long-term detention centres has resulted in concentrations of convicts for whom no serious treatment is available. The long-stay prison of Casabianda accommodates, virtually without treatment, 80 per cent of convicted sex offenders, 75 of them minors. This coincides with the Canadian estimate that more than half of mentally ill patients receive no treatment (Hodgins 1992). Any theoretical discussion of committal to a non-existent system of care would be a mere pretence at finding a solution. The most alarming problem is that of the lack of facilities, and the absence of any treatment for a large proportion of the prison population.

4.2   Confidentiality

The concept of medical confidentiality is obviously required to a high degree in the whole criminal process, and respect for it by doctors is the rule (Restellini 1985). From not denouncing a crime (the Tarasoff case in the United States) to the medical opinion required for the lifting of a psychiatric placement order, by way of the prison psychiatrist 's involvement with the board for the execution of sentences to give his opinion on probation measures, there are numerous occasions for the exchange of information between doctors, judges and prison administrators. In French prisons which have psychiatric services, relations between the psychiatric and prison staff are described as satisfactory by all concerned. However, almost half the psychiatric teams consider that, for ethical reasons connected with confidentiality, they should refuse any involvement with the board for the execution of sentences. There again, it will be the therapist's ethical references, rather than any strict regulation, that will enable him to exchange indispensable information about patients without betraying the confidentiality which is such a decisive factor in treatment.

The problem presents itself rather differently with programmes of treatment applied specifically to certain categories of offenders. The simple fact of belonging to such a category is in itself a label and the medical staff will have to report to the promoters of the programme as to the progress or otherwise of each of their patients. The clinician might be tempted, in the context of this evaluation, to communicate to third parties the intimate thoughts of their patients converted into objective quantifiable "data".

4.3   The technical independence of the therapist

4.3.1   The needs and constraints of independence

Criticism has been levelled at the involvement of psychiatrists in the prison system. Some radical critics consider that psychiatry has no place in the system, its ethical sphere being outside the system. For Fogel (1979), the clinician should act only under contract on behalf of a prisoner, in the same way as a lawyer; deploring the expanding psychiatric system in American prisons, he stigmatises the hypocrisy of linking the duration of a sentence to a sort of good conduct code in compliance with the expectations of therapists. Other critics concentrate on the difficulties or risks inherent in criminological psychiatry: the use of a psychiatrist primarily for evaluation purposes, to the detriment of treatment requirements, and the tendency to sidetrack clinical practice towards a normative function (François 1979).

These criticisms are certainly valid for any treatment programme designed specifically to modify harmful behaviour. The idea of a psychiatrist as a normaliser, an evaluator of dangerousness or a deputy for the judge in determining the length of the sentence, calls for study when it is clearly correlated with the expectation that the clinician should be a lay "arm of the law," or of society, in getting rid of seriously harmful behaviour. One major difficulty is how to define the proper role of a therapy applied in accordance with the rules of the clinician's art, distinguishing it from a "deviation" in the interests of normalisation. This is a major question in any type of psychiatric practice, even in the most democratic countries, and it is still more sensitive in the case of criminal psychiatry, due to the acutely conflicting interests of the individual and the social group. It may call for even greater vigilance with regard to treatment programmes for certain offenders, probably precisely those who are the most stigmatised by the outraged reaction of society.

Certain characteristics of the criminal justice system can tend to limit this technical independence of the therapist. Indeed, this independence can never be absolute and it would be a mistake to believe that the therapist could be in glorious isolation from the context in which he works. The links between judicial institution and clinicians are ambivalent (Legendre) and Bernheim has stressed the notion of the clinician's "double contract": one with the administration (contract to practise), the other being the medical treatment contract. Very often, particularly at times of crisis in an institution, the question of the clinician's technical independence results in power conflicts which unfortunately are more often acted out than verbalised (Real de Sarte 1984).

The clinician must also be able to maintain his intellectual independence. The weight and prevalence of action in the prison environment, to the detriment of verbal communication, the need to be efficient, even discouragement, can sometimes lead the clinician to push his nosographic categories in the direction desired by the judicial authority, or to justify a given penal measure by the necessities of treatment. It must be noted in this regard that therapeutic programmes are all the more instrumental or operative (medication, hormones) when the disorder to be treated is focused on behaviour (the "chemical castration" of rapists, substitute drugs for addicts, etc.). One can speak here of a risk of confusion of clinical and criminal categories when it is the association of a particular form of delinquent behaviour with a means of action said to be specific which would alone organise therapy. The most striking example of this is the statement that prison is in itself therapeutic for the addict in that it forces him to undergo withdrawal symptoms. A therapeutic programme worthy of the name cannot have the sole objective of ending intoxication without dealing with the subject's addictive relationship with his drug, and therefore his total psycho-relational economy.

4.3.2   How to establish technical independence

Genuine treatment institutions can establish their technical independence in various ways depending on the context. In the Pinel Institute clinicians take into account both the criminological aims of preventing re-offending and programme evaluation requirements. The Institute is part of the prison system, but the clinicians' medical views prevail. While agreeing to comply with a strong, even urgent social command, (cf the public status of the sex offender in North America), they obtain substantial resources to develop their clinical work both inside and outside the Institute. Though they are involved in "treating criminals", they detach themselves thanks to the highly developed organisation of the Institute into a diversified but coherent whole, sufficiently substantial in size and scientific weight to impose its technical independence.

Another option, represented by the French SMPRs and in particular the practice followed by BALIER, cuts itself off radically from social demand and considers the clinician as a "psychiatrist working in prison" rather than as a prison psychiatrist (Colin 1993). This independence is sanctioned by the fact that SMPRs form part of the public psychiatric service. The clinician then installs his clinic inside the prison as virtually an extraterritorial unit. He is not directly concerned with criminological aims, and with evaluation only in relation to clinical criteria regarding psychic functioning; he ignores criminological criteria such as predicting dangerousness or the risk of recidivism. His therapeutic tool is not specialised to achieve a specific objective (geared for example to a particular criminological target), but is highly specialised due to the clinical context established in the prison, and is specifically adapted to types of pathologies found in certain offenders. Careful reading of their clinical notes shows that the same pathologies are observed and treated by Dr. Balier and the Pinel Institute.

4.4   The place of specialised therapeutic interventions in the more general context of psychosocial interventions

The purpose of treatment is thus largely defined by, or rather conditional on, the penal process; but the clinician is responsible for establishing his own working context, categories and competence, while subject, as elsewhere in the medical profession, to imposed resources but not to imposed results. He has a mandate from society, but no social commands in the sense of an order placed simply for services. There remains the tricky question of drawing the line between the clinician's field of competence and that of other psychosocial interventions which, though assistance-oriented, reflect neither the same expectations nor the same schedule of conditions. This line is difficult to draw, both because the personality types concerned do not always fall into the clear-cut category of mentally ill subjects, and because any "community" assumption of psychiatric responsibility comprises a substantial component of helping the subject to live in society. Those involved in psychosocial interventions with offenders separate intervention from treatment; they stress that their work is in the nature of guidance, addressed to individuals from whom the most to be hoped is better adjustment to social constraints, not a cure (Prins 1991). Yet studies by prison psychiatrists prove that such states are curable, provided that an adequate therapeutic tool is available. We are perhaps here concerned not so much with techniques or categories as with different degrees of the same proposal to help bring about a change. As regards the working context, it should however be borne in mind that the more the clinician has in hand the patient's subjectivity, the greater the need for him to be able to refer to a theoretical institutional context which will enable him to work out his own responses. Merely applying a technique is not enough.

It is therefore essential to base oneself on the clinical method, and nothing else, in the approach to the pathology to be treated. But the clinician cannot be isolated from the sphere of psychosocial interventions. His skills are highly valuable in throwing light on the psycho-relational implications of the situations encountered by probation service practitioners and other agents in the criminological process. Any type of assistance thus has a clinical aspect, which should be developed in a group supervising or analysing practice with a clinician.

Conclusions

It is clear from the examples of the practice of specialised institutions that the crux of treatment for a specific type of offender is not so much the establishment of a specific category and therapeutic protocol as the institution's capacity and availability actually to provide treatment. This capacity is the really specific need.

The following obvious requirements stem from this observation. Firstly, specialised care can be offered only where an efficient clinical tool already exists: a well-established institution, a diversified team accustomed to the difficulties of prison psychiatry, a mastery of the techniques employed, a pragmatic approach and the rejection of any over-systemisation which would mask the patient behind his symptoms.

Secondly, irrespective of where treatment is provided, prison psychiatry must defend its therapeutic orientation. This cannot be taken for granted, in view of the continuous and varied forms of pressure which seek to force psychiatry to comply solely with the aims of social control, lay emphasis on its evaluation function, relegate it to the status of a regulatory agent as regards tensions within prisons, and generally restrict its technological independence by limiting its possibilities of establishing its own working context. It is only by going beyond these more or less visible limits that prison psychiatry will be able to develop therapeutic action effectively and specifically geared to the psychopathology of its patients; conversely, it is by developing this action that it will be best placed to throw off the greater part of these constraints.

The problem of therapeutic interventions with specific categories of offenders is therefore in the first place to check the validity of clinical categories, and then to create an instrument which will provide modern psychiatric care. The theoretical option providing a vector for this work, and the need for this instrument to comply with judicial and criminological requirements, are of relatively secondary importance.

Basically, the substantial development of psychosocial interventions in the context of probation measures, combined with considerations of economy and the streamlining of methods, have helped to produce a return to the clinical approach, which, together with criminological claims that crime should be "medically" controlled, have been somewhat neglected. The problems of therapeutic interventions with specific categories of offenders are admittedly technical, but above all they are bound up with conflicts in the exercise and recognition of prison psychiatry. By far the most numerous category of offenders in need of care remains that of offenders given no treatment whatsoever, and no technique can succeed in dealing with a whole category of exclusion.

BIBLIOGRAPHY

AUBUT J., 1993, Les théories psychanalytiques. In *Les agresseurs sexuels*, Paris, 1993, pp. 21-34

AYME J., 1993, La refonte de l'article 64 du Code pénal. In *Santé mentale: réalités européennes,* Erès, Toulouse, 1993, pp 271-274

AUBUT J., 1993, La prévention de la récidive: une approche bio-psycho-sociale. In *Les agresseurs sexuels*, Paris, 1993, pp.146-153

BALIER C., 1988, Psychanalyse des comportements violents. Presses Universitaires de France Paris, 1988

BENDJILALI A., 1981, L'histoire du psychopathe et de son passage à l'acte. *Psychiatries*, 1981, 45, pp. 57-63

BENEZECH M., ADDAD M. & al., 1981, Criminologie et psychiatrie. *Encyclopédie Médico-Chirurgicale* (Paris) 37906 A10 — 10-1981

BERGERET J., 1975, *La dépression et les états limites.* Payot, Paris, 1975

BERNHEIM J., 1993, L'expert-psychiatre, médecin du juge ou du détenu ? In *Justice et psychiatrie.* , Association d'Etudes et de Recherches de l'Ecole Nationale de la Magistrature Bordeaux, pp. 41-47.

BERNHEIM J., 1993, Sociothérapie institutionnelle de détenus présentant un désordre grave du caractère: l'expérience de "La pâquerette" à Champ-Dollon (Genève). In *Justice et psychiatrie.* Association d'Etudes et de Recherches de l'Ecole Nationale de la Magistrature Bordeaux, 1993, pp 141-147.

BERNHEIM J., 1986, Etudes sur la responsabilité pénale et le traitement psychiatrique des délinquants malades mentaux: rapport introductif. *Etudes relatives à la Recherche Criminologique.* Conseil de l'Europe, Strasbourg, 1986, vol. XXIV, pp. 13-25

BERNHEIM J., 1980, Ethique en médecine pénitentiaire. D'après un exposé au *Symposium de l'Académie Suisse des Sciences Médicales du 29 Mars 1980* à Bâle. Genève 1980

BORNSTEIN S., COUTANCEAU R., & al., 1993, La situation en France. In *Les agresseurs sexuels*, Paris, 1993, pp. 290-298

BRICOUT J., 1989, Les sociopathies: facteurs familiaux et d'environnement. Etude statistique portant sur 353 dossiers. *Journal de Médecine Légale Droit Médical.* 1989 vol. 32, N° 6, pp.457-487

BUTLER T., 1985, Mental health, social policy and the law. Mac Millan London, 1985

CAMPBELL M., 1993, L'évaluation psychométrique et projective. In *Les agresseurs sexuels*, Paris, 1993, pp. 107-115

CHAFFIN M., 1992, Factors associated with treatment completion and progress among intrafamilial sexual abusers. *Child abuse and neglect*. 1992, Vol. 16, pp 251-264

COLIN M., 1993, En psychiatrie, quoi de nouveau ? In *Justice et psychiatrie* Association d'Etudes et de Recherches de l'Ecole Nationale de la Magistrature, Bordeaux, 1993, pp. 3-9

COLIN M., 1993, Pour une médecine sans rupture entre la prison et la ville.In *Justice et psychiatrie*. Association d'Etudes et de Recherches de l'Ecole Nationale de la Magistrature Bordeaux, 1993, pp. 115-121

CORDIER B., 1991, La délinquance sexuelle: problème de la dangerosité post-pénale. In *La dangerosité"*. Privat, Toulouse, 1991, pp. 85-90

CONACHER G.N., 1988, Pharmacotherapy of the agressive adult patient. *International Journal of Law and Psychiatry,* Vol. 11, pp. 205-212, 1988

COUVRAT P., 1993, Du droit du malade mental aux droits des malades mentaux.In *Justice et psychiatrie*. Association d'Etudes et de Recherches de l'Ecole Nationale de la Magistrature Bordeaux, 1993, pp. 25-35

DEBRAY Q., 1981, *Le pychopathe*. Presses Universitaires de France, Paris 1981

DEBUYST Ch., 1977, Le concept de dangerosité et un de ses éléments constitutifs: la personnalité (criminelle). *Déviance et Société,* Genève, 1977, vol. 1, N° 4, pp 363-387

DUFOUR R.Y., 1989, L'image et le Corps: psychothérapie en milieu carcéral. Paris, 1989, Les Editions E.S.F.

DUNCKER H., 1992, Organisation des soins médicaux dispensés aux criminels dans le cadre de la médecine pénitentiaire Allemande. *Communication aux Journées Scientifiques de l'Institut Alexandre Lacassagne*. Lyon 1992

DUNCKER H., 1990, Approche clinique du problème toxicomaniaque en R.F.A. *Communication personnelle*

EGG R., 1992, Therapy versus penalty: an evaluation study. In LÖSEL F., BENDER D., BLIESENER T.(Eds.), *Psychology and Law*. Berlin De Gruyter. 1992 pp. 175-181

FARRINGTON D.P., 1992, Psychological contributions to the explanation, prevention and treatment of offending. In LÖSEL F., BENDER D., BLIESENER T.(Eds.), *Psychology and Law*. Berlin, De Gruyter, 1992, pp. 35-51

FOGEL D., 1979, Traitement pénitentiaire et contrainte. *Déviance et Société*, Genève, 1979, vol. 3, N° 2, pp. 149-159

GAGNE P., 1993, Le traitement hormonal. In *Les Agresseurs Sexuels*. Paris 1993, pp. 222-234

FRANCOIS J., 1979, Pour une clinique alternative en milieu carcéral. *Déviance et Société*,Genève, 1979, vol. 3, N° 2, pp. 169-178

GARAPON A., 1993, L'obligation de soin. In *Justice et psychiatrie*. Association d'Etudes et de Recherches de l'Ecole Nationale de la Magistrature Bordeaux, 1993, pp. 77-87

GARCIA CARBAJOSA M., 1990, Espagne. In *Législations de santé mentale en Europe*. Paris, 1990, Comité Européen: Droit, Ethique et Psychiatrie, pp.100-134

GAZAN F., 1993, La situation en Belgique. In *Les Agresseurs Sexuels*. Maloine, Paris 1993, pp. 280-289

GAZAN F., 1991, Le traitement des délinquants sexuels: état de la question. *Revue Internationale de Criminologie et de Police technique*, 1991 Vol. XLIV, N° 2, pp. 205-225

GEISSMANN P., 1993, Les grands courants de la psychiatrie et de la psychanalyse contemporaines In *Justice et psychiatrie*. Association d'Etudes et de Recherches de l'Ecole Nationale de la Magistrature Bordeaux, 1993, pp. 11-24.

GIJSEGHEM Van H., 1988, La personnalité de l'abuseur sexuel. Méridien Canada 1988

GRAVIER B., 1986, *Evaluation des psychothérapies en milieu carcéral*. Lyon, 1986, Institut Alexandre Lacassagne.

GUILLOD O., 1986, *Le consentement éclairé du patient: autodétermination ou paternalisme?* Ides et calendes, Neuchâtel, 1986

GRAVIER B., 1993, Le délinquant "fou" en prison. In *Santé mentale: réalités Européennes*. Erès, Toulouse, 1993, pp. 284-288

GUNN J., 1977, Criminal Behavior and mental disorder. *British Journal of Psychiatry* 1977 130, pp. 317-329

HARDING T.W., 1984, Dépression en milieu carcéral. *Psychologie Médicale* Paris 1984, Vol. 16, n°5, pp. 835-839

HARDING T.W., 1990, La santé en milieu carcéral. Institut Universitaire de Médecine Légale. Genève

HEGINBOTHAM C., 1990, Angleterre et Pays de Galles. In *Législations de santé mentale en Europe:* Paris, 1990, Comité Européen: Droit, Ethique et Psychiatrie, pp. 10-66

HENGGELER S.W., MELTON G.B. & al., 1992, Family preservation using multisystemic therapy: an effective alternative to incarcerating serious juvenile offenders. *Journal of Consulting and Clinical Psychology*, 1992, Vol. 60, N° 6, pp. 953-961

HERSCHEL PRINS MPh., 1991, Some aspects of sex offending — Causes and Cures? *Medicine Science. Law*, 1991 Vol 31, N°4

HOCHMANN J., 1980, Quelques aspects cliniques des psychopathies. *Confrontations psychiatriques*, 198O, 18, pp. 59-71

HODGINS S., 1992, The treatment of mentally disordered offenders in Canada. In LÖSEL F., BENDER D., BLIESENER T.(Eds.), *Psychology and Law.* Berlin De Gruyter. 1992, pp. 182-192

KERCHOVE M. van de, 1981, "Médicalisation" et "fiscalisation" du droit pénal: deux versions asymétriques de la dépénalisation. *Déviance et Société,* Genève,1981, vol. 5, N°1, pp. 1-23

KERNBERG O., 1975, *Borderline conditions and pathological narcissism.* Aronson, New York, 1975

LANTERI-LAURA G., 1993, Histoire des idées dans la psychiatrie contemporaine. In *Santé mentale: réalités Européennes.* Toulouse, 1993, Editions Erès, pp. 71-79

LEGENDRE P., 1974, *L'amour du censeur.*Le Seuil, Paris, 1974

LEGENDRE P., 1991, Le pardon. *Revue Autrement* Paris 1991 n° Avril

LEMONDE M., 1993, L'article 64 est-il incurable ? In *Santé mentale: réalités Européennes.* Toulouse, 1993, Editions Erès, pp. 275-279

LEMPERIERE T., 1977, *Abrégé de psychiatrie de l'adulte.* Masson, Paris, 1977

LUNDERVOLD D.A. & YOUNG L.G., 1992, Treatment acceptability ratings for sexual offenders: effects of diagnosis and offense. *Research in Developmental Disabilities* 1992 Vol. 13, pp.229-237

MANOUVRIER L., 1892, Questions préalables dans l'étude comparative des criminels et des honnêtes gens. *Déviance et Société,* Genève, 1986, vol. X, N° 3, pp 209-222

Mc DOUGALL J., 1980, Essai sur la perversion. In *Les perversions: chemins de traverse.* Tchou, Paris 1980

MARY P. & DURVIAUX S., 1991, L'éducation en prison: resocialisation ou occupation? *Revue Internationale de Criminologie et de police technique*, 1991, vol. XLIV, N° 1, pp. 36-42

Mc GUIRE J.& PRIESTLEY P., 1992, Some things do work: psychological interventions with offenders and the effectiveness debate. In LÖSEL F., BENDER D., BLIESENER T.(Eds.), *Psychology and Law.*. Berlin De Gruyter. 1992, pp. 163-174

Mc KIBBEN A., 1993, L'évaluation des fantaisies sexuelles. In *Les agresseurs sexuels*, Paris, 1993, pp.90-97

Mc KIBBEN A., 1993, La classification des agresseurs sexuels. *Les agresseurs sexuels*, Paris, 1993, pp. 58-78

MOLINERO M., 1990, Italie. In *Législations de santé mentale en Europe* Paris, 1990, Comité Européen: Droit, Ethique et Psychiatrie, pp.190-223

MONTMOLLIN M.J., 1985, Un traitement des désordres de la personnalité? L'atelier de sociothérapie du service médical à la prison préventive de Champ-Dollon (Genève): survol de cinq années. *Revue Médicale de la Suisse Romande* 1985 Vol. 105, pp. 65-71

MONTMOLLIN M.J., ZIMMERMANN E., & al., 1986, Sociotherapeutic treatment of delinquents in prison. *International Journal of Offender Therapy and Comparative Criminology* 1986 Vol. 30, pp. 25-34

MULVEY E.P., ARTHUR M.W. & al., 1993, The prevention and treatment of juvenile delinquency: a review of the research. *Clinical Psychology Review* 1993 Vol. 13, pp. 133-167

OTTENHOF R. & FAVARD A.M., 1991, *Nouvelles approches de Criminologie Clinique*. Toulouse, 1991, Editions Erès

PASSET I., 1993, L'obligation de soin: une mesure limite.In *Justice et psychiatrie*. Association d'Etudes et de Recherches de l'Ecole Nationale de la Magistrature Bordeaux, 1993, pp. 93-100

PROULX J., 1993, La récidive. In *Les agresseurs sexuels*, Paris, 1993, pp. 260-266

RAPPARD P., 1981, La folie et l'Etat. Toulouse, 1981 Privat Editeur

RAPPARD Ph., 1993, Raison psychiatrique et rationalité juridique en France et en Europe. In *Santé mentale: réalités Européennes*. Toulouse, 1993, Editions Erès, pp. 261-264

Rapport au Conseil de la Recherche. Ministère de la Justice, 1991, Conditions de vie en détention et pathologies somatiques. Lyon, 1991, Institut Alexandre Lacassagne

Rapport au Haut Comité de la Santé Publique, 1993, *Santé en milieu carcéral*. Rennes, 1993, Les Editions Ecole Nationale de la Santé Publique

Rapport du Comité Interministériel de Coordination de la Santé en milieu carcéral, 1992, Promotion de la santé mentale et organisation des soins psychiatriques en milieu pénitentiaire. Paris, 1992, Comité Interministériel Santé/Justice, dans sa séance du 7 Juillet 1992

REAL DE SARTE O., 1984, Eléments pour une analyse du discours médical en prison. *Déviance et Société*, Genève, 1984, vol. VIII, N° 2, pp. 167-180

Recommandation n° R (82) 17 adoptée par le Comité des Ministres du Conseil de l'Europe le 24/09/1982, 1983, Détention et traitement des détenus dangereux. Strasbourg, 1983, Conseil de l'Europe

RESTELLINI J.P., 1985, Secret médical et patients délinquants. *Revue Médicale de la Suisse Romande* 1985, Vol. 105, pp. 39-44

SCHARBACH H., 1983, Les états limites: approche compréhensive chez l'adulte et chez l'enfant. *Rapport présenté au Congrès de psychiatrie et de neurologie de langue française 1983*. Masson, Paris 1983

SENON J.L., 1993, Dispositif de soins en santé mentale destinés aux détenus d'établissements pour peines. In *Justice et psychiatrie*. Association d'Etudes et de Recherches de l'Ecole Nationale de la Magistrature Bordeaux, 1993, pp. 149-159

TARDIFF K., 1992, The current state of psychiatry in the treatment of violent patients. *News and Views. Archives of General Psychiatry*, Vol 49, June 1992

TRAVERSO G.B. & MANNA P., 1992, Law and psychology in Italy. In LÖSEL F., BENDER D., BLIESENER T.(Eds.), *Psychology and Law*.. Berlin De Gruyter, 1992, pp. 535-545

VEDRINNE J. & ELCHARDUS J.M., Les personnalités du toxicomane. *Confrontations psychiatriques*, 1987, N° 28

WIERSON M., FOREHAND R.L. & al., 1992, Epidemiology and treatment of mental health problems in juvenile delinquents. *Behavior Research and Therapy* 1992 Vol. 14, pp. 93-120

PSYCHOSOCIAL INTERVENTIONS IN THE CRIMINAL JUSTICE SYSTEM

20th Criminological Research
Conference
(1993)

GENERAL REPORT

by
Mr R. HOOD
General Rapporteur,
University of Oxford
(United Kingdom)

Most of the issues raised by the five Rapporteurs have already been discussed in my Introductory Report, and the general tenor of the debate and recommendations for future action and research have been summarised in my Conclusions and Recommendations. This General Report will, therefore, attempt briefly to allude to several problems which will need to be tackled in more depth if psychosocial interventions are to become more widely accepted in the criminal justice system.

The justifications for using such measures do, of course, raise questions of penal philosophy, of individual rights, of broader social obligations, of the validity and reliability of empirical evidence for the effectiveness of such measures, of what constitutes sufficiency of proof, and of how scarce resources should be allocated.

No delegates seriously disputed that the so-called "neo-classical" or "justice model" had the potentiality for limiting punishment through the principle of proportionality: the penalty being never more severe than that which can be justified by the gravity of the offence. Yet, in practice, the emphasis on "deserved punishment", especially when invoked in conjunction with the utilitarian aims of incapacitation (especially for the so-called 'dangerous offender') and general deterrence, had in many countries created a punitive and potentially dehumanising penal agenda.

This has been exacerbated in recent years by the fact that serious discussion of "what works" has been virtually taboo. Witness the quarter of a century since last the topic was seriously addressed by the Council of Europe. Those who have made claims for effective penal "treatments" have been regarded by many criminologists with deep suspicion. Their positive "results" have regularly been ignored or dismissed as the outcome of flaws or biases in the research design or as unwarranted inferences drawn from inadequate data. There has been a tendency to regard them as "special pleading" by persons who have a vested interest in proving that their theories are correct. At best they have been considered to be no more than the inevitable 'fall-out' of random or unrepeatable factors always associated with social experiments.

But resistance to what some have claimed to be the "renaissance of rehabilitation" goes deeper than mere scepticism. It is ultimately rooted in the fear that a resurgence of a rehabilitative penal philosophy would herald the revival of wide discretionary powers over the form, content, duration and conditions of confinement or supervision and surveillance, which would, once again, infringe the liberties and rights of offenders to an unjustifiable degree. Such fears remain real and that is why the delegates to this conference insisted that any form of intervention which might affect these rights must be subject to the safeguards enshrined in the European Convention on Human Rights and in other international standards, such as those recently set out in the European Rules on Community Sanctions and Measures (Recommendation N° R (92) 16). These rules, for example, state that the nature and duration of measures should be proportionate to the seriousness of the offence, that the offender's dignity and human rights should be protected, and that informed consent should be obtained.

There was a strong desire to forge a new balance between the "consequentialist" aim of using punishments to reduce crime and the "desert" or "justice" based approach. Just as psychosocial interventions should not lead to disproportionate punishment and injustice in the administration of the penalty, the emphasis on proportionality and rights should not lead to sterile and potentially harmful forms of confinement and surveillance. Indeed, the view was strongly expressed that, whatever harms offenders may have caused, they were, in general, persons with multiple personal and social disadvantages which the State had a duty to address: at a minimum to ensure that punishment did not add further to such disadvantages. The conference therefore endorsed the view that a *via media* should be fashioned and that the tendency to dismiss rehabilitative efforts as both unattainable and undesirable should be rejected. "Nothing works" was, indeed, a misleading and negative slogan for penal policy to embrace. But so also was the uncritical promotion of "treatment works".

It had not been the task of any of the Rapporteurs at this Conference to explore in any depth whether, and if so how, the resolutions of these tensions and conflicting values might be achieved: apart, that is, from the general appeal to international standards mentioned above. In my opinion, it is time for this issue to be placed high on the agenda of the Council of Europe's deliberations on sentencing and penal policy. All that can be attempted here is an outline of some of the issues which will need to be more closely considered in another forum.

1.   Potentialities for Abuse: The Question of Consent

Before any kind of psychosocial intervention is introduced there should a thorough consideration of all the potentialities for abuse of an offender's right to fair treatment. Legal safeguards must be adequate but so also must be the professional and ethical standards of those who are charged with implementing any measure and with drawing conclusions from the way the offender has responded. The conference was vividly reminded of the possibility of political abuse by an East European delegate who recalled her country's past experiences with non-judicial intervention in maintaining social control, and the abuses of human rights associated with it. Psychiatry had also, of course, been abused in order to silence dissidents. It therefore has to be recognized that the use of psychological methods derived from cognitive-behavioural theory, in order to achieve changes of attitude, patterns of thinking and of behaviour so as to "prepare offenders for living in society", cannot be separated from conceptions of what is regarded as socially acceptable. Such methods have been justified by appealing to the notion that they merely help offenders "to address their offending behaviour" so that they are better equipped in future to make *choices* which might help them to avoid involvement in crime. But does this in reality resolve the issue?

Above all, it has to be remembered that criminal sanctions are, in essence, endured without "consent", even if there might be some room for exercising choice by accepting one sanction or form of captivity rather than another. This is why it was argued that any interventions, in whatever penal context they occur, must be based on consent, preferably through a 'contract' — the offer and acceptance of a service — and made subject to disclosure of information, the reasons for decisions made, and access to grievance procedures and legal remedies. This was also regarded as a necessary corollary for the non-coercive exercise of independent professional skills in a penal environment. Yet those engaged in interventions and research must be aware that it is exceptionally difficult to create the conditions under which consent can be freely given and contracts enforced, without there being some element of duress or fear of advantages forgone. This problem arises in an acute form, of course, when the offender's response to a "service" is used as an indicator of his or her "readiness" to receive privileges, such as allocation to an open institution or home leave or, even more important, when it affects the assessment of readiness for parole. This is especially problematic given the evidence of how inaccurate judgements of future risk can be, especially when they rest on psychiatric diagnoses and other forms of clinical assessment.

Another issue which gave rise to considerable concern was the tendency to call upon the expertise of probation officers, and sometimes clinicians, to gather information about the offender's role in the crime (a form of intrusive psychosocial intervention) in order to help courts to assess the seriousness of the offence. The task here is to understand motivations, expectations, decisions made, and the influence of others etc., in order to uncover the aggravating and mitigating factors which may enable a judgement of responsibility and culpability to be made and proportionate punishment assigned. While some felt that such diagnostic interventions were essential in a desert-based system others believed that it was incompatible with professional ethics to employ such intrusive skills for such a purpose.

2.   Concepts and Criteria

It was clear that little progress would be made in this debate without further clarification of the concepts commonly employed. In particular, the term "treatment" was often used both in its generic sense to mean "the manner of dealing with something" and in its medical sense of "the application of remedies". This latter usage was generally regarded as inappropriate when related to what is essentially a normative behavioural problem, namely the breach of criminal laws. The more neutral term "intervention" should be used, and "treatment" only resorted to in the context of a response to a specific medical condition.

There was considerable disagreement about the criteria which would be appropriate for evaluating an intervention. Some believed that prevention of recidivism was too stiff a test, indeed one that was unlikely to be achieved on a sufficient scale to provide the justification for the expenditure of scarce resources. Rather, they based their case for psychosocial aid on the assertion that the State has a duty to provide ameliorative services so that offenders are not further disadvantaged by the experience of punishment. For example, it was argued that offenders had "a right to help for their drug problem", irrespective of the impact on reconviction. It was sufficient if interventions limited the negative effects of long term confinement, including the prevention of suicide and deliberate self-harm; if they produced a less-coercive and less oppositional institutional culture; and if they created a safer environment for both prisoners and staff. In dealing with mentally abnormal offenders the objective of psychiatry in the penal setting should be the alleviation of symptoms and, if possible cure. The avoidance of reconviction was considered merely a subsidiary bonus: the relationship being strictly doctor-patient not doctor-criminal.

It was also argued that a sufficient criterion would be evidence that offenders had changed their attitudes, expressed more socially acceptable values, and were better able to function in socially acceptable ways, irrespective of subsequent reconviction. Several delegates stressed the importance of taking account of the subjective meaning of the experience to those who had undergone any intrusive intervention. Indeed it was argued that interventions can only be successful when the subject accepts the legitimacy of the action being taken.

Yet there was a strong body of opinion which insisted that the ultimate justification for the use of any intervention in the criminal and penal process must be its measurable impact on crime — including a reduction in the 'quality' or frequency of offending. This is because, apart from "desert" based arguments, all justifications for imposing punishment (rather than offering assistance) are essentially "consequentialist" and must therefore be evaluated in relation to their consequences for crime control.

But this does not mean that various measures of reconviction are the only criteria than can be used. Evaluations can also be made of the extent to which a programme of intervention achieves the goals set for it in terms of service delivery; the extent to which it is able to achieve savings in the use of expensive resources, particularly imprisonment or high security conditions; and the extent to which it eases collateral and unnecessary pains on offenders, their families and victims. Both cost-effectiveness and cost-benefits must be borne in mind.

This was a well-worn discussion. None of it was new. But the fact that it occurred, yet again, underlines the continuing necessity for all those engaged in this field to make clear the objectives of interventions, the precise nature of the service intended to be delivered, and the criteria to be employed in assessing whether such objectives have been achieved. Lack of clarity on these fundamental issues makes it exceptionally difficult to compare the outcomes of different studies.

Difficulties were also experienced in relation to distinguishing the many connotations of the terms "restoration", "compensation", "restitution", "mediation", "reconciliation" "rehabilitation" and "reintegration". This made it particularly hard to determine the aims and content of various programmes which seek to take into account the victims of crime as well as the offenders. There was, therefore, uncertainty as to the criteria against which the performance of such interventions could be assessed. Is the aim primarily to satisfy the victim? To achieve "resolution" of offender-victim conflicts? To promote offender rehabilitation through a form of non-exclusionary "shaming" ? Or is it primarily to ease the burdens on the normal machinery of criminal justice?

3.   When does an Effect become Worthwhile?

In assessing interventions aimed to change the attitudes and behaviour of offenders it became obvious that there should be no "great expectations". Two reasons were given. First, the influence of natural processes, such as maturation, as well as a host of individual and social factors are so great that, in relation to them, it would be surprising if brief interventions — like most cognitive behavioural courses — had anything more than a marginal effect. Secondly, in other areas of intervention, notably in medical research, the size of effect produced by particular preventive or curative remedies is often no more than about 10 percentage points. This is no greater than the overall size of the effect found in meta-analyses of offender-orientated programmes, yet medical treatment programmes would be based on such a finding.

An 'effect size' of 10 percentage points is, of course, the average obtained from meta-analyses of a wide range of studies carried out on different populations in a variety of settings. It provides an indication of what might be achieved by a general application of an interventionist approach. And, indeed, an overall fall of 10 percentage points in the rate of recidivism from say 50 to 40 per cent (which is, of course, a 20 per cent reduction), should not be lightly dismissed, for it is well known that recidivists are responsible for a disproportionate amount of offending and of the costs falling on the criminal justice system.

But what must be aimed for is a maximisation of effects through the understanding of which types of interventions have the largest positive impact on particular types of offenders and in what penal and organisational settings. And, of course, it is just as important to avoid the "mis-allocation" of offenders to measures which may prove disadvantageous and counterproductive.

Careful study of which types of programme are associated with positive effects does suggest that cognitive-behavioural methods may have the greatest potential, but this can only be confirmed if there are well-conducted replications in many countries. Before such methods are introduced it is incumbent on those who promote them, including psychiatrists, to produce a greater amount of hard evidence that their methods do, in fact, consistently and reliably produce the results claimed.

4.   What Standard of Proof is Required?

In fact, it was apparent that far too little is known at present about the causal sequences or interactions which are associated with producing lower than expected reconviction rates. It was argued that the great advantage of the cognitive behavioural approach was precisely that it was not dependent on an individualised psychological model of criminality, but compatible with sociological theories such as differential association, subcultural values, access to legitimate and illegitimate opportunities, and calculation of risk. This may be so, but it does not guarantee that any particular social learning programme will be compatible with the criminal justice context within which it is carried out.

Interventions often consist of a number of elements, and researchers must make greater progress in identifying which aspects of them have a positive and which might have a negative impact and in what circumstances. To what extent are the positive results a product of the fact that a proportion of experimental interventions will always have a marginally greater impact, because of the incentives they provide for pro-social behaviour? There is a need to show that results are reproducible in non-experimental settings.

Two facts stand out. First, even in those interventions which have produced the largest positive effects, the impact has been more significant when measured in relation to changes in expressed attitudes and moral reasoning than when recidivism is the sole criterion of success. Secondly, any lowering of rates of recidivism is more likely to be a "delay effect" than a "desistance effect". After about four years the differences favourable to "intervention groups" compared to "control groups" tends to disappear. This suggests that, while interventions may have an impact on attitudes towards criminal behaviour and legal rules, they are, over time, swamped by the realities of the limited legitimate opportunities and other pressures in the post-intervention situation. There is therefore a need for a style of intervention which will include relapse prevention strategies. But how can this be achieved without prolonging State intervention beyond any period which can be justified by the seriousness of the offence?

The conference was also made aware that different inferences can be drawn when interventions are associated with lower rates of reconviction. It may be, for example, that assignment to a "programme" is associated with favourable decisions made at a later stage about offenders — say, not to prosecute or to avoid imprisonment — which have a greater impact on the prospect of avoiding further reconvictions than the original intervention itself.

It is apparent that these problems cannot be explored without an investment in longitudinal research designs which follow cases through the process of intervention and for a lengthy period afterwards. In other words, intervention strategies need to be understood within the context of criminal and non-criminal careers and of the way in which judicial intervention takes place. Whether randomisation is a pre-requisite for such research, given the legal and ethical problems when interventions might produce negative as well as positive effects was a question upon which different views were strongly expressed. In my own view, the insistence on pure random designs would be stultifying.

Very little progress will be made, therefore, until there is a very considerable investment in the implementation of psychosocial programmes alongside properly designed and controlled evaluative research.

5.   Allocation of Resources

High quality resources are scarce within the penal sphere and are likely to remain so. This naturally raises the question of how they should be allocated. This was discussed particularly with reference to mediation programmes which have largely been aimed at "the shallow end" of the criminal justice system which deals with juvenile petty offenders. Properly conducted mediation, as opposed say to a caution, or a monetary penalty, is costly. Should it not therefore be reserved for more serious cases? If so, should it always be carried out within the criminal justice system, with full and free consent being obtained from both victims and offenders — which, of course, would not be easy to guarantee if the alternative was prosecution and criminal stigmatization.

The question "How far can one go?" in promoting mediation between offenders and their victims inevitably led to the question of whether it would be appropriate as the sole response to a serious offence. Some argued that it was undesirable that it should be, because that would lead to inconsistencies in the response to offences — depending on the willingness of the offender to participate — and would produce unequal treatment of offenders and victims and a sense of injustice. Nor should it be allowed to invert the victim-offender roles, so that the victim became doubly victimized through being regarded as a "clinical instrument" for the reformation of offenders. There was also the possibility that mediation would merely be added to existing methods, thereby increasing the weight of social control. It was clear that there were major issues to be resolved before priorities in the allocation of mediation resources could be established.

There is a tendency to assume that interventions will be more effective in non-custodial settings and therefore to give priority to them. Yet serious offenders are much more likely to be imprisoned to mark the gravity of their offences. If effective interventions could be devised for them, this would, in crime control terms, be a major advantage in limiting the need for long-term confinement for incapacitative ends. The greatest "pay-offs" appear to be most likely with those at the mid-point of their career, when of course, offenders are faced with stark choices, in relation to loss of conventional roles and reputations or the acceptance of definitions as "real criminals". It will take a sea-change to convince governments that this is where substantial resources should be allocated.

6.   Conclusions

In the currently prevailing punitive climate there are far too few measures available to assist prisoners to help themselves, especially given the multiple social problems, including mental instability and deficient social skills, which so many of them display. The conference wholeheartedly endorsed the conclusion that the aim must be greatly to raise the quality of services offered to offenders in order to make the criminal justice system more humane and efficient, while at the same time increasing its effectiveness (in a variety of ways) without leading to the abuse of human rights. The fact that this was thought to be no pipe-dream is what made this conference so memorable.

PSYCHOSOCIAL INTERVENTIONS
IN THE
CRIMINAL JUSTICE SYSTEM

20th Criminological Research
Conference
(1993)

CONCLUSIONS AND RECOMMENDATIONS

by
Mr R. HOOD
General Rapporteur,
University of Oxford
(United Kingdom)

CONCLUSIONS

In recent years a growing body of evidence has challenged the claim that "nothing works" in the field of psychosocial interventions which aim to reduce recidivism. In particular, new forms of intervention have been developed which claim to be better grounded on criminological knowledge. Further, models of intervention based on a concern to address the victim-offender relationship have taken root. These developments needed to be assessed in their own right and in the context of the growing demand for legal safeguards and for proportionality between crime and punishment.

The conference acknowledged that "nothing works" had been a misleading formulation. It had before it sufficient evidence, from meta analyses and other studies, to show that some interventions were associated with a significant effect on rates of reconviction as well as various other criteria. The size of the overall effects calculated from meta analyses was, however, uniformly modest (about 10 percentage points, but no more modest than in some medical research). This was to be expected given the many other influences which shape offenders' life experiences, attitudes, opportunities etc. Even so, the effects have been much more substantial when cognitive behavioural approaches were applied to appropriate offenders. Nevertheless, it was recognised that caution in drawing inferences is called for: the effects could be due not to the intervention as such but to selection and/or experimental effects or to different discretionary decisions and/or influences in the post-intervention period, etc. Bearing this in mind, it was clear that it would be equally simplistic to replace the "nothing works" slogan with the bold generalisation that "treatment works".

The medical concept of "treatment" was regarded as inappropriate (even in the psychiatric sphere) to describe models of social learning which relate to harmful behaviour, when this so obviously depends on social definitions and values. It was agreed that "psychosocial interventions" could refer to a wide variety of services for offenders and victims and that such interventions could serve many purposes, not only the reduction of recidivism. Examples were: assessing responsibility and culpability, providing help to the disadvantaged, restoring mental health, improving the institutional climate, lessening victimisation and suicide, and, in the case of mediation, satisfying victims' needs and feelings and assessing the meaning of mediation to the parties involved. There was much debate on the extent to which recidivism (despite well-known flaws) should be regarded as the acid test of effectiveness.

Concern was expressed as to whether the emphasis on effectiveness would reproduce the familiar problems of unbridled discretion and lack of respect for offenders' rights associated with the discredited 'rehabilitative ideal'. It appeared, however, that many new types of intervention were based on a recognition of the need for voluntary consent (in so far as that is possible when under a penal sanction), on teaching offenders to exercise their own choice and fitting them to do so, and on the notion of a 'contract' for a service offered. Providing that this is adhered to, there is no necessary incompatibility with a system based on proportionality and respect for rights. Indeed, given the many personal and social handicaps which recidivists are known to have, it was argued that the State has a responsibility to provide such opportunities for change, always bearing in mind, of course, that they should not be applied coercively. In other words, it might be possible to achieve an equilibrium between the concern to assist offenders to avoid crime and the concern to protect them from arbitrary and repressive abuse of power.

It was difficult to reach a consensus on the meaning and purposes of mediation, reparation and reconciliation, and even more difficult to establish their place in relation to the criminal process. Fear was expressed that this approach was being too much confined to the diversion of petty forms of delinquency and there was a desire to explore its potentiality within the criminal justice system — either as an alternative, or a complement, to traditional sanctions.

The conference also addressed the perennial issue of the practicalities of delivering high quality psychosocial services, including diagnostic and assessment facilities, to offenders and victims. It was recognised that success is ultimately dependent on the appropriate structures being in place, notably: an adequate and efficient organisation, sufficient resources, trained and motivated staff, and a suitable environmental setting.

RECOMMENDATIONS

1. The conference strongly emphasised that the recourse to, and the implementation of, psychosocial interventions should be guided by respect for fundamental legal safeguards as enshrined in the European Convention on Human Rights, and, in particular, by the common principles regarding penal policy among member States of the Council of Europe as set out in the European Prison Rules (Recommendation N° R (87) 3) and in the European Rules on Community Sanctions and Measures (Recommendation N° R (92) 16).

2. The conference also provided sufficient evidence to warrant a much greater investment in research to evaluate psychosocial interventions. Governments should devote the substantial resources required so that research can address more adequately the issues raised by this review of the current state of knowledge. In addition, all agencies which seek to intervene in offenders' personal and social functioning should be required to set up systems to enable their actions to be monitored and evaluated. This applies to victim oriented programmes as well as to psychiatric services. The conference recommends in particular that:

2.1 the Council of Europe take initiatives to promote analyses of what mediation schemes comprise and evaluations of their contributions both within and outside the criminal justice system;

2.2 research be carried out on the 'contents' of and processes involved in psychosocial interventions, particularly social learning programmes, in order to evaluate both positive and negative factors and outcomes.

2.3   more research be undertaken on the processes leading to offenders refraining from crime or relapsing into recidivism. This will need the application of longitudinal and, wherever possible, experimental research designs. In particular, it would have important implications for after-care services;

2.4   attention be directed to what offenders believe their own needs to be and to their views on the extent to which interventions meet these needs. Particular emphasis should be paid to their perceptions of the fairness of their treatment in its widest sense;

2.5   more information be gathered about the circumstances in which, and the reasons why, offenders 'drop out' or 'hang on', and what the consequences are for them and for the system of assessment which allocated them;

2.6   adequate (i.e. complex) measures be developed so as to make it possible to assess from various perspectives the costs and benefits associated with various interventions, with the aim of maximizing the quality of services provided.

3.   Finally, in the context of the rising political support for more punitive and austere penal measures, the conference has demonstrated that a more constructive response to criminality and the problems of offenders and victims should not be dismissed as ineffective and unattainable. Indeed, the Council of Europe should promote the development of such measures.

Sales agents for publications of the Council of Europe
Agents de vente des publications du Conseil de l'Europe

AUSTRALIA/AUSTRALIE
Hunter publications, 58A, Gipps Street
AUS-3066 COLLINGWOOD, Victoria
Fax: (61) 34 19 71 54

AUSTRIA/AUTRICHE
Gerold und Co., Graben 31
A-1011 WIEN 1
Fax: (43) 1512 47 31 29

BELGIUM/BELGIQUE
La Librairie européenne SA
50, avenue A. Jonnart
B-1200 BRUXELLES 20
Fax: (32) 27 35 08 60

Jean de Lannoy
202, avenue du Roi
B-1060 BRUXELLES
Fax: (32) 25 38 08 41

CANADA
Renouf Publishing Company Limited
1294 Algoma Road
CDN-OTTAWA ONT K1B 3W8
Fax: (1) 613 741 54 39

DENMARK/DANEMARK
Munksgaard
PO Box 2148
DK-1016 KØBENHAVN K
Fax: (45) 33 12 93 87

FINLAND/FINLANDE
Akateeminen Kirjakauppa
Keskuskatu 1, PO Box 218
SF-00381 HELSINKI
Fax: (358) 01 21 44 35

GERMANY/ALLEMAGNE
UNO Verlag
Poppelsdorfer Allee 55
D-53115 BONN
Fax: (49) 228 21 74 92

GREECE/GRÈCE
Librairie Kauffmann
Mavrokordatou 9, GR-ATHINAI 106 78
Fax: (30) 13 83 03 20

IRELAND/IRLANDE
Government Stationery Office
4-5 Harcourt Road, IRL-DUBLIN 2
Fax: (353) 14 75 27 60

ISRAEL/ISRAËL
ROY International
PO Box 13056
IL-61130 TEL AVIV
Fax: (972) 349 78 12

ITALY/ITALIE
Libreria Commissionaria Sansoni
Via Duca di Calabria, 1/1
Casella Postale 552, I-50125 FIRENZE
Fax: (39) 55 64 12 57

NETHERLANDS/PAYS-BAS
InOr-publikaties, PO Box 202
NL-7480 AE HAAKSBERGEN
Fax: (31) 542 72 92 96

NORWAY/NORVÈGE
Akademika, A/S Universitetsbokhandel
PO Box 84, Blindern
N-0314 OSLO
Fax: (47) 22 85 30 53

PORTUGAL
Livraria Portugal, Rua do Carmo, 70
P-1200 LISBOA
Fax: (351) 13 47 02 64

SPAIN/ ESPAGNE
Mundi-Prensa Libros SA
Castelló 37, E-28001 MADRID
Fax: (34) 15 75 39 98

Llibreria de la Generalitat
Rambla dels Estudis, 118
E-08002 BARCELONA
Fax: (34) 34 12 18 54

SWEDEN/SUÈDE
Aktiebolaget CE Fritzes
Regeringsgatan 12, Box 163 56
S-10327 STOCKHOLM
Fax: (46) 821 43 83

SWITZERLAND/SUISSE
Buchhandlung Heinimann & Co.
Kirchgasse 17, CH-8001 ZÜRICH
Fax: (41) 12 51 14 81

BERSY
Route du Manège 60, CP 4040
CH-1950 SION 4
Fax: (41) 27 31 73 32

TURKEY/TURQUIE
Yab-Yay Yayimcilik Sanayi Dagitim Tic Ltd
Barbaros Bulvari 61 Kat 3 Daire 3
Besiktas, TR-ISTANBUL

UNITED KINGDOM/ROYAUME-UNI
HMSO, Agency Section
51 Nine Elms Lane
GB-LONDON SW8 5DR
Fax: (44) 718 73 82 00

**UNITED STATES and CANADA/
ÉTATS-UNIS et CANADA**
Manhattan Publishing Company
468 Albany Post Road
PO Box 850
CROTON-ON-HUDSON, NY 10520, USA
Fax: (1) 914 271 58 56

STRASBOURG
Librairie Kléber
Palais de l'Europe
F-67075 STRASBOURG Cedex
Fax: (33) 88 52 91 21

Council of Europe Press/Les éditions du Conseil de l'Europe
Council of Europe/Conseil de l'Europe
F-67075 Strasbourg Cedex
Tel. (33) 88 41 25 81 - Fax (33) 88 41 27 80